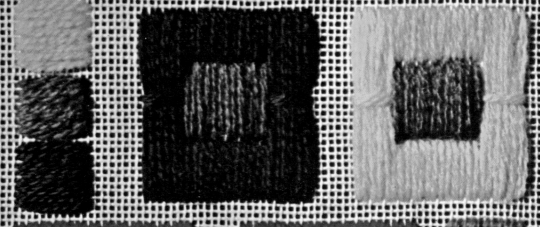
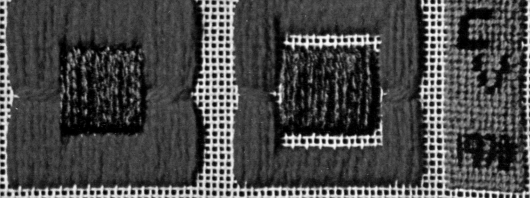

Needlepoint for Everyone

By the same authors

NEEDLEPOINT MADE EASY

Needlepoint for Everyone

MARY BROOKS PICKEN and DORIS WHITE

with Claire Valentine

HARPER & ROW, PUBLISHERS • NEW YORK, EVANSTON, AND LONDON

Dedicated to

Dr. Howard Rusk, doctor, teacher, humanitarian,
in appreciation of his great works
in therapy for the physically handicapped

and

With gratitude to the great and to the unknown of
past generations, through whose efforts and innovations
we have received our heritage of needlepoint,
and with acknowledgment to those enthusiasts of the present
who have made needlepoint a creative art form
of today, we dedicate this book
to the needlepointers of the future.

Contents

Introduction by Russell Lynes • 1

Our Heritage • 3

Gracie Mansion, Sturbridge, Boscobel, Mount Vernon, Williamsburg

Blair House • 9

Needlepoint Essentials • 13

Just Starting? • Accomplished Needlepointer? • Buying Needlepoint • Choice of Design • Canvas • Yarn • Needles • Measuring for Needlepoint • Materials for Needlepoint • Threading the Needle • Starting and Ending a Strand of Yarn • Filling in Around a Design

Design and Color • 33

Reducing or Enlarging a Design • Transferring a Design to Canvas • Centering a Design • Plain or Fancy Stitches • Coloring or Painting a Design • Working a Design • Color

Canvas Stitches • 53

Continental • Basket Weave • Petit Point • Regular Half-Cross • Simplified Half-Cross • Elongated Half-Cross • Bargello or Flame • Encroaching Gobelin • Brick • Diagonal • Chevron • Parisian • Tramé • Ripping Out Needlepoint Stitches • Piecing and Enlarging Canvas • Enlarging with Fabric

Left-Handed? No Problem! • 77

Left-Hand Continental • Left-Hand Petit Point • Left-Hand Basket Weave • Left-Hand Diagonal • Left-Hand Half-Cross Stitches

Blocking • *Mounting* • *Finishing* • 86

Rehabilitation and Recreational Therapy • 91

Frames • Working with a Frame

Interior Design • 95

Benches • Chairs • Stools • Cushions Unlimited • The Personal Touch • Bell Pulls • Luggage Racks • Card Table Covers • Rugs • Screens • Wall Panels • Pictures • Mounting Chair Seats

Fashion Accessories • 107

Bags: Daytime, Evening, Travel • Luggage • Needlepoint Mounted on Wicker Bag • Brief Case • Book Cover with Handles • Address Book • Memo Pad • Closet Accessories • Waistcoats and Vests • Cummerbund • Slippers • Hats • Small Personal Accessories • Dog Coat

House and Home • 117

Needlepainting

Samplers • *Mottoes* • *Monograms* • 125

Alphabets • Family Record Samplers • Family Tree • Wedding and Birth Samplers • 19th Century Samplers • Mottoes • Marking Canvas for Lettering • Baste Marking • Transferring a Name to Canvas • Handwriting • Highlighting a Design • Letters or Numerals Made with Backstitches • Computer Numerals • Monograms

Devotionals • 139

Planning Committees of Parishioners

Teaching • 150

For Children • 153

Men and Needlepoint • 159

The Hobbyist and The Collector • 167

Advertising & Publicity Via Needlepoint • 179

Museum Treasures • 183

Cutting and Sewing Fashion Accessories • 198

Fold-under Finish • Compact Slip-case • Eyeglass Case • Needle Book • Clutch Bag • Book Cover with Carrying Handles

Symbolism • 200

Bibliography • 203

National Directory of Art Needlework Shops • 204

Acknowledgments • 207

Index • 211

Color insert follows page 88.

Introduction

UNTIL I READ THE PROOFS of *Needlepoint for Everyone,* I did not know that for more than twenty years I have been using "Penelope" canvas and that I have been plying a needle (many needles; I lose them) in the "continental" stitch and the "basket weave." It is nice to learn after many millions of stitches what it is that I have been doing. I've invented a technique (or so the authors generously contend in the chapter "Needlepoint for Men") but basically I am a one-stitch needlepointer.

One of the great pleasures of this pastime is how far you can go with how little basic skill. Compared with painting in water color or acrylic or oils, needlepoint is for people who are all thumbs. The materials can't run away with you; the wools come in a range of colors that satisfies the most demanding tastes for the outrageous or the subtle. The canvas determines the size of the stitch; the needle is blunt so that it is almost impossible even to prick your finger. I consider myself something of a virtuoso at needlepoint, but I can scarcely sew on a button and I certainly couldn't hem a napkin. Smoothness of surface comes with practice, but anyone can learn the rudiments (if not the refinements) of needlepoint in an hour.

When I started doing needlepoint many years ago as therapy (now I do it for pleasure), the authors' previous book did not exist, and I had to learn a great many things by trial and error that are clearly and precisely described and diagrammed here. Some helpful objects, like the waterproof felt pen (so useful for putting designs on canvas) did not exist. The general level of needlepoint design to be had from wool-work shops was appalling. I was lucky enough to get several of my friends who are artists to design chair seats and other pieces for me, and I eventually discovered that it is possible to improvise designs as one goes along, based on the verticals and horizontals of the canvas—all sorts of geometrical figures, like those of a kaleidoscope, in glowing or retiring colors. And all of this can be done with the simplest of basic techniques on the same kind of canvas. Curiously, this is a handcraft in which manual dexterity is the very least of one's needs; anyone (as the title of this book implies) who has eyes and fingers, and, of course, a great deal of patience can do needlepoint. It is not an art or a craft for anyone in a hurry.

But needlepoint has many advantages over many other handcrafts. It is not antisocial; it does not hinder conversation. It is flexible and adaptable to time and to use. I used to be a Sunday painter, or weekend artist, but unless I had several hours to set up, paint, and clean up it was not worth doing; you can pick up needlepoint and work on it for five minutes or several hours: it is there when you feel like it for as long as you feel like it, and you can carry it with you. It is companionable. The results can be (and often are) not only satisfying but useful, and its possibilities are endless.

Needlepoint for Everyone is what I should have started with, but which, many years later, I am now delighted to contribute to and to possess. It is not only a primer for the beginner (which I am not) but a reference book for the expert which, if I live long enough, I hope to be.

RUSSELL LYNES

Needlepoint for Everyone

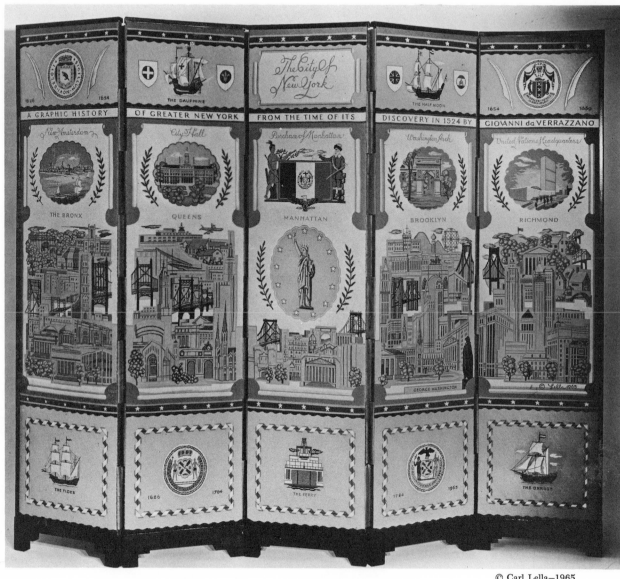

© Carl Lella—1965

A graphic history of Greater New York is shown on this beautiful
screen which decorates Gracie Mansion, home of New York City's mayor.
The vignettes at the top of the middle section of the screen are done
in full color on an ivory background. They
show important incidents in New York City's history,
namely, the settlement of New Amsterdam,
City Hall, the purchase of Manhattan, the Washington Arch,
and the United Nations Headquarters.

(*continued at bottom of opposite page*)

AMERICAN
20th Century

Our Heritage

ALTHOUGH NEEDLEPOINT, WHICH IS EMBROIDERY ON CANVAS, was a type of needlework highly developed by the English, little was brought to America by the first colonists. The early settlers had to make much of the cloth that they needed for garments or household use. They used the native berries and other plants to dye and re-dye fabrics for re-use.

Patchwork developed from this frugality. It is the one needlework peculiarly American.

The canvas and wools used for needlepoint had to be imported, so except for the few who could afford a fairly expensive hobby, needlepoint was not done to any extent in the United States until the late 18th and 19th centuries.

Because needlepoint was considered a formal type of needlework, it was used with the most formal furniture styles. Each needlepoint example shown in this chapter is from a historic residence and reflects a phase of our American heritage.

Today we are continuing this historic process by making needlepoint for use in our churches or as museum pieces or to be left as heirlooms.

(continued from previous page)
The top and bottom panels show a number of the Great Seals of the City of New York, the sailing ships of the early explorers of this region, and the Staten Island ferry.
The center panels illustrate more than sixty landmarks which encompass the five boroughs of New York City.
The purpose of this ambitious project was to give the viewer a vivid picture of the early history and continuing growth of this great metropolis.

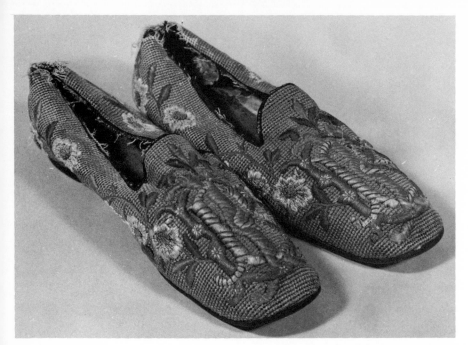

AMERICAN
19th Century

A man's bedroom slippers
lined with white kid.
The needlepointed
slippers have an overlay
of embroidery done in
rich colors. Very likely a
pattern from one of
the ladies' books of this
period was used.

This fringed cushion was one of ten designed
and personally worked by Martha Washington at
the age of sixty-nine. It is on view
at Mount Vernon, Virginia. In this period many hard
chairs needed their own cushions in the
interest of seating comfort.
This attractive shell design would suit many
contemporary homes. If you would like to duplicate
it, see reference on page 203.

AMERICAN
18th Century

4

AMERICAN
Late 18th Century

Boscobel at Garrison, New York, is the restored
home of States Morris Dyckman, 1755–1806. The restoration
was financed by Mrs. DeWitt (Lila) Wallace of *Reader's Digest*.

This rug in the Ashlar Room is 9 by 18 feet in size and was
worked on 12-inch squares. A floral spray sets off the
center of each square, and the
background is done in brown and red.

A needlepoint rug worthy of becoming an heirloom.
It features a floral center and border;
cornucopias full of flowers are the corner motifs
of the center section. The rug is
perfectly done with rich, colorful yarns.

ENGLISH
Mid 18th Century

AMERICAN—18th Century
Philadelphia 1725

This needlework slipseat for a Queen Anne
side chair is from Colonial Williamsburg.
The daughter of Governor William Keith
of Pennsylvania is said to have executed
this design of stylized flowers.

ENGLISH—Early 17th Century

During this century men and women
often used a box such as this to hold jewelry
or intimate toilette items.
The lining was of silk, and sometimes
a mirror was secured to the inside of the lid.

The needlepoint was done in a design
suitable to the owner. Occasionally a quotation
would be worked on the band of the cover
which might also include the owner's name.

The inscription on this box reads:

A wonder strange yet wonder true
Is here presented to your view
For he alone which I thus paint
Was King, Confessor, Martyr, Saint   AE33

ENGLISH—Early 18th Century

Walnut wing chair. Note the perfection
of upholstery—an important item.
Needlepoint beautifully worked deserves
the utmost in mounting when you realize
how long it will last and how richly mellow
it will become as the years go by.

7

Blair House *The President's Guest House*

AMERICANS CAN BE TRULY PROUD OF BLAIR HOUSE. This 19th-century home, diagonally across Pennsylvania Avenue from the White House, is used to entertain visiting dignitaries to the United States.

Blair House is really two houses in one: the original Blair home built in 1824 and an adjoining house, built just before the Civil War for the Blair's daughter, Elizabeth Blair Lee, wife of Samuel Phillips Lee, a cousin of Robert E. Lee. The two houses are now connected by doorways cut through the adjoining walls on all floors, making one spacious, charming home. The house contains a priceless collection of portraits and English and American furnishings of various periods. A collection of Lincolniana adds a great deal of interest to the house.

On October 29, 1942, Blair House became the property of the Government of the United States and the official guest house of the nation when President Roosevelt approved its acquisition as a historic monument. Kings and queens or heads of state may be entertained here with the formality suited to their positions in their own countries. These dignitaries may also entertain or schedule conferences in Blair House should they so desire.

There are two dining rooms in Blair House. The photograph on the opposite page shows the Blair-Lee dining room with Chippendale-type chairs, each seat covered in needlepoint. A close-up of the design is on page 10. The chair seats, needlepointed by wives of congressmen and cabinet members, took one and a half years to complete.

Above: On the end of the table is a beautiful covered
dish, one piece of the Lowestoft porcelain
used as inspiration for the chair-seat design.
The decorative wreath is worked in several shades
of blue against a white background.

Left: This attractive bench
is used in front of
the fireplace in the
President's library.
The colors are greens,
golds, and white with
red accents.

Linen, cotton, and wool
are the predominant
decorative fabrics used
in these quarters.
The needlepoint pieces
serve as appropriate
highlights throughout.

Bedroom
The lion statue,
of Bennington pottery,
is a dominant feature of
this room where kings and
other heads of state reside
when in the United States.
The design on the
gold-fringed pillow, with
background of red, was inspired
by the lion statue.
It is an outstanding
piece of needlepoint.

Library-Study
The needlepoint on this armchair
is a duplicate of the original
cover. After many years of use
the original Blair piece
was carefully removed and sent
to England where every detail
was meticulously copied.

The chair shows vividly the
possibilities of color in
needlepoint. The many hues
are clear and bright.

11

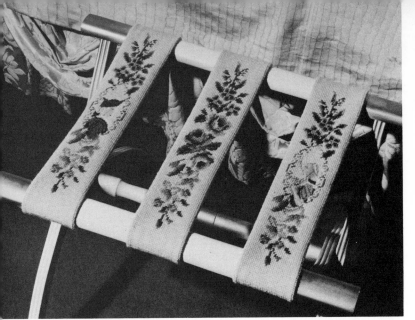

Left:
Second Floor—Queen's Suite
Since silk is the decorative fabric used here, the only needlepoint found is the white luggage rack with the colorful floral sprays. A charming colonial profile is centered on each side strip. The same needlepoint design is duplicated on the luggage rack in the President's room, except that there the background is black.

Below:
The pole screen, used to hold back the heat, to prevent drafts, or just for ornament, is from the original Blair home. The colorful bouquet of flowers is highlighted by the dark, ornate border.

Below:
Third Floor Sitting Room
For use by a visiting Prime Minister or a person "second-in-command." The Blair family's glass collection is shown along with an interesting needlepoint chair from the original Blair home.

Needlepoint Essentials

Just Starting?

RELAX—YOU ARE ABOUT TO ACQUIRE A LIFELONG HABIT that will not only help you to forget everyday tensions, but will also result in a completed work of art. It will be useful as well as beautiful.

Before you pick up a needle we suggest that you take the time to read through the following pages so that you can decide what your first project will be.

You will also learn which basic materials you need to do your first needlepoint project, and where and how to buy materials.

Accomplished Needlepointer?

HAVE YOU MADE SO MANY pieces of needlepoint that you feel there are no new fields to conquer?

Then browse through the pages of this book. See the variety of techniques done by men, starting on page 159. Interested in religious symbolism? See page 138. The needlepoint expert with free time might consider organizing or joining a church or temple needlepoint project as outlined on page 149.

Many of you may presently be involved in helping a local hospital or rehabilitation center, or plan to do something along this line. If so, the chapter starting on page 91 may give you inspiration.

Are you a frustrated teacher—with nothing to teach? Why not start a course in your club, organization, or religious group by following the outline on page 151.

The individualist, who likes to develop her own ideas, should refer to the chapter starting on page 33.

For some new and original items that are enhanced by needlepoint see the photographs on page 106.

Buying Needlepoint

NEEDLEPOINT DESIGNS can be purchased:

—With *design completely worked,* and only the background to be filled in. These needlepoint pieces usually have a motif centered on the canvas. The design is worked in the continental stitch, or for a few fine details, in the continental with petit point.

—With *designs worked in tramé.* The yarn colors are the guide to the distribution of color when working over the long stitches with needlepoint stitches. See illustration on page 72. The yarn needed to complete the item is usually included in the cost of the purchase.

—With *design painted on the canvas.* The painted colors indicate the yarn colors to use in the working of the needlepoint. The yarn needed to complete the item is often included in the cost.

—As a *design chart.* In the chart each square represents one needlepoint stitch, and each color is indicated by an individual symbol, number, or letter. See example on page 49.

The needlepoint designs listed above are stock items, but not all types are necessarily available from all sources.

Made-to-order designs are available at the needlework specialty shops. These are "painted on canvas" designs with selected yarn supplied to complete the piece.

First Purchase. If you are buying your first needlepoint piece, take extra time to select your project, as it may determine whether needlepoint will become a pleasurable hobby or just a sometime happening. Reading this book and studying the illustrations should help

Design motifs
worked completely
in petit point.
Background to be
filled in either
all petit point
or all gros point.

you to decide what you would like to make and how to use it.

Visit an art needlework department or a specialty shop, and take the time to browse through their stock of needlepoint designs. Unless you are already adept with a needle, and have a creative art background, we suggest that your initial venture be a piece of canvas with the design already completed. Filling in the background, as well as placing stitches in and around the design area, will give you the opportunity to practice some of the essentials of this art. Refer to *Choice of Design* on page 16.

Buy an item available on medium-size canvas—10 or 12 threads to the inch. See chart on page 20. Although the same general principles apply to any canvas size, the finer canvas requires more patience than the larger sizes. See below about kits available with all materials included to make a completed needlepoint item. One of these may just fill your present need. Usually these kits include everything needed to finish the item completely. Check the contents so that you can buy anything that is not included. Having everything at hand is one way to insure your finishing the project once you start.

If you decide to purchase the design and yarn separately, be sure to buy sufficient yarn to complete the background. See page 22 for *Basic Yarn Formula* and page 23 for *Background Color*.

Working and finishing your first needlepoint project will give you an idea of what you want to do next.

Needlepoint Kits. Several manufacturers make kits that sell in a very wide range of prices, many of them very reasonably priced. These

Design worked in gros point with center of lower flower petit pointed. Background is complete.

packages are put up in different ways and include various materials. Some items have the design already worked with only the background to be filled in. In others, the canvas has a painted or stamped design with assorted colored yarn in addition to the background yarn to complete the needlepoint. A needle is usually included in the package.

Picture kits come with and without frames. Kits for small personal items such as eyeglass cases or wallets may include the lining fabric.

Examine some of these kits. You may find one that is exactly to your taste! Or buy a simple kit for a beginner. It may be the start of a whole new outlook for the recipient.

Choice of Design

INSPIRATION FOR DESIGNS now comes from every section of the globe, because of today's widespread interest in needlepoint.

At one time many fine needlepoint pieces originated on the small island of Madeira. The art reached such a high level of perfection because generations of mothers passed on their techniques and enthusiasm to their pre-teen daughters.

There are many steps in the production of a beautiful needlepoint piece before it can be purchased. The photographs, taken in Madeira, show only three of the steps:

1. Designer creating a floral design.
2. Sample makers working design from original art.
3. Home workers embroidering needlepoint designs.

Manufacturers are now obtaining needlepoint pieces with finished motifs from many other sources. Many of the newer devotees of this art prefer to work the whole design themselves, so the range in designs of painted canvas grows and grows. You will find designs on canvas in all shapes and sizes, in all styles and colors to suit every taste. Certain design motifs have year in and year out appeal. Floral motifs are always in favor. Other subjects go in or out of fashion just as clothes do.

Certain animals and birds are favorite subjects. If you do not find the one you want when shopping, it can be made to order by a specialty shop. For this reason the same subject will often be found in a variety of design styles. For example, the owl photograph gives five interpretations of the same bird. You

might like to use an owl design, but still not care for any of those shown. This picture will help you to visualize how designs differ when done by various artists. These owls are but a single example.

In addition to the variations in styles of design, you will find many similar designs, or the same design used to decorate a wide range of items. The illustration below shows needlepoint butterflies, combined with different flowers, used as a chair seat, mounted for a handbag, and framed for wall decoration. When you visit your needlepoint center, many other design comparisons can be seen. You will also find an interested and talented sales person who will be glad to find just the design you need for a specific purpose.

Canvas

Canvas, Yarn, and Needle Chart

On pages 20 and 21 are actual-size photographs showing groups of canvas, yarn, and needles.

Page 20 illustrates some single-thread canvas; page 21, double-thread canvas.

These few examples will help you understand the relationship between the size of the canvas mesh, the weight of the yarn, and the needle size.

Quality is the most important factor in buying needlepoint canvas. Your finished work will last as long as the canvas foundation. The finest canvas available is made of cotton and is imported from England, France, Germany, and Hong Kong.

Qualities to Look for in Good Canvas

1. Evenly spaced meshes.
2. Flawless threads (no knots or lumpy sections).
3. Polished semi-stiff finish adds body and prevents yarn from catching in meshes.

Types and Color

Double-thread canvas (Penelope canvas)—is most often found in an ecru color but it is also made in white. Alternating large and small meshes are formed in weaving. Every two vertical threads are woven closely together but the horizontal threads are evenly spaced. (*Below left*)

Selvages indicate the side edges. The top and bottom edges should be hemmed or bound.

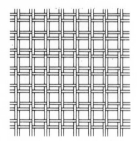 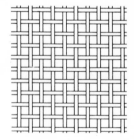

Single-thread canvas (mono-canvas)—is available in white, yellow, or ecru. The meshes are uniform in size because vertical and horizontal threads are evenly spaced in both directions. (*Above right*)

This evenly woven canvas has no up and down. You can start work from any edge or in any direction.

Sizes of Canvas Mesh

Petit point canvas—20 meshes to the inch and finer. Single-thread and split mesh double-thread canvas.

Gros point canvas—10 to 18 meshes to the inch. Single thread.

Gros point canvas—8 to 12 meshes to the inch. Double thread.

Quick point canvas—3 to 7 meshes to the inch. Double thread and single thread.

Rug canvas—any of the sizes listed above, except petit point, can be used to make a rug. The choice of canvas will depend on the size of the rug to be made. Quick point sizes are used most often.

Width of Canvas

24 inches for finer canvas.
24 to 36 inches for most types of canvas.
36 to 40 inches for rug canvas.

Right Side of Canvas

Needlepoint canvas does not have a right and wrong side because of its special finish which makes it the same on both sides. Therefore, the side of the canvas on which the design is painted, inked, or traméd becomes the right side. If a design is already worked, the right side of the stitches determines the right side of the canvas.

Determining Amount of Canvas to Purchase

Before purchasing canvas, determine the size of the object to be covered. See *Measuring* on page 24.

After making a paper pattern of the object to be covered, add 1 to 3 inches all around.

Size of design. The design selected should be in proportion to the size of the object to be covered.

For example: A small chair requires a small and/or delicate design. Large or heavy furniture should have an impressive design.

Area to be worked. When the design is centered on an object, or a border design is used, at least 1 to 3 inches of background area should be visible around the outside edge.

Allover and repeat patterns that cover the entire surface of the object should have about 1 inch of background around the outside edge.

Allowance for shrinkage, mounting and finishing. To the background area beyond the design that will be visible after mounting add at least 1 inch of worked canvas on all edges plus a minimum of 2 inches of unworked canvas.

The rule above applies generally. For example: less allowance is needed when working on very small objects and special accessories. See the individual item for instructions.

Finishing Canvas Edges. Canvas purchased with a worked motif often has a selvage edge on both sides and hems at top and bottom. If the piece of canvas you plan to work on is not finished on all edges, use one of the following methods to bind off:

1. Make a plain hem.
2. Finish with bias binding.
3. Apply masking tape.
4. Add a line of quick-drying liquid glue.

Masking tape, either paper or plastic, can be used to bind edges, but care must be taken when blocking. The tape becomes loose when wet and will not hold the tacks properly.

Use this method for needlepoint pieces that do not pull out of shape and require minimum blocking.

Glued canvas edge gives greater strength to the edges by gluing threads together.

Place a line of liquid glue around edge of canvas two or three meshes from inside edge of hem, bias or masking tape. Allow to dry thoroughly before starting needlepoint stitches.

Marking Area to be Worked. Designs are not always centered exactly on the canvas. Before marking the area to be worked, count each mesh in single-thread canvas (count large meshes in double-thread canvas) to the right and left of the design. There should be an equal number of meshes on each side, and an equal number above and below the design. Diagram **A** shows how to count the meshes in each direction.

It is important to check the design placement on every piece of needlepoint you are going to make.

This same principle applies to motifs you work yourself on painted canvas. After finishing the motif, check meshes as instructed above before proceeding with the background.

After you determine the area to be worked in needlepoint stitches, including meshes to be worked beyond visible surface, add allowance for shrinkage, mounting, and finishing; then outline the entire area with pencil. Double-check to be sure size is correct, then mark with a double-thread basting stitch, India ink, or a waterproof dry-marker pen. Test any marker you plan to use, on the outer edge of the canvas or on a separate piece, to make sure it will not bleed or run when dampened.

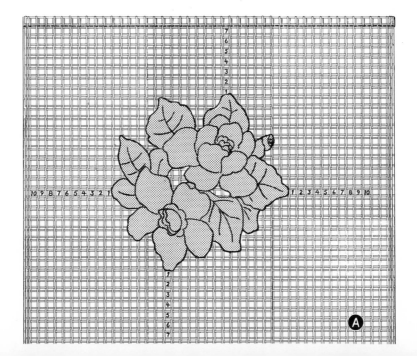

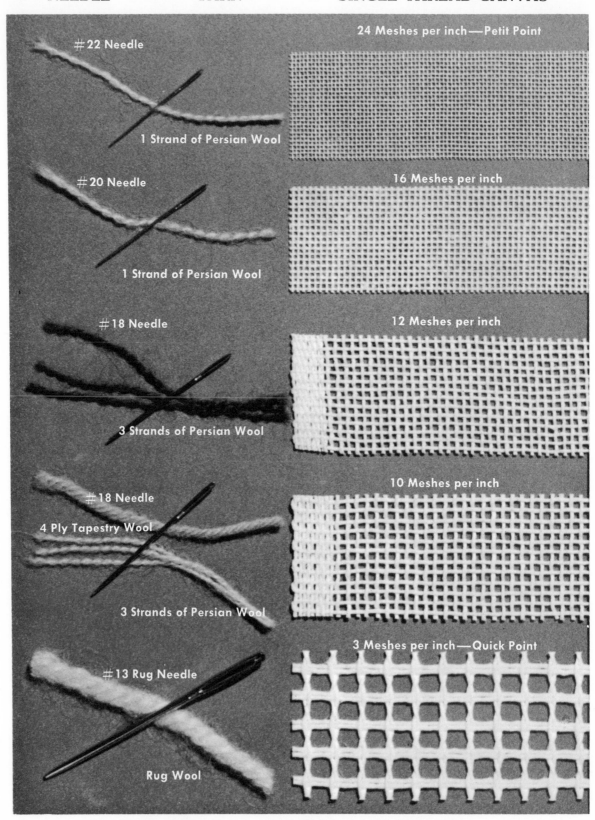

#22 Needle

1 Strand of Persian Wool

24 Meshes per inch—Petit Point

#20 Needle

1 Strand of Persian Wool

16 Meshes per inch

#18 Needle

3 Strands of Persian Wool

12 Meshes per inch

#18 Needle

4 Ply Tapestry Wool

3 Strands of Persian Wool

10 Meshes per inch

#13 Rug Needle

Rug Wool

3 Meshes per inch—Quick Point

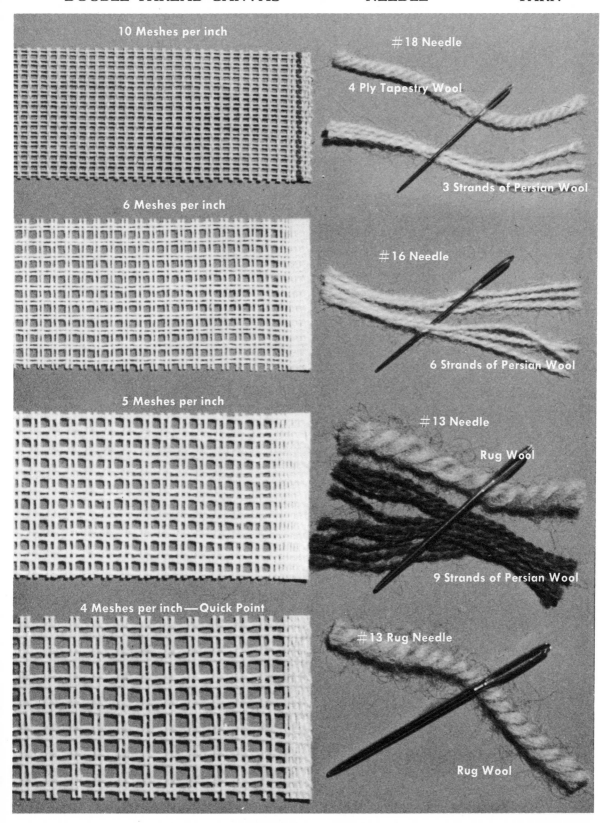

10 Meshes per inch

#18 Needle

4 Ply Tapestry Wool

3 Strands of Persian Wool

6 Meshes per inch

#16 Needle

6 Strands of Persian Wool

5 Meshes per inch

#13 Needle

Rug Wool

9 Strands of Persian Wool

4 Meshes per inch—Quick Point

#13 Rug Needle

Rug Wool

Yarn

NEEDLEPOINT YARN is made of long-fibered virgin wool which does not pill easily. It is fast dyed, mothproofed, and spun to last for years of service.

Although you may experiment with other wool yarns or with yarns made of mercerized cotton, nylon, and silk, for long wearing quality and best canvas coverage nothing is better than the wool yarns made especially for needlepoint.

Yarn Requirements

Consider the following points before you start calculating the amount of yarn needed.

1. Tension exerted while working the stitches.

When a person is tense or nervous very likely the needlepoint stitches will be tight and the yarn will not cover the canvas completely.

If you find this happening as you work, sit back and relax. Slip the tip of the needle under the tight stitches and fluff them lightly. As you continue your needlepoint try to keep both yourself and the stitches relaxed.

2. Size of canvas mesh determines the strands of yarn required.

3. Type and quality of yarn used.
  (a) Weight of yarn, if thick or thin.
  (b) Number of strands per length.
  (c) Yards to a skein or a pound.

Tapestry yarn is available in 40-yard skeins. Sometimes it can be found in 100-yard skeins.

Persian and *Penelope* yarns are usually sold by the pound but are sometimes available in 200-yard skeins.

4. Color of yarn selected.

Dyeing affects yarn's loftiness or covering quality. Darker shades often do not fill in as well as lighter colors. When this happens, pamper the darker yarn across the canvas by not pulling it too taut.

5. Size of design area has to be figured when determining yarn required for background area only. Usually a design covers about one quarter of the canvas.

Multiply the length by the width of the design to obtain the approximate area in square inches which the design covers. Subtract this figure from the number of square inches in the entire piece. See *Measuring* on page 24.

For example:

Canvas area is $14'' \times 16'' = 224$ sq. inches
Design area is $8'' \times 9\frac{1}{2}'' = 76$ sq. inches
Background area is $\qquad 148$ sq. inches

Many experienced sales people can measure yarn literally by sight. As such an expert person may not always be available, the basic formula that follows is recommended.

Basic formula for determining the quantity of yarn needed for a piece of needlepoint:

1. Number of strands in length of yarn.
2. Measure lengths or yards of yarn used when working 1-inch-square area of needlepoint stitches.

Strands of yarn 16 to 18 inches long are usually easiest to handle.

Multiply the number of canvas inches to be worked in a particular color by the number of lengths or yards of yarn used for 1 square inch.

Note: When you divide the strands for fine canvas you need less yarn and when you add a strand or two you need more yarn.

Persian or Penelope yarn (3 ply). The number of strands usually needed for a specific size canvas when using either of these yarns is shown below:

MESHES (PER INCH)	NUMBER OF STRANDS USED	NEEDLE SIZE
24 and 18	1 strand	23 or 24
14	2 strands	20
12	3 strands	21 or 22
10	3 strands	18

Tapestry yarn (4 ply) 40-yard skeins. When using this yarn on canvas with 10 meshes to the inch the amount needed varies with the stitch used.

Continental stitch averages 1¼ yards to the square inch. Multiply the total number of square inches by 1¼ and divide by 40 to get the number of skeins required.

For example:

To cover area—20″ × 20″ = 400 square inches
Multiply by   1¼ = 500 yards
Divide by 40 = 12½ skeins

Purchase a minimum of 14 skeins of the same dye lot. This allows for errors, loss of yarn, etc. If possible, store remaining yarn as shown on page 105, to have it readily available when required.

Half-cross stitch averages 1 yard to the square inch. Divide the total square inches to be covered by 40 for number of skeins needed.
    For example:

To cover area 20″ × 20″ = 400 sq. inches
Divide by 40 = 10 skeins

Purchase minimum of 12 skeins of same dye lot and store as described previously.

As each stitch requires more or less yarn the best method of determining the amount needed is to work 1 inch of each stitch and calculate as described in the Basic Formula. Always buy slightly more yarn than the amount figured. Store for future use.

Dye lot. The slightest variance in color will be noticeable on the surface of the finished work.

Make it a point to purchase at one time from the same dye lot all the yarn required to complete background area of any piece you work.

Background Color. Choose a background color that will allow the design to either dominate or recede. For best results, the background color should contrast with the outer edge of the worked design by being in a lighter or darker yarn to set off the design.

All beginners should practice about 1 inch of whichever stitch they plan to use, in order to get the feel of each stitch.

Work the stitches outside the outlined area, if there is enough space on the canvas. If the outline is close to the canvas edge, use a separate piece of canvas of exactly the same thread count.

Separating Strands of Yarn. The size of the canvas selected determines the number of strands used when working each needlepoint piece. See page 20. Persian (hairy) and Penelope (smooth) yarns have 3 strands (3 ply)

twisted loosely together. Tapestry yarn has 4 strands (4 ply) twisted tightly together.

Separate the number of strands required at one end of the yarn and hold with the fingers of one hand. Push the remaining strand or strands down until they are separated from the other strands as in diagram below.

Needles

HISTORY TELLS US that the metal needle came into use during the reign of Queen Elizabeth I, but the crude needles she used for her needlepoint cannot be compared with the finely crafted needles available today.

The needles used for needlepoint are sold in packages labeled "tapestry." These are special long-eyed needles, usually with a blunt point. However, the needles used for very fine petit point stiches often have more tapered points.

The inside area of the long eye is especially smooth so that yarn will not fray while in work. The extra length of the eye makes it easy to thread thick yarn, while the blunt needle point slides easily in and out of the canvas meshes. This point does not seem to catch in the stitches of a previous row as easily as the sharper pointed tip.

Measuring for Needlepoint

THE MEASUREMENTS NEEDED are determined by the object to be covered and the manner in which the piece will be finished.

Finishing can be done by

1. Pulling edge under or over to be tacked or glued.
2. Tacking and gluing flush with edge.
3. Tacking to edge with decorative tacks.
4. Taking seam allowance either by sewing or gluing for finishing accessory items.

Picture Frame—Turn frame to back; measure from top to bottom and from side to side. Place end of tape or ruler inside of frame where glass fits. Make paper pattern.

For *oval* or *round* frames take glass out of frame to use as a guide for making pattern. Lay glass over a piece of brown paper. Keep pencil perpendicular and draw around outside edge of glass. When cutting out paper pattern, cut about ⅛ inch inside pencil line.

Cushions

Knife edge. Measure across cushion from edge to edge and add seam allowance.

Box edge. Measure across cushion from edge to edge and add seam allowance. Then measure length and width of boxing, the narrow strip which joins the top and bottom of cushion.

These principles of measuring apply to any shape of cushion.

Furniture. Before measuring an upholstered seat on a chair, stool, etc., be sure that any repairs to springs or padding have been done beforehand.

Slip-seat. When measuring the type of seat which fits into the frame, remove the seat from the chair. Measure from back to front and from side to side. If seat is shaped, take two or more measurements each way as illustrated. Add ½ inch to 1 inch all around so that edge of needlepoint can be turned to underside and tacked. If seat is thick across front, mark for mitered corners as instructed below.

Seat with springs. To fit a pattern for a shaped seat as shown below, use a piece of muslin instead of brown paper because the

muslin can be fitted smoothly. Cut the muslin a little larger all around than the chair seat. With a soft pencil mark a center line on both the horizontal and vertical threads of the muslin. With chalk or pins mark the centers of the chair seat both horizontally and vertically. Lay muslin over chair seat, matching the exact centers where the lines cross. Match the lines in both directions, first placing a pin at back and front of seat, then at each side. Smooth muslin from center outward, placing pins about 2 inches apart on the vertical center line.

Make a slash in muslin at each back corner to enable you to work around uprights of chair back. Mark around back frame with a pencil. Carefully clip muslin at curves and turn edges under so that you can fit them around the frame more easily. Measure across back of chair to see that vertical line is centered.

Mitered corner. On front corners be sure the fold is straight up and down and turns toward side. Measure across front of chair to see that the vertical line is centered. Make any adjustment necessary for a smooth fit. Pencil mark around the lower edge of seat. Remove muslin from chair. With your tape measure check the size of the muslin pattern with the measurements of the chair—from front to back and from side to side. The muslin should be ad-

justed so that it is the same as the chair. Make the muslin symmetrical on both sides. Mark the corners carefully.

Because cloth can be pulled on the bias it is more satisfactory to use a paper pattern to lay on the canvas. The outline will be more accurate. Make a duplicate pattern on brown paper with the vertical and horizontal lines exactly the same as on the muslin. Cut the paper pattern on the finished edge, omitting the seam allowance, or turn under. Draw a broken line ½ inch below center horizontal line. (See below.) Draw an 8-inch circle in center of pattern as indicated. Use this as a guide for proper placing of design motif on chair seat. See *Marking Area to be Worked* on page 19. Mark horizontal and vertical lines through center of design motif. Pin paper pattern over canvas matching the two vertical lines and matching the *broken* horizontal line on the pattern to the horizontal basting on the canvas. In addition there should be at least ½-inch margin all around on the canvas for blocking and finishing. Use waterproof India ink or waterproof marker to outline the paper pattern on the canvas. The paper pattern can be used as a guide when blocking the needlepoint.

Handbags and Luggage. See page 115.

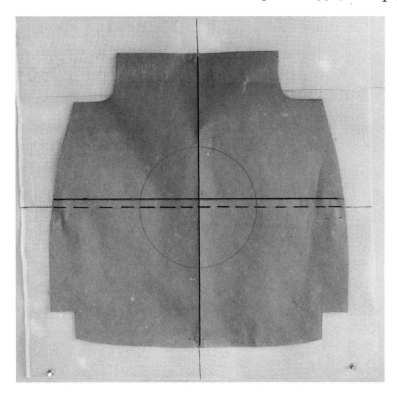

Materials for Needlepoint

Basic Essentials

Object to be made or covered.

Ruler—18-inch is practical. Yardstick is useful when making large patterns.

Nonstretch tape measure.

Paper for pattern—brown wrapping or heavy white bond.

Pencil—#2 or softer.

Waterproof India ink and fine brush.

Dry-marker pen—waterproof type. Test every marker you purchase on a sample of needlepoint canvas. Let dry thoroughly, then wet canvas to see if color bleeds.

Glue—quick-setting, clear-drying.

Canvas, yarn or floss.

Needles, thimble, scissors.

Container to store or carry needlepoint.

Optional
Frame for stretching canvas. Needle threader.

Essentials for Making Your Own Designs and Applying to Canvas

Graph paper—opaque and transparent, acetate film (available at artists' supply shops.)

Pencils and waterproof India ink.

Crayons, colored pencils and/or pastels in assorted colors.

Dry markers in assorted colors.

Oil paint in assorted colors, Japan thinner and/or turpentine, stiff brushes.

Optional
Reducing glass, magnifying glass, pantograph.

Essentials for Removing and Replacing Stitches

Small pointed scissors.

Tweezers.

Crochet hook.

Essentials for Blocking

Board—heavy plywood larger than canvas to be stretched (heavy enough not to warp).

Muslin to stretch over board.

Wrapping paper.

Pencil.

Rust-proof tacks.

Bowl for water and sponge.

Essentials for Mounting

Upholstering—

Object to be upholstered.

Rust-proof and/or decorative tacks.

Hammer.

Black cotton or nylon fabric for covering bottom of upholstered item.

Knowledge of upholstering.

Patience and great skill.

Unless you can do a professional-type job, have your needlepoint finished and mounted by an experienced person in this field.

Mounting Handbags or Luggage—Should be done only by professional bag makers.

Making Pillows

Forms in shape desired—square, round, triangle, bolster, etc. Stuffed or foam rubber.

Sewing machine, needle and thread.

Mounting Fashion Accessories and Other Small Items—Essential needs vary with the manner in which item is finished or mounted.

Sewing Essentials for Finishing Fashion Accessories and Other Small Items

Pins, needles, and thread.

Lining fabric or felt.

Steam iron, press cloth, brown paper.

Threading the Needle

Length of Yarn to Use in Needle. The proper length of yarn to use is optional with each individual. Experiment with various lengths to see how well the yarn covers an area of a particular piece. Use the length that fills in evenly and covers the canvas completely.

Experienced workers use the following as a guide in deciding the length of yarn to use:

Fine canvas—shortest length
Medium canvas—medium length
Heavy canvas—longest length

Hold the eye end of the needle between thumb, and third finger of right hand (left hand if left-handed).

A. Use the needle as a bridge by dropping 3 inches of yarn across it, and hold against needle with index finger.

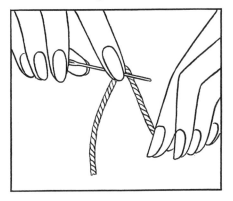

B. Make a small loop around needle by pinching the yarn tautly between thumb and forefinger of the opposite hand.

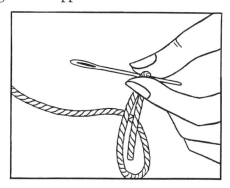

C. Withdraw the needle, keeping the yarn gripped firmly between your fingers, with the small loop just visible.

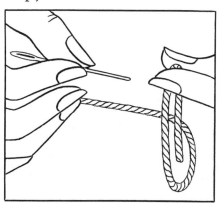

D. Set the eye of the needle over the small loop, and force the wool gently *up* through the eye, relaxing the pinch gradually.

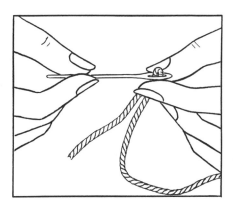

E. With the loop pull the doubled yarn through the eye of the needle. This method of threading is easy on the eyes, yarn, and disposition. It works every time.

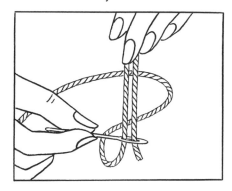

Paper Method of Threading. Use a narrow strip of paper (narrow enough to fit eye of needle) over the end of yarn when threading short ends into the needle.

See page 93 for illustrations and further details.

Note: Never work with more than 2 or 3 inches of yarn through the needle. Constant pulling of doubled-over yarn through canvas creates thin stitches in completed work.

When yarn twists while it is being worked, the tension can be relieved simply by dropping the threaded end of the yarn and letting it unwind by itself.

Starting and Ending a Strand of Yarn

THERE ARE A NUMBER OF WAYS to fasten a strand of yarn when doing needlepoint stitches.

Several factors determine which you use:
—the stitch you are doing.
—what you are making.
—how it will be used.
—which method you find best for you.

Running Stitches Outside Working Area. Two or three stitches are run in-and-out of the canvas meshes outside the outlined area to start each strand of yarn. End each row of stitches with the same number of running stitches.

This gives a smooth, unridged finish all around a piece of needlepoint and makes a good flat edge for mounting.

Most of the illustrations in the chapter on stitches show this method. See page 54.

Running Stitches Inside Working Area. Also called *worked-over end*. Run needle in-and-out of a few canvas meshes inside the outlined area so running stitches end with needle in position to start first needlepoint stitch.

Use this method when needlepoint is to be glued to an object. It is also used when developing designs which have motifs of the same color scattered over the canvas.

Waste Knot. So called because it is a temporary knot. It is cut off when no longer needed.

Knot end of yarn. On front of canvas, insert needle five to ten meshes from working corner. Where knot is placed depends on stitches being started.

Work over excess yarn on back as stitches fill the canvas. Cut knot off when the stitches on front reach it.

To see illustration of this knot refer to *Basket Weave Stitch* on page 56.

Starting and Ending at Various Points on Back of Canvas

A. When coming to the end of a strand of yarn draw needle through to underside. Turn canvas over and, working on wrong side, weave needle over-and-under every other stitch just completed, for about 1 inch to anchor end.

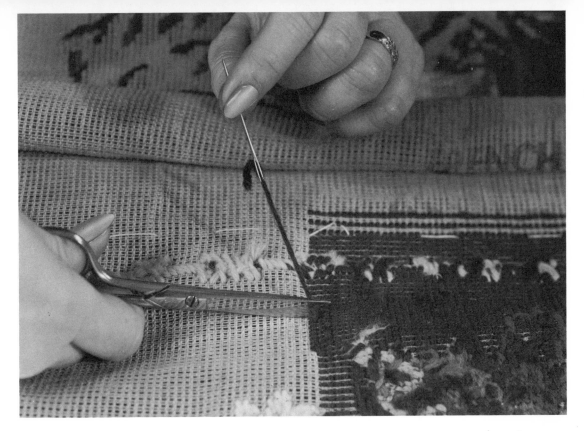

B. Clip yarn neatly on back to prevent yarn you are working with from becoming entangled.

C. Start opposite previous ending, and weave needle with new strand of yarn over-and-under every other stitch for about 1 inch.

Note: When working one way only across canvas and making a solid color background, it is advisable to vary the yarn lengths to avoid starting and ending in the same place. This can cause a ridge that is discernible from the right side.

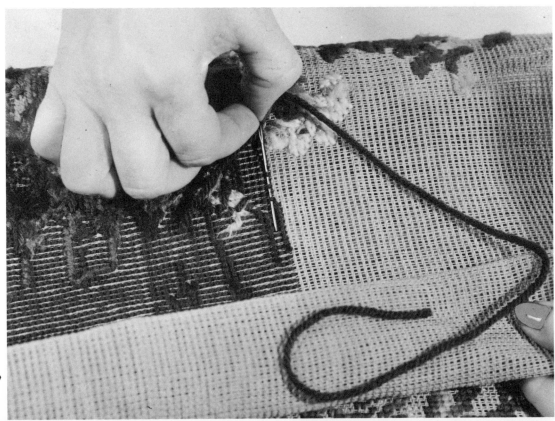

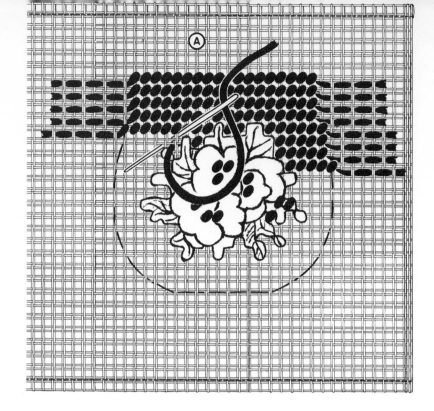

Filling in Around a Design

WHEN STARTING A BACKGROUND, most of us are prone to fill in the small areas in and around the design motif first, and then start the rows of stitches from the outside edge of the canvas.

Do not do this. You will enjoy filling in the background, and it will be less monotonous if you alternate between the long rows of stitches and the few stitches needed to fill in around the motif.

This can be done by starting at the corner of the outlined area (which corner depends on the stitch you are using for the background) and completing at least three rows of stitches. This procedure helps develop a

rhythm for the stitch being done.

Start another row of stitches and end the row while there is still enough yarn to complete a dozen or so stitches. Use the short needleful to fill in some areas around the design. This will give you a change of pace. Now, continue with a few rows of background stitches, using another short length to fill in a few more small areas.

Be sure the background stitches match the slant of the stitches in the design.

A illustrates how the continental stitch is used to fill in and around a design. It also shows that the stitches worked inside the design are made exactly the same as the others.

Gros Point Background Around Petit Point Design on Double-Thread Canvas

Many people prefer to accentuate a petit point design by working the background in and around the design with the larger continental stitch. The contrast between the size of the two stitches creates a three-dimensional appearance that enhances the beauty of the piece. See photograph **B**. Use the continental stitch around the petit point design as far as there are two canvas threads each way to allow for the larger stitch. Also use the continental stitch in the open areas of the design when possible.

Petit point is most painstaking and should be used to cover all single threads around the design. See page 23 for *Separating Yarn*.

For greater ease in working close to a petit point design, insert the needle one mesh to right in row above, over single thread; pull needle through to the wrong side; now bring point of needle up in mesh directly left of mesh where yarn is drawn to right side. This takes more time than a one-motion pull-through, but in small pieces around the design this is necessary as the petit point meshes are so small and close together.

Use continental stitches around a gros point design, making sure the background stitches slant in the same direction as those in the design.

C illustrates how the simplified half-cross stitch is used to fill in around a design. To fill the space below the design, work from the bottom up. When you reach the design, draw needle to the back and run it under threads of the design. Cut the yarn. To continue above the design, anchor your yarn under the design yarn—wrong side, of course. Continue working to top of canvas as in preceding rows. Begin again at the bottom and continue this row until you reach the design. End yarn as in previous row, then begin again at upper edge of design and work toward top of canvas as before. Continue with your needlepoint until all the marked area is completed.

If you are left-handed, see page 84.

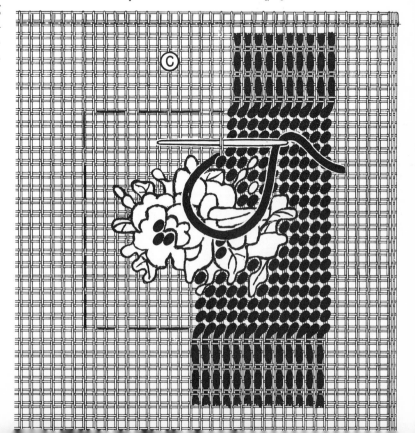

Holding Canvas in Work

THE PHOTOGRAPH SHOWS THE CANVAS rolled up from the bottom while the piece is being worked in the simplified half-cross. As the row of stitches goes above the center of the piece, roll the canvas *from the top down*. This keeps the canvas out of your way as you work, and the roll can be held easily in your free hand.

The direction in which a stitch is worked usually determines which edge of the canvas is rolled; down from the top, up from the bottom, or in from either side.

Roll edge under so the right side of the piece is always on the outside. Use a safety pin near each end to keep finished work rolled.

Protect Needlepoint from Soil While in Work. This is especially important if the background is a delicate color, or you are doing a design in pastels.

Use a lightweight hand towel or a piece of plastic to cover finished work as it is rolled.

Lay edge of covering an inch or so from working area, smoothing it over the area already finished. Roll the covering and canvas together, and pin ends of roll as described previously.

Out-of-Shape Needlepoint

Some stitches, such as the basket weave and simplified half-cross, seem to have less tendency than others to pull canvas out of shape while in work.

However, no matter how lopsided canvas becomes while working it, if the stitches are properly made, this crooked appearance will not affect the finished product.

The piece shown here is worked perfectly; each stitch has been set in place on the canvas with perfection, but it was worked in the continental stitch which tends to pull the canvas out of line. Blocking as shown on page 86 will rectify this condition promptly and restore the canvas and stitches to their proper angle.

Design and Color

In today's society self-expression is becoming increasingly important to the individual. Needlepoint is an art form ideally suited to creative self-expression.

A few years ago an American painter and designer, Natalie Hays Hammond, became interested in doing needlepoint. There are few people capable of following her method of doing canvas embroidery because the entire design has to be visualized, both in detail and color, before starting to work. Each picture, or panel, was worked directly on canvas without any preliminary drawing, either on paper or on canvas. Only by developing each idea directly on the canvas could this artist achieve the final desired result.

All her designs reflect Miss Hammond's interest in certain themes. Some of the groups of "variations on a theme" include symbols, animals in a farmyard, open and shut books, blueprints, and scenes of ancient ruins. One of her skyline designs is shown framed on the back end paper.

The continental stitch (gros point) was used exclusively, and each design has a contemporary feeling no matter what the subject.

Many factors determine the kind of art or design which you prefer. You will find innumerable books available on design and color which can be used for reference. Any period design or style can be translated into needlepoint, although some designs are easier to stitch than others. Each design is modified slightly because the stitches are made in square meshes on the canvas. See diagram on following page.

For those who prefer to purchase designs for working, we have outlined sources and available types on page 14. For those who would like to add a personal touch, but still would not like to make the entire design, we suggest adding a border (page 40) or a contrasting background (page 41).

Often a person may decide to make her own designs because she cannot find designs to suit her taste or needs. Design variations and how to start are outlined in this chapter.

Design

A GREAT DEGREE OF INDIVIDUALITY can be expressed through needlepoint because of the many avenues of approach open to you.

Rather than start from scratch, you may adapt an existing design to your own use in various ways. Use a single motif in a repeat design (see diagrams on page 37). Or form a section of a design into a new shape, or by just changing the color scheme get an entirely different design effect.

You can develop a design from any period in history, although your research will show that some periods are better documented than others. Consult your library and museum for information.

Use needlepoint to record an event, or to make a sampler, a prayer, or a motto. See page 125 for ideas.

Use nature as a souce of inspiration. Start with a photograph in color or black and white. It can be a landscape, seascape, floral bouquet, or a portrait of a person or an animal. Turn to page 116 to see how others have needlepointed a favorite view.

Purely imaginative or abstract designs can be drawn, from which color roughs can be made in a variety of art mediums. See page 38.

Greeting cards, calendars, magazines, china, antique prints, or tapestry and decorative fabrics are some of the things which can inspire needlepoint designs. Children's coloring books are a good source for simple designs that can easily be transferred to canvas.

Stencils can be used as the basis for developing design ideas. On page 136 we show how an alphabet stencil was used for initials.

The *cut paper method* is an ideal way for people who cannot draw to create designs. Simple shapes can be cut from paper and moved around to make designs either on a large sheet of paper and traced on the canvas to make a pattern, or the shapes can be traced directly on the canvas. A package of children's construction paper will provide enough material for many ideas plus the advantage of working out the design in color. See page 44 for suggestions on cutting.

The following design principles are the ones we consider to be most important to our subject.

Proportion and scale—the relation of the size of a design to the canvas area or object it is to decorate; also the relationship of one element of a design to other elements of the same design. Proportion and scale also apply to the relation of needlepoint to the size of a room in which you are planning to use it.

Balance and unity are achieved by placing all design elements so as to obtain a harmonious and pleasing whole. The distribution of color is an important factor in the balance and unity of a design.

Rhythm in a design suggests movement, and adds dimension by repeating shapes and/or colors in a pattern pleasing to the eye.

Symmetry refers to a pattern or design that is the same on both sides of a vertical center line. See top design on opposite page. Symmetry can also refer to a design that is the same on four corners. See border design on page 126.

Asymmetrical designs have different shapes on each side of the motif, but they will still be balanced by the grouping of the shapes and/or colors.

Graph Paper

A paper used by architects and graphic artists, it is printed with fine lines which form even squares. It can be bought from artists' and architects' supply stores, and it is available in single sheets, pads, and rolls. All types are made of an opaque paper, but sheets and pads are also available in a slightly transparent paper. They are made in the following sizes or scales:

$$4 \times 4 \text{ squares per inch}$$
$$5 \times 5 \text{ squares per inch}$$
$$8 \times 8 \text{ squares per inch}$$
$$10 \times 10 \text{ squares per inch}$$

Usually the small squares are marked off

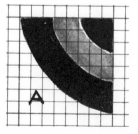
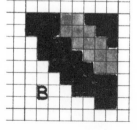

into 1-inch squares with a heavier line which makes it easier to count.

A. You can make a sketch of your design directly on the graph paper, or rough it out on tracing paper and then square it off on graph paper. **B** is squared off, and it helps you to see how curves and various shapes change as they are blocked in. (See opposite page.)

The paper with the larger squares (4 × 4 and 5 × 5) is good to use when planning a design for the heavier rug canvas. For medium- and small-scale designs use 8 × 8 and 10 × 10 in order to keep the design areas more compact.

Mylar or acetate film, printed in 1-inch squares divided into quarters like 4 × 4 graph paper, can be obtained with a blue, orange, or black grid. It comes in small sheets or by the yard.

The film is smooth on one side and textured on the other. The smooth side gives the film its transparency, and the textured side permits you to draw on it with a pencil when desired. Handle it in the same manner as described above for graph paper, or use it for tracing from original sources.

If you want to copy a piece of needlepoint without making a tracing, lay the film over the original, and tape it down with masking tape. The printed lines divide the design into squares which are easy to follow when transferring the design to canvas.

Protecting books, prints and other documents when tracing designs. If you use tracing paper to copy a printed design, there is a strong chance that you will damage the original with the pencil or pen point. To avoid this possibility use a piece of heavy, clear acetate under the tracing paper to prevent any impression from going through to the original.

Tapestry or Needlepoint. Canvas work was called "tapestry" originally because the early designs always produced an embroidery that looked like the woven tapestries. Many of the illustrations in the museum chapter beginning on page 183 shows the similarity of needlepoint panels to tapestry panels.

Rosetta Larson, the designer, updated wall panels in contemporary designs to be used as hangings in the same manner that antique tapestries were used. A beautiful example of

her work is illustrated on pages 116 and 117.

The chair above shows how individual motifs can be combined for a very decorative design. All the motifs were copied from an antique tapestry, reduced in size and simplified. The animals and birds are silhouettes. A minimum of detail was used in the flowers and mounted figures.

For the seat design, the motifs on one side were reversed and used on the opposite side with the exception of two motifs which can be seen near the back edge of the seat.

An antique tapestry was also the inspiration for the decorative chair covering of stylized floral motifs, below.

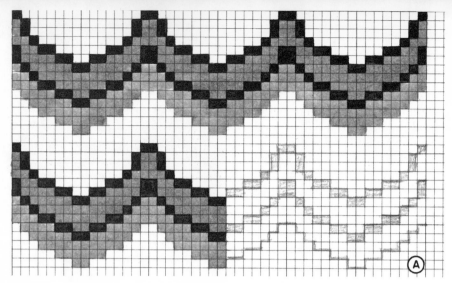

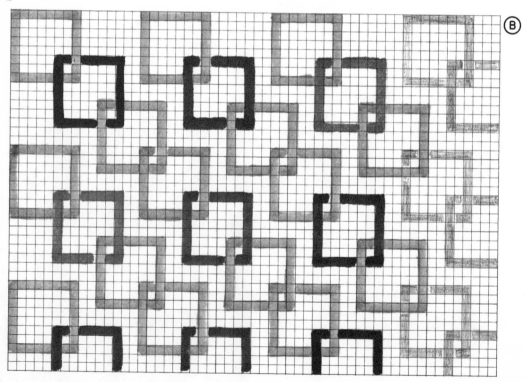

Repeat designs are those developed by repeating one or two motifs, or design units, in a regular sequence. This type of pattern is used for borders, stripes, geometric effects, and floral motifs in spaced allover designs.

Plan the design on graph paper so that it will fit the area to be worked. It is easier to change the spacing on paper than on canvas. However, if you are planning a random stripe, and it is not important where the color or pattern breaks, lay out the design directly on the canvas. "Random" can apply either to the width of the stripes or how the color is repeated or both.

Geometrics, stylized florals, and other simple motifs usually develop into repeat designs. These allow great freedom of expression and application. Often the same design can be used for either a large or small item just by using a coarser or finer canvas and yarn.

Use bold motifs for large-mesh canvas. The 10 mesh to the inch canvas can be used for many items while the fine petit point canvas is used for delicate designs and small items.

A shows a horizontal stripe design worked on graph paper, showing both color and stitch repeat.

B shows a square or block motif used in an endless chain. This is an example of design that can be developed in a wide variety of effects depending on how the color or colors are distributed.

Allover designs can be handled in three ways:

C. "One-way" means that the motifs are evenly spaced with "heads up." All motifs run in the same direction.

D. Up-and-down patterns alternate the top and bottom of a motif across the design.

E. Scattered patterns repeat the same motifs, but over a wider area than the patterns described above. The numbers in the diagram indicate where the same motif is repeated in exactly the same position. The broken outline shows a blocked-in area with motif (1) repeated at about the same distance from the four corners.

To cover a larger area with the same size motif repeat the various motifs on the sides for added width, and on the top and bottom for added length. The uneven shadows indicate where the motifs were added to both sides.

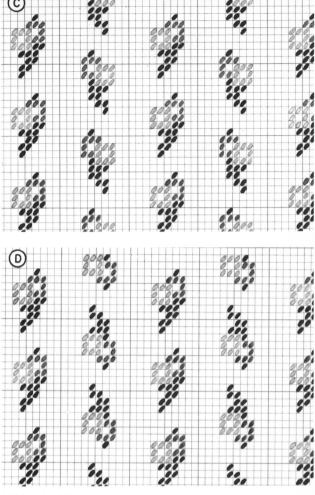

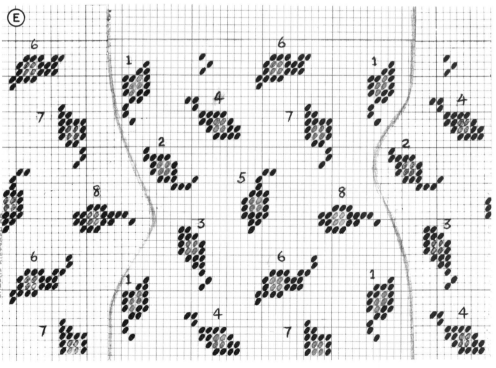

A

Design Variations

Design Variations of the Same Subject. Almost any subject or idea can be developed into a design to suit your taste. Most of us have a tendency to visualize certain subjects in one style or pattern, but many subjects which might seem "old hat" can be developed into a design with a contemporary feeling. The illus-trations on these two pages show variations of one subject.

The Lion and the Lamb. Isaiah's Old Testament prophecy has been interpreted in many ways by artists throughout the centuries past. The 19th-century American painter, Edward

B

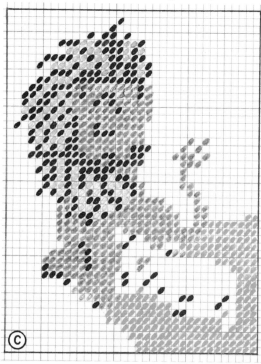

C

Hicks, painted about a hundred versions of "The Peaceable Kingdom" which included the lion and the lamb, among many animals.

Here we show a few versions of the subject to aid you in visualizing how to interpret a theme of your own choice.

A shows a sketch of the subject before it is transferred to canvas. It is a good example of a simplified design for needlepoint. The lion's mane is stylized, and the rest of the body acts as a background for the white lamb. This sketch can be developed in greater detail, depending on the final size, and the color will add dimension and interest to the design.

B shows a drawing that was used for a Christmas card. **C** shows this grouping squared off on graph paper as an example of how much it has to be modified to be usable on canvas. If this design were to be used larger, more detail could be added which would help the shading,

especially in the lamb. A curly effect similar to the first illustration could be used here.

In **D** the lamb has a smooth outline, but its wooly coat is given detail by using shades of gray or pale yellow inside the outline.

E shows a type of detail in the lion's head that could be used in any of the other designs shown.

Making Duplicate Designs. Duplication of a design usually occurs in making patriotic or national organization emblems—Republican, Democratic, Masonic, Shriner, Girl Scout, and many others.

If you need to repeat a subject and are allowed some freedom in reproducing the design, try to find a variation as shown with the two eagles below. Each of these designs could be framed or used in other ways.

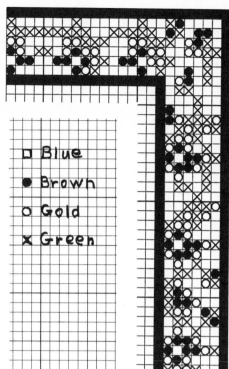

□ Blue
● Brown
○ Gold
x Green

Border Designs. A variety of effects can be obtained, depending on the type of border used.

You can frame the design by using several rows of stitches around the outside edge in a color that contrasts with the background. Dimension can also be added by using a stitch that contrasts with the background stitch.

Above left: A narrow, geometrical border within the background area is the same on the top and bottom edges. However, the sides, which match, are a slightly different repeat.

Above right: A section of a four-color border laid out on graph paper with a color chart. This border is shown complete on page 126.

Below: A border of scroll motifs adds flair to a

floral design. A two-toned effect can be obtained by using a darker color for the background outside the scroll than you use inside. See the bench at top of page 96.

Below right: Featherlike scrolls make a 2-inch

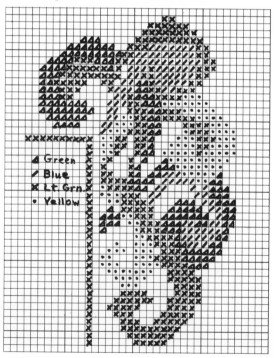

▲ Green
╱ Blue
x Lt Grn.
• Yellow

40

border. This style of design could be used to border an otherwise plain cushion. Enlarged greatly, it would make an effective rug design.

Except for the simplest designs, it saves time to lay out all borders on graph paper before starting to work on canvas.

Below left: When planning to use any diagonal border effects, always plot the corners on graph paper because the opposite corners always vary in some way.

Background Design. Photograph below shows how interest and dimension can be added to a single motif by making a patterned background instead of filling in with a single color. The checkerboard background was added because after the floral motif had been finished, it looked too delicate for the cushion for which it was intended.

This type of pattern is planned and blocked-in like any other design except for one difference: the background has to be worked around the motif.

Start by tracing the outline of the motif and the outside outline, or edge of the finished item. For a pattern similar to the checkerboard, both side edges should be divided identically; the top and bottom edges should be divided in the same manner.

The design chart below shows how the background can be divided more casually for an irregular, striped effect. Use the darkest color across the center area, and graduate the lightest colors toward the top and the bottom.

A diagonally striped background can be made by using the diagonal stitch in two or three tones of the same color. See page 67.

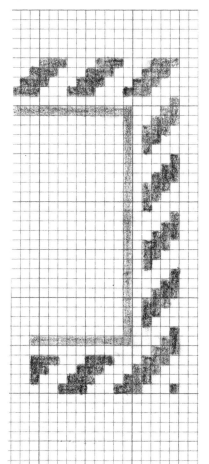

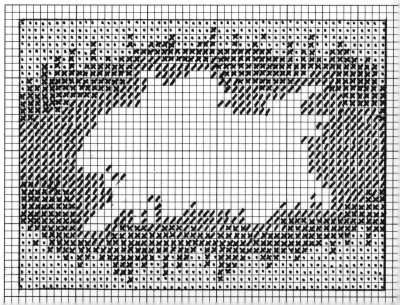

The Nude Human Figure is not easy to use in needlepoint because of the lack of fluidity in canvas stitches. When the figure is clothed, it is easier to illustrate because angular lines and draping effects can be used.

The needlepoint of the statue of David is shown actual size in the photograph, above left. The finely modeled nude figure and the arched dome are composed almost completely of curves. Only by using the finest canvas and the tiniest stitches is it possible to reproduce such a theme in needlepoint. A person having the combined skills of an artist and a master craftsman would be the only one able to do such a fine piece of needlepoint. It would be hard to find an antique needlepoint piece that could match this one in workmanship.

"Four Seasons" is a wall hanging with four figures that are impressionistic in style. In other chapters of this book you will find various approaches to the handling of figures in needlepoint.

Silhouette profiles or figure outlines are a simplified way to handle human subjects on canvas.

To make a silhouette tack a piece of paper against a door or wall. Have a person stand at a distance from the paper with a very strong light behind him. Adjust the light so that his shadow falls on the paper. Move the person and the light back and forth until you have the size and detail you want.

If you portray the head only, more detail can be shown than if you were to do the entire figure. It is important to add interest to the silhouetted figure by showing motion or action. A seated figure is best in profile, with the feet, hands, and arms placed in interesting positions. Figures shown full length can be standing with legs apart, jumping, dancing, or jogging. Because a design such as this is made in flat tones, the outlines can be exaggerated.

Reducing or Enlarging a Design

Photostats. The easiest and quickest way to have a motif or design made to the desired size. The cost depends on the amount of reduction or enlargement required. Check the Yellow Pages of your phone book to see if this service is available in your community.

Squaring a Design. Trace the design on transparent graph paper or on plain tracing paper. Draw an outline (square or oblong) on the outside of the design so that all details are inside the box. If tracing paper is used, divide the outline box into equal squares. The size of the squares depends on the size of the design. Use ¼- or ½-inch squares for a small design; use ¾- or 1-inch squares for a medium size and for most general use. Larger squares can be used for very large designs.

On another piece of graph paper or tracing paper, outline the area of the new size desired. Then divide the new area into the same number of squares as the original. If the new size is larger, the new squares will be proportion-

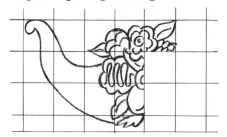

ately larger; if the new size is smaller, the squares will be proportionately smaller. Transfer the design inside each original square to the corresponding square of the new size.

Pantograph. This is a practical tool to have on hand, especially for those who plan to do many of their own designs. Instructions are included with the instrument, showing how to use it for reducing, enlarging, or making same size copies of drawings, photographs, etc. It consists of a tracer point, **A,** placed over the original art or photograph which follows the outline while you move a lead pencil, and **B** at another point to make an outline on paper of the drawing in the new size.

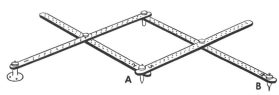

The cost of a pantograph depends on its size and the material of which it is made (wood, metal, or plastic).

Graph Paper. Any design can be reduced or enlarged by using the various sizes of graph paper available. **A** shows a motif outlined on 10×10 paper; **B** shows a reduced version made by dividing each square of a 4×4 paper into thirds so that there are 12 stitches to the inch; **C** shows an enlargement of the same motif made by counting out the same number of squares on 8×8 paper.

If you have a petit point design which you would like to work on larger canvas, trace the design on transparent graph paper having small squares. Count the number of stitches on the crosswise and lengthwise edges, and mark them off on graph paper having larger squares. This shows what the new size will be and which canvas can be used for it. See canvas comparisons on page 20.

After you have roughed out the general outlines of the design, you can use symbols and/or colors to indicate the color breakdown. Use the chart on page 49 as a guide.

Transfer Design Direct to Canvas. The principle above also can be used to transfer a design from one size of canvas to another by counting the stitches and canvas threads as you work. Use this method for simple designs only, unless you are an experienced needlepointer and have tried other methods.

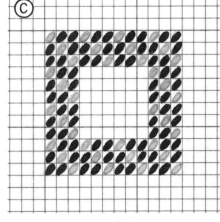

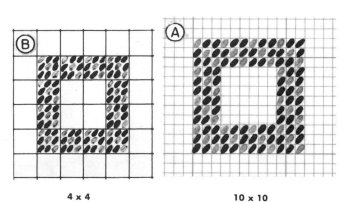

4 x 4   10 x 10   8 x 8

43

Transferring Design to Canvas

IN THE PRECEDING CHAPTER are listed the equipment and materials needed for needlepoint. Again, we wish to stress the importance of using waterproof India ink, dry markers, and oil paints because, when the canvas is blocked, it has to be dampened or made very wet. If the materials used to transfer or outline designs are not colorfast, they will bleed into the wool yarn.

Reversing a Design. Make a tracing of the design then turn face down over paper or canvas, and go over the outline from the wrong side of the tracing paper.

Carbon paper. Use a nonsmudging carbon such as dressmaker's carbon. Lay canvas on a flat, smooth surface. Keeping the threads straight, use masking tape to hold canvas in position. Lay designs right side up over the canvas, center lines matching. Tape top corners, and insert carbon paper face down between the design and the canvas. Smooth carefully, and tape the other corners so that there is no shifting while you work. Use a medium-hard pencil to trace over the design. After the carbon and design are removed, go over the outline on the canvas with ink or paint to make the outlines clearer.

Stencils. Ready-made stencils can be used directly on canvas. These are usually simple motifs or letters and numerals. After you have determined the position of the design, the stencil can be laid directly on the canvas, and the outline made or the motif filled in.

Cut-paper. Simple shapes can be cut out of newspaper or construction paper. Motifs can be cut from children's coloring books, greeting cards, or similar sources. Paper, folded so as to give multiple layers, can be used for cutting several petals, leaves, etc. in one operation.

Templates are master patterns or stencils used for making uniform outlines on canvas to an exact size when a large number of cushions are to be made. See kneelers in *Devotionals*, beginning on page 141. Draw an accurate outline on stiff, heavy paper or cardboard. Cut away the inside area; the framelike pattern which remains is used as a guide for developing designs and marking the correct outlines.

Drawing on the canvas can be done by tracing over the design or drawing directly on the canvas. Lay the design (drawn on either graph paper or tracing paper) face up on a light-table or against the glass of a window facing the sunlight. Tape in place with masking tape. Place canvas over the design, matching the center lines and the outline of the design. Tape canvas so that it is flat and smooth.

With a medium-hard pencil trace all main outlines of the design; then put in whatever details you need. If you prefer, trace only the main outlines, then remove the canvas and design from the glass, and draw in the details freehand.

After the outlines have been perfected, go over the pencil lines with a fine brush and India ink, or oil color, or use a fine dry marker. Add the color detail as you prefer.

Slides can be projected onto a large sheet of paper taped to a wall. Outline the main details in pencil on the paper. This is an excellent way to enlarge a scene which is to be transferred to canvas. See the example on page 118.

Centering a Design. On page 19 we show how to center a finished motif. This same principle applies to all designs. In most cases the optical center is halfway from side edge to side edge, and is approximately ½ inch to 1 inch above the center from top to bottom. The exceptions are those items which may be viewed from four sides, such as benches and stools.

Most allover or repeat designs have to be centered in order to look well balanced.

Plain or Fancy Stitches?

The beginner should resist the temptation to use a variety of stitches in a single piece even though she is an experienced embroiderer. For example, in crewel embroidery most of the stitches are surface decoration while in needlepoint the yarn is worked into the canvas, which makes it look more like fabric.

Detailed motifs usually look best when done in the simple or plain stitches.

Bold or flat designs can be done in fancy stitches. The more elaborate stitches add dimension and texture interest to the surface.

When using a variety of stitches for a single design, it is helpful to make a pencil or crayon rough indicating the stitches. In this way you can see the relationship between the angles of the stitches before starting to work. On page 46, combining of some stitches is outlined.

A design or motif can be done in a simple stitch; then a fancy stitch can be used for the background. The reverse is also true; a motif developed in several fancy stitches will contrast well with a plain stitch background. The kneelers shown on page 145 were handled in this way.

Stripes. Some stitches automatically make stripes, but you should plan the number of stitch rows for each color. The diagonal stitch is always on the bias; the bargello is usually done in peaks of various heights, and the chevron is a horizontal, zigzag stitch.

Children will enjoy doing the diagonal stitch because it works up quickly. They can even start drawing on graph paper by indicating the color stripes, and then follow the graph as they work on the canvas. See the stripe variations on page 67.

Coloring or Painting a Design

AFTER THE DESIGN OUTLINE has been transferred to canvas, color can be added by one of the following methods. (If you plan to follow a design chart, see instructions on page 50.)

Wax Crayons. Simple designs and bold effects can be colored with wax crayons or pencils. The colors are set on the canvas by going over the colors with a dry iron, using light pressure.

Oil paint should be used when very fine detail has to be shown, or when a wide range of color is needed. It can be used on all canvas, but the paint must be thinned so that it will not clog the meshes.

Turpentine and/or Japan drier can be used as a thinner. If turpentine alone is used, the canvas will take at least forty-eight hours to dry.

Japan drier darkens the color slightly, but when a small amount is used with the oil paint, the canvas will dry in twenty-four hours or less.

Try thinning the oil color with a little of both drying agents to get a drying time between the two mentioned above. Test the paint combinations on canvas scraps until you find the one you prefer.

Use stiff brushes so that the thinned paint coats the top surface only and does not go through to the underside. Use a fine brush for detail and a slightly wider brush for filling in larger areas.

Never start to do the stitches until you are sure that the canvas is completely dry.

Dry markers are practical to use on canvas because they dry instantly, but you may find that their color range is too limited for your needs. Your primary concern when you buy dry markers is that they are waterproof. Test each type of marker by using it on a scrap of canvas. Let ink dry, then wet the canvas thoroughly. After it has dried completely, check the canvas scrap carefully to see if the marker color has run.

If you like working with markers, keep two types on hand—the pencil or pen type for fine work and the larger type for filling in flat areas.

Tramé can be used instead of oil paint or dry markers to show the areas of color with the colored yarn itself on Penelope or double-thread canvas.

Outline the design with pencil on the canvas, then fill in with the correct colored yarn, using the tramé stitch as instructed on page 72. Alternate the rows of these underlay stitches so that when the final stitches are worked, ridges do not show on the surface of the needlepoint.

design) are worked first because they are the focal points and are most important; then the background is filled in.

In instances where the motifs are outlined it may be best to work the outlines first, and then fill in the details of the motifs.

Undefined Areas. When a design has color areas that are not sharply defined, the approach used will vary with the design. The steps followed in the making of one such design are described below.

Working a Design with an Indefinite Outline. The design for the jacket of this book was inspired by a color photograph of the interior of a cave showing stalagmite and stalactite formations.

Top: The original drawing was done with pastels, a good medium to use when the colors blend together and have indefinite shapes without sharp outlines.

Transfer the outline to canvas with pencil, then use dry markers for colors. Apply colors lightly for this type of design because, as you work, the various stitches may overlap the color outline.

Working a Design

You can start to work a needlepoint design in several ways, depending on how the design is laid out and what stitch or stitches you plan to use.

The principal motif or motifs (scattered

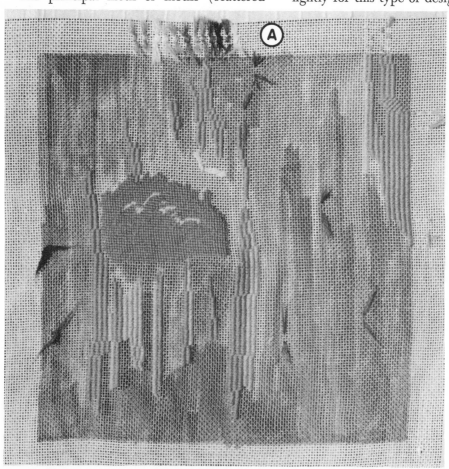

Bottom—opposite page: Petit point stitches were used for the oval shape centered just to the left of the vertical center. Although this is the focal point of the design, the shape could not be completely filled in until the points overlapping the bottom and left edges were worked in the elongated half-cross.

Bottom: All the elongated half-cross stitches were worked next because they covered so much of the canvas. The brick stitch, which gives texture contrast above the petit point stitches, was done next. The encroaching Gobelin stitch gives good vertical accents because the greens blend together. A few petit point stitches were used at those points of the design which needed a very fine highlight of white.

The *top right* picture shows the back of needlepoint. When working this type of design, finish off the ends of the yarn by running the needle under stitches on the back of the area just completed. This method makes it easier to remove stitches if you have to correct a mistake or change a stitch or two. Cut end of yarn close to the back of canvas so it won't be caught into another color as you work.

Yarn Samples as a Color Guide. In photograph (**A**) short lengths of the yarn colors are tied to the canvas across the top edge. Strands of wool can also be tied at various points of the design if it helps you to visualize the distribution of the wool colors.

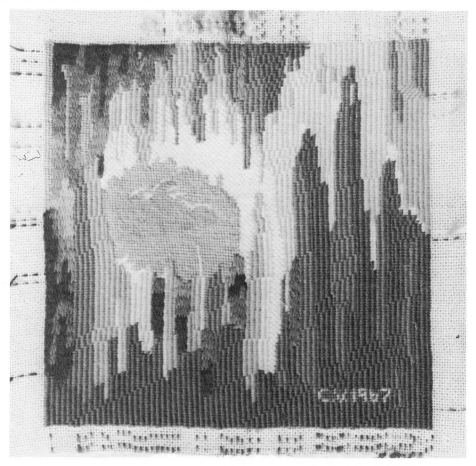

Design Chart

THIS TYPE OF CHART can be purchased, or you can develop your own design in this technique.

The color key shows that there are thirteen colors, each represented by a different symbol. Use these symbols as a guide to marking your own design chart.

Lay the design chart under tracing paper or transparent graph paper, and make a rough color layout by blocking in the largest areas of color. This will help you to visualize where the colors will be when you are working on the canvas. Use colored pencils or magic markers.

Chart on opposite page has 64 stitches across and 132 stitches down. If you use #12 single-mesh canvas to make this design, make a pencil outline 5½ inches wide and 11 inches long. Then count the canvas meshes across the top edge and down one side edge to see that the mesh count is the same as the stitch count on the chart.

As you count the meshes, mark off every 12 threads outside of the pencil outline. This will correspond with the small lines outside of the design area. With a pencil follow a thread across the canvas at each of these points. Lay a ruler across the design chart at these points to help you to see where the colors change.

After checking the size of the outline, check the placement of the outline on the canvas. Make sure that it is centered and that there is at least a 2-inch margin on all four edges. Mark the vertical and horizontal centers of the design area, making a line of basting stitches in both directions.

Starting to Work the Design. The Madonna and Child was worked in the continental stitch on single-mesh canvas. The focal point of this design are the figures of the Madonna and Child, and all other details are considered as background.

If this is the first time you have followed a design chart, we recommend that you start to work on the canvas by filling in the figures first. After this area is filled in, it will be much easier to do the background details. Refer to page 28 for instructions on starting and ending a length of yarn.

Madonna blue is the color which covers the largest area in this design, but because the figures are outlined in black and the blue robe is broken into folds by black lines, it will be easier to do the black yarn stitches around and in the figures of the Madonna and Child. Then fill in the blue and the red robe colors, followed by the facial features, brown hair, and the white. Follow this by doing the black outlines in the background, and then fill in the rest of the colors.

If you are experienced at following a design chart, you probably have developed your own routine. There is no reason to change your way of working unless the above suggestion seems easier to do.

Metallic thread. We mention this here because it could be used on the foregoing design in the halos, which are worked in gold-colored wool. If you would like to add a metallic quality here, work some gold metallic thread over the wool stitches.

On finer canvas a gold silk or cotton thread can be used as an underlay for gold metallic thread.

If you wish to use silver metallic thread, work it over white for a polished effect.

Details Added with Cotton or Silk Thread

Sometimes there are details in a design that are not sufficiently prominent. Details can be lost to view when wool colors are very close in color value. The same thing can happen when the overall design is either bold in concept or compact in space. In either case, after the design is completely worked in wool, the extra-fine details are embroidered over the wool with strands of silk or cotton thread, usually with a backstitch. The antique guns and clock on pages 172 and 173 are two examples of this embroidered detail.

Outlining. There are times when the colors to be used for the motif and the colors for the background blend so closely that it is hard to distinguish the design. An outline can be used to separate the colors or to add depth to the design. The colors generally used for outlining are black, brown, white, or beige.

On page 146 the Ark screen shows outlining used to give uniformity to all the motifs.

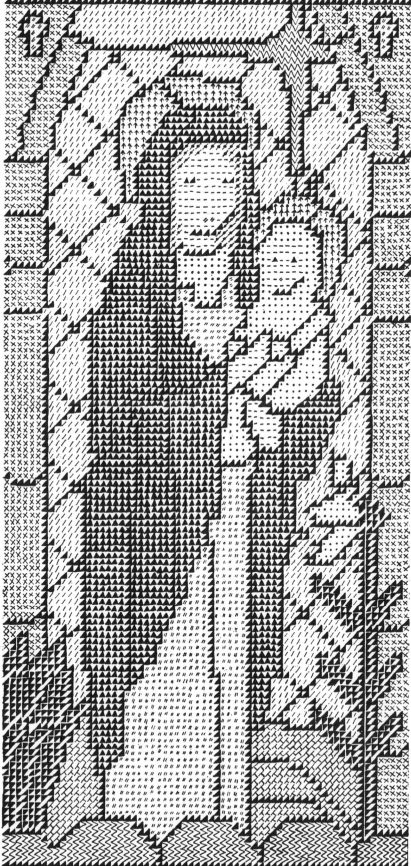

Colour Key

Colour	
Black	◩
White	⊡
Sky Blue,	◪
Halo Gold,	⬆
Leaf Green,	◪
Stone Grey,	⊠
Madonna Blue	⬓
Field Green,	◩
Straw,	▷
Star Yellow,	⋁
Robe Red,	⫽
Hair Brown,	◪
Flesh	⊟

Color

Our world would be extremely drab and uninteresting if everything around us were in neutrals such as grays or beiges.

Who has not experienced a lift in spirit on viewing a field of wild flowers with a backdrop of green trees, or a snow-capped peak against a blue sky?

The colorful poster beckons us to travel, and the magazine photograph frequently serves as the inspiration to sew or to cook.

In the past, most needlepoint was regarded as sedate embroidery, mostly because of lackluster color combinations. Happily, this is no longer true. Zingy colors are now available in a wide range of wool yarns.

Color exerts a powerful influence on our lives even though we may not consciously be aware of it. We can only cover a few aspects of this most complex subject.

Primary colors, yellow, red, and blue, are the basic colors; they are the source of all other colors. Oil paints and dry markers are available in sets of assorted colors. You can start with a basic assortment (twelve colors), and add any additional colors you may need as you do more and more of your own designs.

Secondary colors are the three colors between the three primary colors—violet, orange, and green. The arrows on the color circle indicate which two primary colors are mixed together to make one of the secondary colors.

Intermediate colors are colors that come between each of the primary and secondary colors. The name indicates how the two colors are combined. Violety red contains more red than violet; red violet is evenly divided, and reddish violet contains more violet than red.

Complementary colors refer to any two colors which together combine all the primary colors. Blue and yellow together make green; green's complementary color is red (directly opposite on the color wheel). The arrows indicate the other complementary colors.

Although complementary colors harmonize well, they tend to be very sharp in their pure form. Usually a tint or shade of the complementary color is used with the primary color for a more pleasing effect.

When you want to use your favorite color in its brightest, purest form, plan a complementary color combination.

Tone is a term used interchangeably with other color terms, loosely referring to the qualities of color. For example, one hears of a deep tone or a light tone, a bright tone or a dark tone, a monotone or a grayed tone.

Hue is the quality that distinguishes one color from another, and gives the color its name. Red and purple are different in hue, but they both may have the same value. Red remains the name of the hue whether it is light, dark, or grayed.

Primary Colors

RED

BLUE

YELLOW

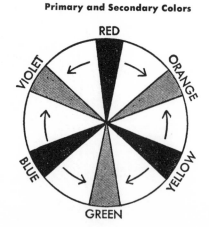

Primary and Secondary Colors

RED

VIOLET

ORANGE

BLUE

YELLOW

GREEN

Value refers to the lightness or darkness of a color. The lighter the color, the higher is its value. The term "value" has nothing to do with the intensity of a color, but refers solely to the gradations between the extremes of light and dark.

Tints are produced by adding white to a color thereby making it lighter. **Shades** are exactly the opposite; black is added to make a color darker.

Pastels are colors high in value, obtained by adding white. They are also called tints, pale colors, or delicate colors.

Warm and Cool Colors. Red, orange, and yellow are warm; green, blue, and violet are cool. The warm colors are known as advancing colors; the cool colors are called receding colors.

Grayed colors are obtained by adding a touch of their complementary colors in proportion to the extent to which you wish to subdue them.

Monotone refers to a color scheme done in various shades and tints of a single color.

You can gain experience in handling shading effects by working a design in four or five tones of one color, such as light blue, medium blue, royal blue, and very dark blue. Do not be subtle when using two or more values of a color. There should be definite contrast or the ombré will be difficult to distinguish.

Bright colors look darker when they are worked into the canvas.

Dark shades in large areas have a tendency to pick up dust, which makes them look gray. **Lighter shades** do not have this fault.

A **color family** refers to related colors such as real or true red, blue-red or red-violet, orange-red, and grayed red. It also includes tints and shades of these colors.

Natural colors include earth color, grass, trees, flowers, sky, and sea. Frequently we visualize a color differently than it is because there is such a great variation of color in nature.

Background colors are usually selected in values which allow the design to dominate or recede, depending on the effect desired. Use a background color that contrasts with the outer edge of the motif. It should be either lighter or darker to set off the design. The exception occurs when the motifs are outlined. See *Outlining* on page 48.

For several decades after Queen Victoria's bereavement, a black background was considered the proper one for most needlepoint. This can be seen when examining many of the pieces in museum exhibits. Black is still used, but as a part of strikingly modern designs.

Today, both light-colored and brilliant-colored backgrounds are favored for home decorating. The choice depends on personal preference. Off-white and any of the pale tints

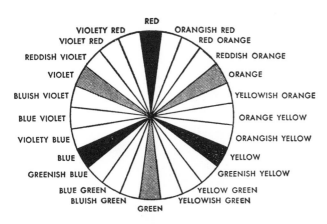

Intermediate Colors

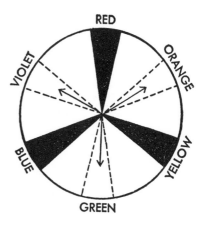

Complementary Colors

have an air of femininity; bold-colored backgrounds can be used for more contemporary settings.

When you are planning a color combination, take into consideration the fact that colors definitely affect one another. A color may make the adjoining color more vivid or it may subdue it. A motif composed of light colors will look lighter against a dark color than against a white background.

Lighting conditions also affect the appearance of a needlepoint design. Wool yarn absorbs the light because of its soft texture. We have stressed the need for evenness of workmanship because any variation in tension will be seen in the finished piece of needlepoint.

Color and Period Furniture. For various periods you will find the photograph and print collections of museums to be invaluable. Study pictures of furniture of the period in which you are interested; they illustrate the type of design and color combinations suited to a particular era.

Interior Design. When making a design for a room in your home, select yarn colors that will complement the color scheme. Needlepoint should be distinctive, but it should still fit its setting.

Dining chair seats can have the same design with a different color background for each, or each chair can have a different design, but with the backgrounds made of the same color.

Gifts. Always consider the color preference of the recipient when planning a gift of needlepoint.

Color Cards. Yarn color cards can be seen wherever needlepoint supplies are sold. If a specific color is not on hand, it can often be specially ordered for you.

A color card of any type (paints, decorative fabrics, plastics) can be helpful when you are developing a design at home. Many color cards are available in shops upon request; many can be obtained from manufacturers upon written request. See offers of color cards in home decorating magazines.

Dyeing Wool. There are people who like to do everything from scratch! If you would like to dye your own wool yarn, see page 206 for a supplier of the necessary materials.

Color Chart—Front End Paper

Penelope wool was used to make the color bands on single-thread canvas.

Left-hand side: Each color band shows a tint, the pure color, and a shade. The three wide bands to the left are the three primary colors. The wide bands to the right are the secondary colors, and the narrow bands in between are intermediate colors.

Right-hand side: *Top row*—A cool color family of five blues; a warm color family of five reds. *Second row*—Five brilliant colors and five pastels. *Third row*—A range of neutral browns and grays. The blocks were made just to show various color effects.

Canvas Stitches

DON'T BE CONFUSED by the number of needlepoint stitches shown on the following pages. As a matter of fact there are many other stitches which can be done, but we have concentrated on those which are basic and can be used and combined for almost any effect you want.

Some people enjoy using only two or three stitches for their projects, while others may combine many different stitches in one piece for a change of pace.

Some needlepoint stitches have contradictory names. This is understandable when you consider the various sources from which needlepoint has developed. Stitch names have also been influenced by names used in other forms of needlework. The cross-stitch in linen embroidery is made in the same way as the cross-stitch in needlepoint. Needlepoint is canvas embroidery, so the stitches used on canvas can also be called canvas stitches.

If you are to enjoy this craft, it is essential to be able to do the basic stitches well. These include the continental, bargello or flame, half-cross, and basket weave, and we urge you to try each stitch, step by step, as presented in this chapter, even those of you who are already familiar with some of these stitches. It is possible that you may find a quicker, easier way to do a stitch which you have used previously.

Mark a small area (like the ones shown in the following diagrams) on a piece of canvas and practice the individual stitches. It will help you to decide which stitches will be most enjoyable to do.

Please note: The instructions on the twenty-one pages which follow are for right-handed needleworkers. If you are left-handed, see page 77.

Continental Stitch

MANY NEEDLEPOINTERS PREFER THIS STITCH. It is considered one of the best stitches for developing design areas, as well as for filling in backgrounds. It can be used on both single- and double-thread canvas. Always work from right to left. To start and end a stitch use the method you prefer. See instructions for starting and ending on page 28. All the stitch illustrations show the running stitch outside of the outlined area.

Double-thread canvas. Work through large meshes, over double threads as illustrated below on left. *Single-thread canvas* is shown on right.

The illustration below shows the top crosswise edge turned under and hemmed by machine. The basting stitches show the "outlined area." When working on single-thread canvas it is easier to indicate the outlined area with pencil or ink rather than thread. See page 61.

1st Row—Start on front of canvas at the upper right corner, outside the outlined area, with running stitches. See **A** in diagram. Draw needle to front of canvas in first mesh of area to be worked. Insert needle one mesh to right in row above, and with one motion bring point of needle up in mesh directly left of first mesh where yarn is drawn to front. See **B**. Continue across row, repeating the stitch to end of outlined area, ending with needle on front of canvas. Then make running stitches to end row as in **C**. Cut yarn.

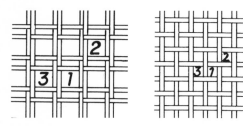

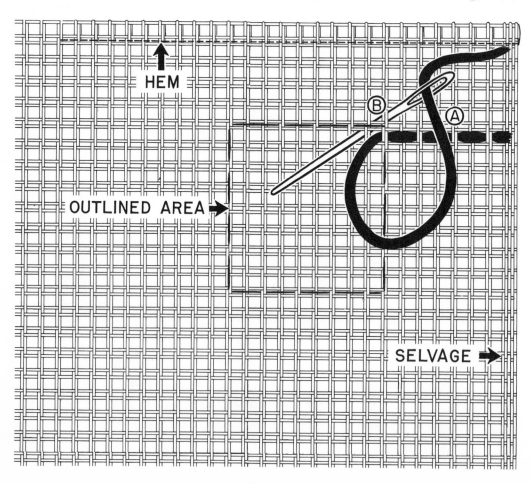

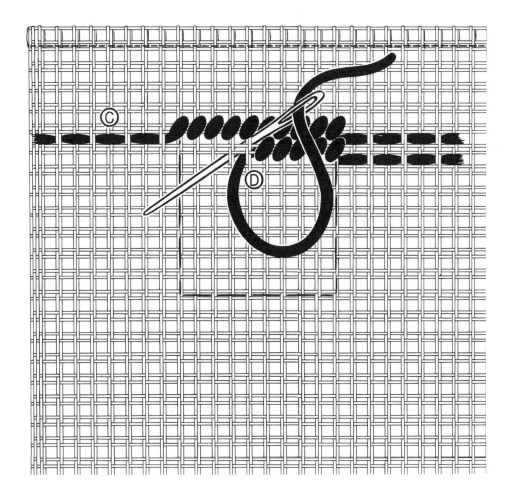

2nd Row—Start on front of canvas with running stitches as for first row. Draw needle to front of canvas in first mesh of area to be worked. Insert needle one mesh to right in row above (in same mesh as stitch in previous row). Repeat same as for first row. See **D**. End row with running stitches. Cut yarn.

Continue working each row in the same manner until the entire outlined area is filled in. Refer to page 30 for *Filling in Around the Design,* using the continental stitch.

Right: This photograph shows how the continental stitch looks on the wrong side.

Petit Point Stitch, which is a smaller version of the continental, is shown on page 58.

Basket Weave Stitch

THIS IS ALSO KNOWN as the *bias tent* stitch. It is the stitch preferred by authorities who do ecclesiastical needlepoint. It can be worked on both single- and double-thread canvas. For starting the yarn see *Waste Knot* on page 28.

Double-thread canvas. Work through large meshes, over double threads.

Single-thread canvas. Work over single threads in same way.

Diagram A—Draw the needle to front of canvas in first mesh to be worked, in upper right corner of outlined area. Insert needle one mesh to right in row above, draw needle to front of canvas in mesh 2 directly left of bottom of stitch 1. Holding needle vertically, insert needle one mesh to right in row above, and draw needle through at mesh 3.

Diagram B—To complete third stitch, insert needle one mesh to right in row above, draw needle to front in mesh 4.

Diagram C—Holding needle horizontally, insert needle one mesh to right in row above, draw needle to front in mesh 5 to complete fourth stitch. Continue up row with needle in horizontal position to complete fifth and sixth stitches.

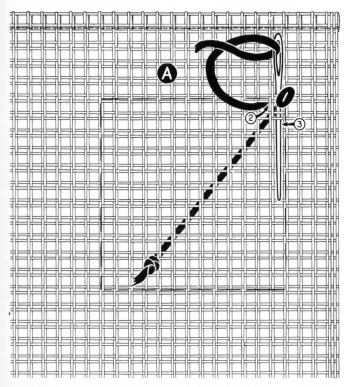

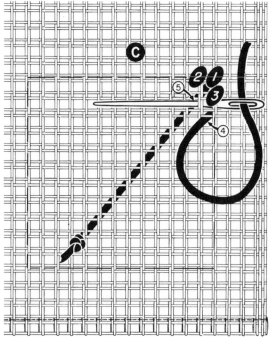

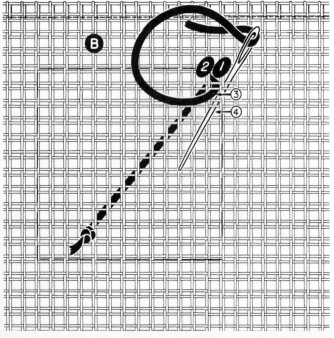

Diagram D—After stitch 6 is completed in top row, draw needle to front in mesh 7. Holding needle in vertical position, insert needle one mesh to right in row above to complete seventh stitch.

Proceed down canvas as shown in **Diagram E**. After completing stitch 10, insert needle horizontally to complete stitch 11. Then proceed up canvas.

56

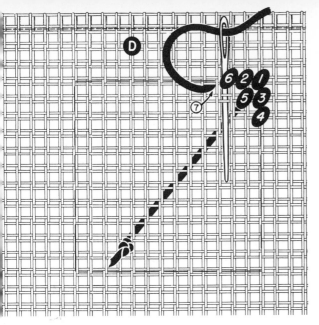

The needle is held horizontally when working up the canvas, and vertically when working down. Always alternate an *up row* with a *down row*. Continue this procedure until outlined area is completed.

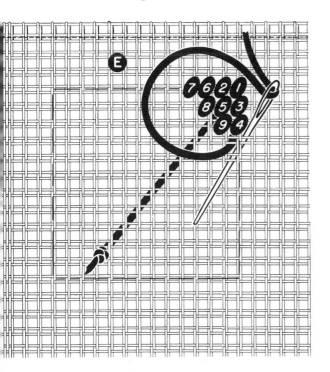

Ending a Length of Yarn. It is safer to stop work at the middle of a diagonal row rather than to stop at the bottom or top of the outlined area. Then you will always know in which direction you are going. Always continue stitches from where you leave off. Do not go to another part of the background.

Below: Photograph showing how the basket weave stitch appears on the wrong side.

Diagram F—The secret of maintaining the count for this stitch is to *always make two stitches next to each other horizontally on the top row of your work* as at 1–2, and *two stitches on the right-hand outer edge of your work* as at 3–4.

Continue to work up the canvas, inserting the needle horizontally, to make stitches 5 and 6.

Insert needle vertically to make stitch 7. Continue down the canvas in same way to make stitches 8, 9, and 10.

Insert needle horizontally to make stitch 11. Continue up canvas in same way to make stitches 12, 13, 14, and 15.

Insert needle vertically to make stitch 16 and continue down canvas as previously instructed.

Continue to alternate an up row of stitches with a down row. Always make two stitches together on the right before starting an *up row*, and two stitches together at the top before starting a *down row*.

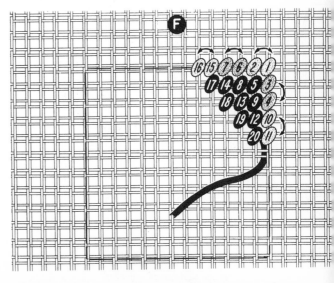

Petit Point Stitch

THIS STITCH CAN BE USED for either design or background area. Petit point refers to the size of the stitch to be worked on the canvas. The number of meshes per inch determines whether the stitch is petit or gros point. Most experts agree that a stitch is petit point size when worked on canvas which is 20 meshes to the inch or finer.

Work a petit point stitch exactly the same as the continental stitch on page 54 except that each stitch is worked over single, not double, threads. See *Separating Yarn* on page 23, usually necessary when doing finer stitches.

Either single- or double-thread canvas can be used for this stitch. See comparison below.

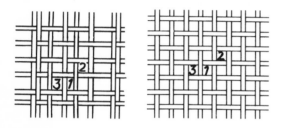

Double-thread canvas—**Diagram A** shows how the threads are separated in double-thread canvas while at work.

Single-thread canvas—**Diagram B** shows how petit point stitch is worked exactly the same as the continental stitch.

Filling in and Around a Petit Point Design—with Petit Point Stitches. Because petit point meshes are very fine and close, we recommend that stitches close to the design be worked with distinct up and down movements rather than drawing the needle through with one motion. This is the same method used when working needlepoint on a frame. See page 93.

With Gros Point Background on Double-Thread Canvas, work the continental stitch as close to the outer edge of petit point design as possible. Also fill in the open areas in the design with the continental stitch. Whenever a full gros point stitch cannot be made next to the petit point design, work petit point stitches in the background color to fill the area. This creates a three-dimensional effect.

Appliqué Petit Point. In this process very fine canvas is applied right over the regular canvas. Then it is worked with the tiniest possible stitches (over fifteen hundred to the square inch). These stitches are worked through both canvases. Because the stitches are so fine, details that heretofore only a paint brush could achieve become possible to the needlepointer. Rarely is this technique used, and then only by highly skilled specialists in this work. The stitches are made to produce facial expressions which compare favorably with those in paintings. This type of needlepoint was used for the heads in "The Last Supper" shown on page 148.

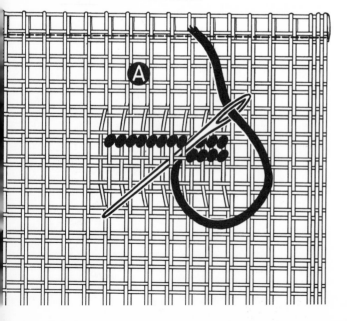

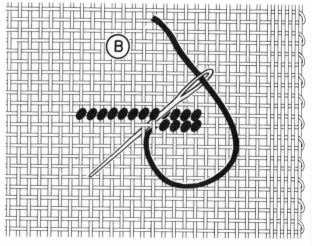

Half-Cross Stitches

These stitches are grouped together because of their similarities: regular half-cross, simplified half-cross, and elongated simplified half-cross.

Regular Half-Cross Stitch

This stitch can be worked on both single- and double-thread canvas.

Double-thread canvas—working through large meshes, over double threads.

Diagram A—Start in the upper left corner of canvas with running stitches outside outlined area. See instructions on page 28. Draw needle to front of canvas at 1, insert point of needle down in 2, with one motion draw needle out in 3. Continue across canvas in same manner

(needle down in 4, up in 5, down in 6, up in 7, and so on). Finish with running stitches as at start. Cut yarn.

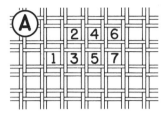

Diagram B—Make each succeeding row by returning to left side of canvas and working each row exactly the same as first row, inserting needle one mesh to right and above in same mesh as stitch in previous row.

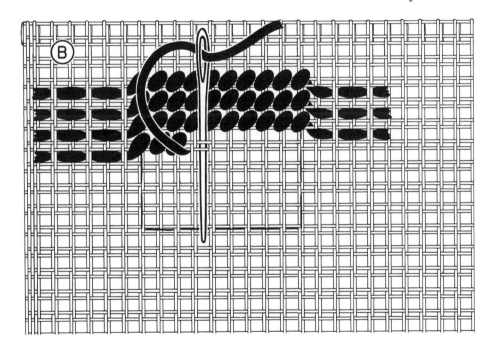

Left: Photograph shows how back of canvas looks when worked in the regular half-cross stitch.

Note: If you are now using this stitch and are right-handed, try turning the piece around for more comfortable working so that you work across from the right lower corner. This allows your yarn to loop below your hand and saves one motion with each stitch.

Simplified Half-Cross Stitch

This stitch has been adopted by many in place of the regular half-cross because it allows a more comfortable position for the hand, and tends to let the yarn fall in a natural untwisted loop below the hand while working. This helps to retain the original fluffy quality of the yarn.

When the simplified half-cross is worked in one direction, as recommended, it is easier to block and more uniform in appearance. In addition it is a stitch that works up quickly. Use only on *double-thread canvas*. Work through large meshes over double threads. Always start from lower right and work straight up canvas. Start on the front of canvas with running stitches below outlined areas.

Diagram A—Draw needle to front of canvas in first mesh of area to be worked.

1st Row—Insert point of needle one mesh to right in row above, and with one motion draw needle through mesh to the left. Work with needle in horizontal position so that you make a slanting stitch on front of canvas, and a straight stitch on back. Continue this stitch to top of outlined area. Draw needle to right of canvas and end with running stitches.

Diagram B—Make running stitches directly left of first row. Draw needle up in first mesh of area to be worked.

2nd Row—Insert needle one mesh to right in row above (in same mesh as the stitch in previous row). Draw needle through mesh directly to the left. Continue to top of outlined area, and end as for first row. Refer to **C** on page 31 for *Working in and Around Design* with simplified half-cross stitch.

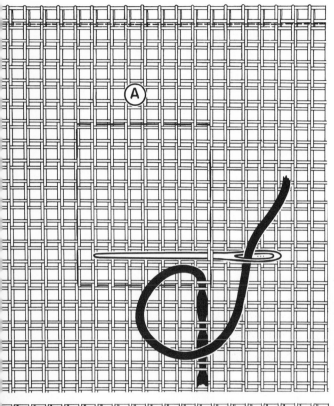

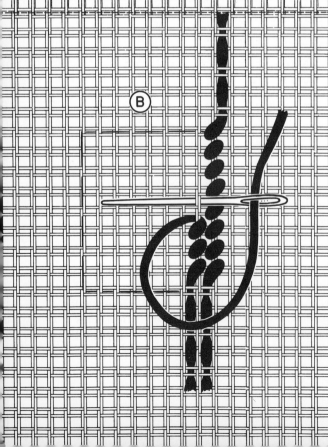

Elongated Simplified Half-Cross Stitch

This is a variation of the preceding stitch developed so it could be worked on a single-mesh canvas. It is worked in exactly the same way except that the horizontal needle is inserted under *two* single threads instead of a set of double threads.

Diagram A—Start with running stitches and draw needle to front of canvas in first mesh of area to be worked.

1st Row—Insert needle *two* meshes to right in row above and bring point of needle up in second mesh directly to the left. Continue this stitch to top of design area. Finish with running stitches. Cut yarn.

Diagram B—On front of canvas, skipping one mesh to left of first row, make running stitches in line with first row. Draw needle to front of canvas.

2nd Row—Insert needle two meshes to right in row above (in same mesh as stitch in previous row). Draw needle through second mesh directly to the left. Continue to top, and end as for first row.

This is both easy and interesting to work. See the effect obtained with this stitch in the photograph used for this book jacket. A black and white reproduction is shown on page 47.

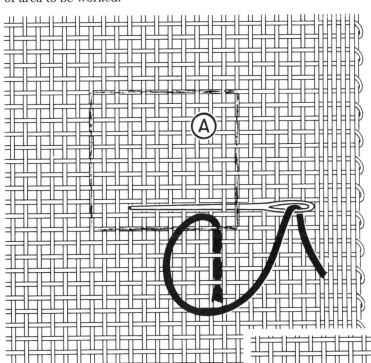

Opposite page: Photograph shows how the back of the canvas looks when worked in the simplified half-cross stitch.

61

Bargello or Flame Stitches

THE NAME "BARGELLO" applies to a group of designs in which the stitches are worked on counted canvas threads. This type of stitch has been done since needlepoint first began, and has various names. It not only works up quickly and is fun to do, but it is effective on a wide range of sizes and canvas. See photographs on page 64.

This stitch can be used on both single- and double-thread canvas.

If the design is worked out on graph paper first, it will be easier to do this stitch on canvas. Determine the height of the peaks so that you will know when to start working downward. This straight vertical stitch is worked in diagonal groups of stitches (each stitch over a selected number of threads) to form peaks or "flames" across the canvas.

Bargello or Florentine Stitch

In this design version each stitch covers the same number of threads in all rows. The only change is in the color of the yarn.

Diagram A—From left to right, work diagonally in vertical stitches over the selected number of threads. Each successive stitch is one thread higher than the preceding stitch until peak is reached. (The peak in illustra-

tion is three stitches wide). Working downward on the right, repeat the same number of stitches as are on the left. Continue to alternate groups of stitches up and down across the width of design.

Diagram B—With another yarn color, start second row on left, working each stitch over the same number of threads as in first row all the way across. All succeeding rows are worked in the same manner.

"Long" Bargello or Flame Stitch

In this version the design effect is more pointed, and each row of crosswise stitches is worked over a *different number* of threads.

1st Row—The straight vertical stitch is worked from left to right over three threads, each succeeding stitch *two* threads higher than the preceding stitch until peak is reached. Working downward on the right, repeat the same number of stitches as are on the left. The peak of the next group of stitches can be lower (as shown in **C**) by making one less stitch before starting downward. If you want the second peak to be higher, go up an extra stitch or two before starting downward.

Continue alternating groups of stitches

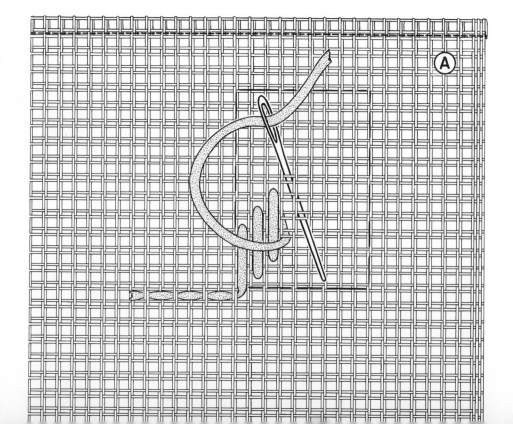

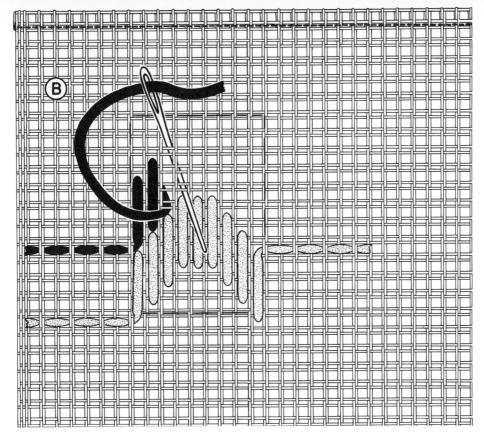

across width of design. The "peak" of each group can vary in height.

2nd Row—With another yarn color start at left as for the first row, but make stitch over five threads and each succeeding stitch over five threads, making an even row of stitches above the first row.

3rd Row—With still another yarn color start just as for previous rows. The stitches shown are again worked over three threads, a repeat of the first row. You can change the length of the stitches in this row if you wish, making them shorter or longer. Continue with rows in various lengths of stitches until desired area is filled. To complete the top and bottom edges, fill in the empty triangles with rows of stitches, working from one section to the other by carrying the yarn under the points. (D)

You should now understand how bargello works on a repeat design formula. The first row of stitches determines the depth and variations of the points; the colors selected for each row determine the final overall effect.

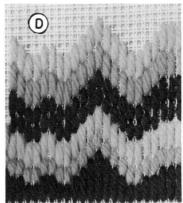

(continued on following page)

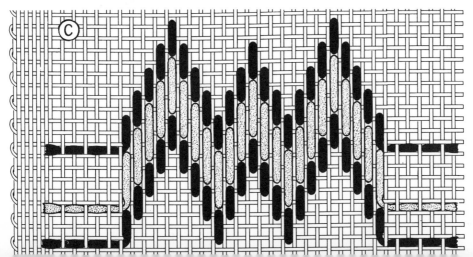

63

(*continued from previous page*)

Irregular or Uneven Bargello. This is a variation of the other two types. It is worked in the same manner as instructed previously except for one change. The first row is developed in stitches of *varying* length, instead of uniform length. Each additional row is also done with stitches of varying length. The overall effect is more uneven than the regular bargello. Photographs on pages 90, 91 and 106 show this stitch in use.

Above: This photograph shows an effect that can be obtained with the irregular bargello.

Encroaching Gobelin Stitch

THE GOBELIN STITCH IS A VERY OLD STITCH having several variations. We show the encroaching stitch because it works up quickly in large areas and is beautiful for subtle shaded effects.

It can be used on both single- and double-thread canvas. Always work from left to right and down from the top of canvas.

Diagram A—Start with running stitches five meshes below upper left corner. Draw needle to front of canvas in first mesh to left of outlined area. Insert needle vertically five meshes above and one mesh to right. Continue across canvas in same manner. End with running stitches and cut yarn.

Diagram B—Start the second row only four meshes below, but insert the needle one mesh above bottom of stitch in first row. See 1. Continue across canvas in same manner.

It may be hard to see where the ends of the stitches overlap until you have worked a few rows. See use of this stitch in photograph on page 47.

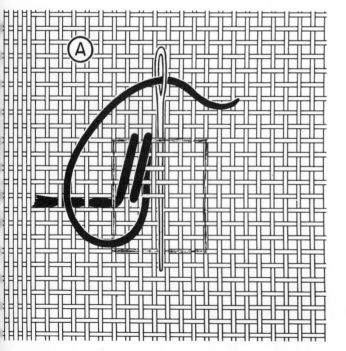

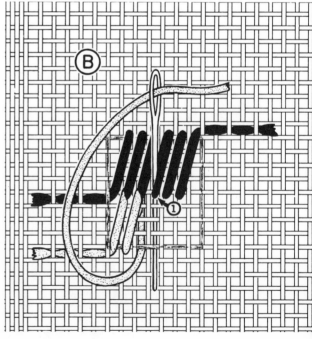

Brick Stitch

THIS IS ALSO CALLED the alternating stitch, which indicates the way in which the needle alternates when making the stitches. Because the brick stitch is small in size it can be used as a background in small areas, and it helps add dimension to adjoining stitches. Each row is worked in an opposite direction, alternately.

Use on single-thread canvas.

Diagram A—Start with running stitches. Draw needle to front, two meshes below upper left corner of outlined area. Insert needle two meshes above, and draw diagonally down through one mesh to right, stitch 1. Insert needle as illustrated, and draw through to make stitch 2.

Diagram B—Insert needle two meshes below, and draw diagonally up one mesh to right for stitch 3.

Diagram C—Insert needle two meshes above and draw diagonally down through one mesh to right for stitch 4. Insert needle two meshes below and draw diagonally up through one mesh to right for stitch 5. Insert needle two meshes above and draw diagonally down through one mesh to right for stitch 6. Insert needle two meshes below for stitch 7. Draw needle to front of canvas two meshes directly *below* stitch 7.

Start second row of stitches working from right to left. Insert needle above (in same mesh as bottom of stitch 7) and draw diagonally down one mesh to left for stitch 8.

Diagram D—Insert needle two meshes above (in same mesh as bottom of stitch 6) and draw diagonally down through one mesh to left for stitch 9. Insert needle two meshes below, and draw diagonally upward one mesh to left for stitch 10. Continue to alternate up and down until row is finished with stitch 14.

Starting with stitch 15, alternate up and down in same manner as top row.

See how this stitch works up as a background on page 47. The attractive compact case holder on page 106 was worked in this stitch.

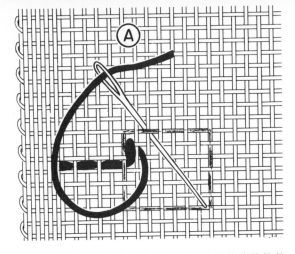

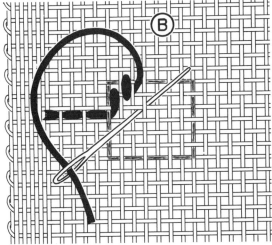

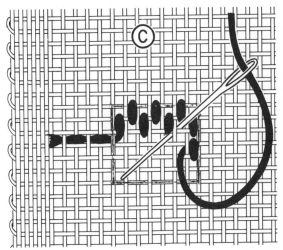

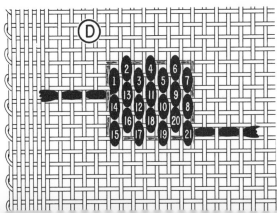

Diagonal Stitch

THIS IS A FASCINATING STITCH to do because of the varied effects that can be obtained with color. It is lovely when done with two or three shades of the same color, and it is beautiful when done in a rainbow of colors. It is a stitch that adapts itself to geometric motifs in a most pleasing way. This stitch can be used on both single- and double-thread canvas.

Double-thread canvas: Work through large meshes, over double threads. Start on the front of the canvas below the outlined area in the lower right corner with running stitches as shown.

Diagram A—Draw the needle to the front of the canvas in the first mesh of the area to be worked (see 1). Insert point of needle one mesh to right in the row above (see 2), and with one motion bring needle out at 3. Insert point of needle down in 4, up at 5.

Diagram B—Continue diagonally across until the top row of the outlined areas is reached. Finish with running stitches, and cut yarn.

Diagram C—Start each row from the lower right corner in same manner as first row. Always begin each new row to the left of the previously completed row.

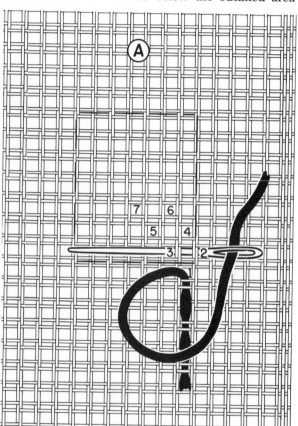

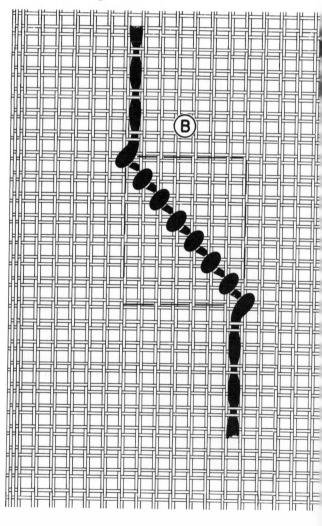

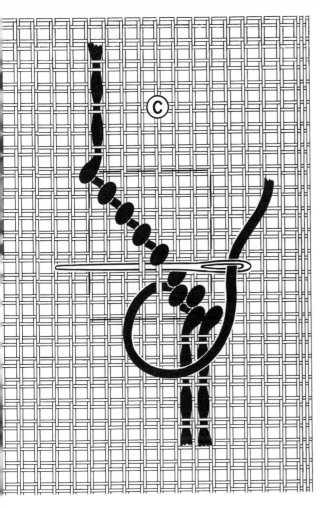

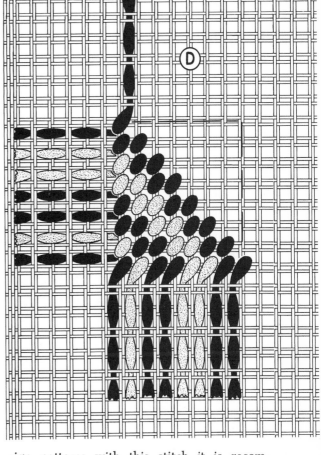

Diagram D—Continue working until entire left outlined area is completely filled in. Reverse your canvas so that the top is at the bottom. Follow directions from beginning to end exactly as for first half of canvas. Turn diagram upside down to see how upper half appears finished.

To obtain both unusual and consistent de-sign patterns with this stitch it is recommended that you *work one way only* as instructed above.

The photographs below show three design variations. The running stitches along side and bottom edges are included because they can be used as a guide to the number of rows used per color.

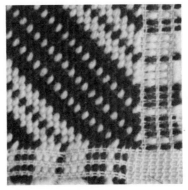

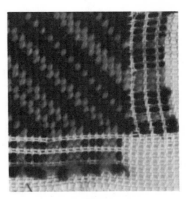

Chevron Stitch

THE CHEVRON STITCH IS SO NAMED because it is composed of a series of diagonal stitches meeting at an angle. The rows of diagonal stitches are worked vertically with every second row slanting in the opposite direction. The front surface of the canvas is covered with long stitches, while the wrong side has mostly short stitches.

In the diagrams the stitch is shown being worked on double-thread canvas with the needle inserted vertically under two close horizontal threads, and *only in large meshes*.

This stitch looks best when three strands of Persian wool are used for working. The wide range of colors in this yarn gives you the opportunity to create many interesting color effects.

Diagram A—Start at upper left corner with running stitches. Draw needle to front through first large mesh.

* Insert vertical needle downward *under*

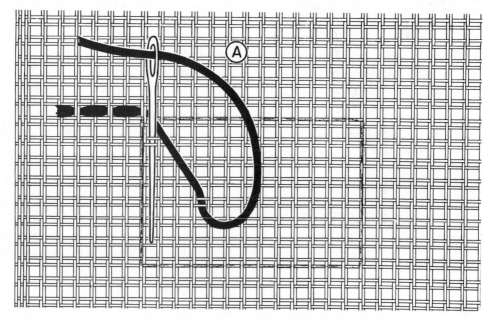

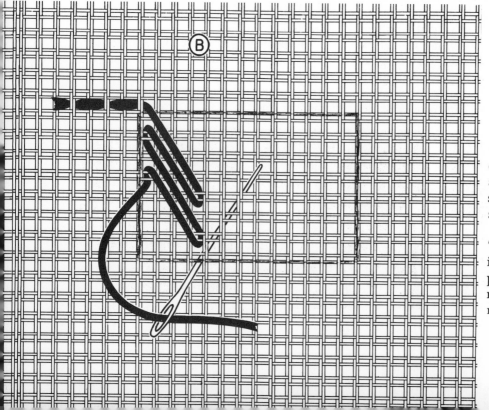

NOTE:
* Single asterisk indicates where to reread and repeat certain steps in making this stitch.

** Double asterisks indicate the second place to reread and repeat certain steps in making this stitch.

68

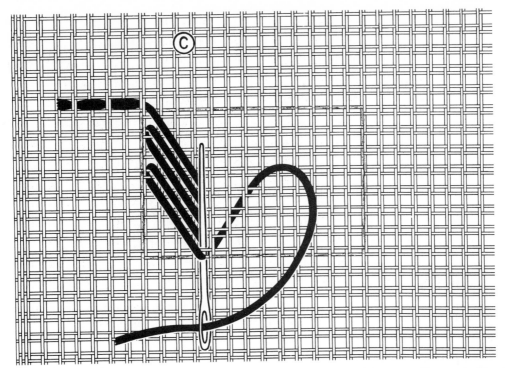

double threads, five meshes down and four meshes to right of outline.

Go left—directly below top end of first stitch, insert needle vertically and draw to front of canvas.

Diagram B—Holding needle vertically, continue to make short stitches downward under double threads, alternating diagonally up (left), and down (right).

** When end of stitch (right) is close to bottom of outline, insert needle *diagonally upward* as shown and draw needle to front four meshes up and three meshes to right.

Diagram C—Holding needle vertically, insert upward into bottom mesh and draw needle through so this stitch overlaps the end of stitch on the left.

Go right—insert needle *vertically upward* under double threads in mesh directly above end of previous stitch.

Diagram D—Holding needle vertically, insert in mesh on right so ends of stitches overlap in center. Draw to front at 1.

Go right—insert needle upward in second mesh below outline and draw to front in first mesh.

(continued on following page)

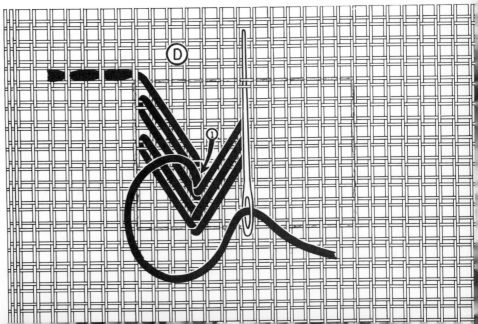

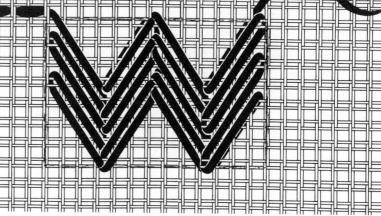

Diagram E—Go left; insert needle in same mesh as end of opposite stitch. Draw needle to underside.

Go right (yarn is under canvas). Draw needle to front in top mesh.

Continue diagonally up and down as instructed from * (page 68) until stitches on left side of second point are complete.

Follow instructions beginning at ** (page 69) for stitches on right side of second point.

Left: The photograph shows the horizontal zigzag stripe obtained by making rows of different colors across the canvas. All stripes are.random; there is no specific color repeat or number of stitches repeated. The piece includes a row of single stitches and a row seven stitches deep.

This illustrates the needle case cover before it was finished to look like photograph on page 106.

You will find this stitch is fun to work once you get the rhythm of it. Try more than one sample until you see how to combine the colors you want to use.

Photographs below illustrate the Parisian stitch.

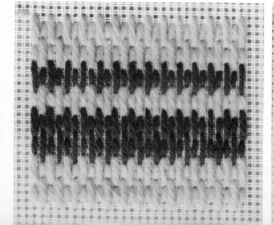

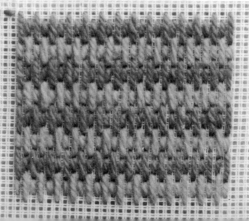

70

Parisian Stitch

THE PARISIAN IS A COMBINATION of long and short upright stitches worked horizontally across the canvas in alternating rows. Use a full strand of yarn so as to cover the vertical canvas threads.

An effective geometric stripe is obtained by alternating two colors. To obtain wider stripes, make two or more rows in a single color. See photographs on page 91. When worked in a single color on fine canvas, the rows of upright squares make a most attractive background.

This stitch can be used on both single- and double-thread canvas. On *single-thread,* alternate stitches over two meshes and four meshes. On *double-thread,* alternate stitches over one mesh and three meshes.

Diagram A—Make running stitches to left of upper corner of outlined area and draw needle to front of canvas. Insert needle two meshes below and draw diagonally up one mesh right and one mesh above where yarn comes out.

Diagram B—Insert needle four meshes below and draw diagonally up one mesh right and one mesh below where yarn comes out. Continue to end of row, alternating short and long stitches. When making last stitch in row, insert needle straight downward and draw to front four meshes below.

Diagram C—Insert needle four meshes above (in same mesh as bottom of short stitch) and draw diagonally left two meshes below. Insert needle two meshes above and draw diagonally left four meshes below. Continue alternating long and short stitches until end of row. For third row follow instructions given for row 1.

(Bottom of opposite page)

Far left. This photograph shows the stitch worked in random rows of color as: 2 light, 1 dark, 1 light, 2 dark, 2 light.

Near left. Shows the same stitch but the colors are alternated in single rows.

71

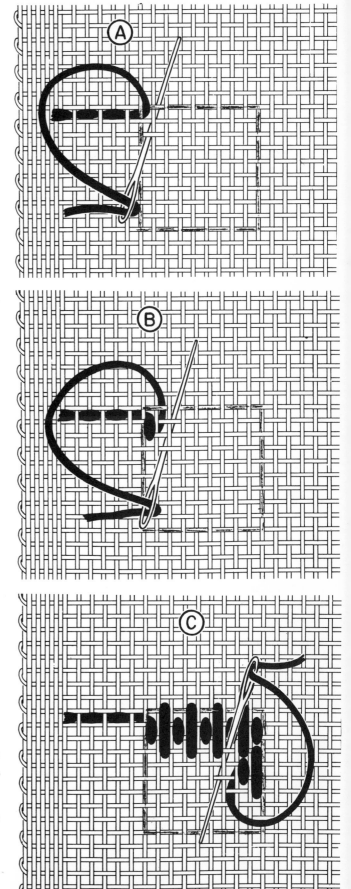

The photograph below
is an actual size section
of a scene done in tramé.
The entire scene, titled
"View of Delft,"
is shown on the left.

Tramé

TRAMÉ IS AN UNDERLAY of colored yarn thread placed over the horizontal meshes that are close together in double-thread canvas. The purpose of tramé is to indicate the design and change of colors on the canvas. In this case yarn is used instead of painting the canvas.

Use the regular half-cross stitch to work over the tramé. The number of stitches of

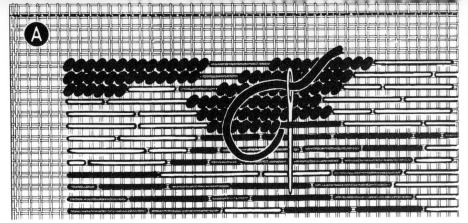

each color will vary in each row, so it will save time to continue from row to row with the same color yarn. Do this by turning the canvas upside down when the color ends in one row so you can continue working the stitch from left to right in the next row.

Turn the canvas for the following row and continue doing this until all the stitches in one color are filled in or you come to the end of a strand of yarn.

Start with another color yarn and work the stitch in the same manner.

Diagram A shows tramé being worked over with the regular half-cross stitch. It is worked from the upper left corner of canvas across to right with the needle placed in a vertical position for each stitch. This illustrates how the colors are scattered over the area.

When purchased, all tramé pieces come complete with appropriate colors and amount of yarn required to needlepoint over the tramé underlay.

Often the finer details such as faces or small figures are already done in petit point.

Ripping Out Needlepoint Stitches

In some instances you may be rushed or become tense while working a piece of needlepoint. If this should happen, you may find some stitches are either too tight or too loose. Do not let a few stitches impair the beauty of your finished needlepoint. Remove the imperfect stitches carefully and then replace them.

Slip a crochet hook under the undesirable stitches to loosen them. Then slip one point of a pair of sharp-pointed scissors under next to crochet hook and snip one stitch at a time until you have cut a few of the stitches you wish to remove. Be careful not to cut your canvas. Pull out the short yarn pieces with your fingers or with a pair of tweezers. When removing stitches, rip out the half-cross from the right side, as in **A**; the continental should be ripped out from the wrong side.

When ripping a row of stitches, cut a stitch or two in the center of a line and carefully draw out the balance of stitches to be removed until there is a short length of yarn on each end.

To thread the short length of yarn into the eye of the needle, cut a piece of paper about 1-inch long and narrow enough to go through the eye of the needle. Fold in half crosswise and lay the ripped end of yarn in the folded paper. Slip the paper and yarn into the eye of the needle. See **B**. Now you are ready to put the needle through to the wrong side and fasten off the yarn, just as though you were terminating the yarn in a row.

When replacing the stitches, be sure to match the adjoining stitches exactly in slant and size.

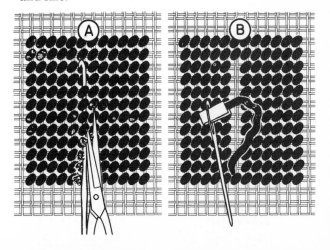

PIECING IS RECOMMENDED primarily to join rug sections, to lengthen a piano bench cover, or to enlarge any canvas which is too small for the object to be covered.

When and Why You Would Piece or Enlarge Needlepoint

1. You may have completed a piece of needlepoint without a specific use in mind and then decided to cover an object larger than the needlepoint.

2. The original piece was measured incorrectly and does not cover properly the object for which it was intended. It is essential that sufficient yarn be purchased from the same dye lot to complete the entire enlarging project.

3. When an older piece of needlepoint is to be revamped to fit a new object, fabric piecing is recommended because of the difficulty in matching new yarn to the older, exposed yarn.

Overlap Piecing

How to piece. Obtain canvas of the same type, quality, and mesh count as the canvas to be pieced. This method can be used on either single- or double-thread canvas. On double-thread canvas work your stitches in the same mesh as the original stitch.

If the continental stitch is used, work in large meshes. If petit point stitch is used, by

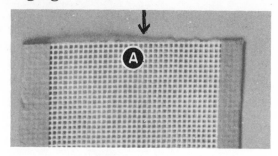

splitting the double threads work the overlapping meshes with the petit point stitch.

For extra strength while working stitches, bind side and bottom edges of piece of canvas to be added to the original piece. Run a thin line of quick-setting, clear-drying glue across the top edge. See **A** above. The glue will keep the canvas from fraying while the needlepoint stitch is worked over this row to join the two pieces together. Overlap glued edge of canvas about 1 inch over canvas to be pieced, carefully lining the meshes up one over the other. Keep the overlapping edge two or three rows from the original worked area. Pin, then baste from side to side. See photograph **B**.

Starting at edge of original needlepoint work toward the overlapping canvas, making the same stitch as used on the original piece. See photograph **C**.

When working across the canvas edged with glue use the "frame method" of inserting the needle up and then down in two dis-

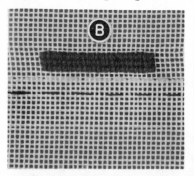

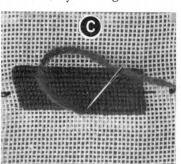

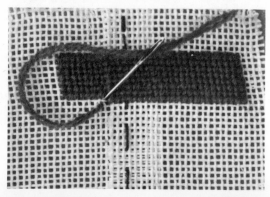

Photograph **D** shows the wrong side of the horizontal piecing.

Left: This photograph shows how vertical overlap looks from the right side.

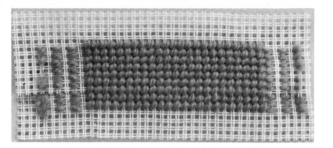

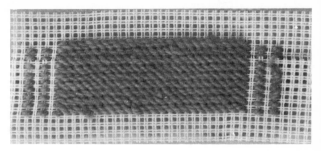

tinct motions for each stitch. See page 93.

This is important because the overlapping meshes can be *thrown out of line* if this row of stitches is worked the usual way—pulling needle through two meshes with one motion.

Working stitches through the 1-inch overlapped canvas will insure strength to the joined pieces. Continue working stitches beyond overlap just as for regular needlepoint until desired size is completed.

Reblock the entire canvas for a professional finish. See *Blocking* on page 86.

Above left: Horizontal overlap piecing on double-thread canvas worked with the continental stitch. *Above right:* How the wrong side appears.

Below left: Vertical overlap piecing on double-thread canvas worked with the simplified half-cross stitch. *Below right:* The wrong side.

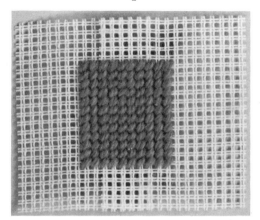

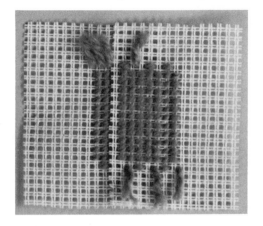

Abutted Edge Piecing

This method of piecing is recommended for:
1. Double-thread canvas when worked horizontally. To piece vertically is difficult on double-thread canvas. When necessary the best method to use is *Enlarging with Fabric*, page 76. Or use the *Overlapping* method shown on opposite page.
2. Single-thread canvas when worked either horizontally or vertically. For this type of piecing be sure canvas to be added has exactly the same size mesh as the original piece. Meshes to be joined together must be lined up perfectly one over the other so stitch can be worked exactly as on the original. The illustrations shown are of double-thread canvas joined horizontally to add length.

Overcast separately the seam edges of two identical pieces of canvas. Place the right side

of these two overcast pieces together to make a seam. Be sure the meshes match perfectly and appear as one. Pin, then baste the canvases together taking about a ⅜-inch seam. Use a strong linen thread or a thread drawn from the canvas.

Backstitch over the vertical threads as at **A**, using a distinct up-and-down movement in making the backstitches. A single thread of each piece will be drawn together and appear as at **B**. Press seam open. Treat the right side

(*continued on following page*)

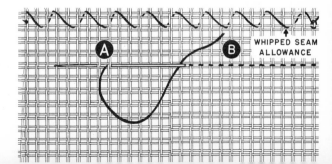

WHIPPED SEAM
ALLOWANCE

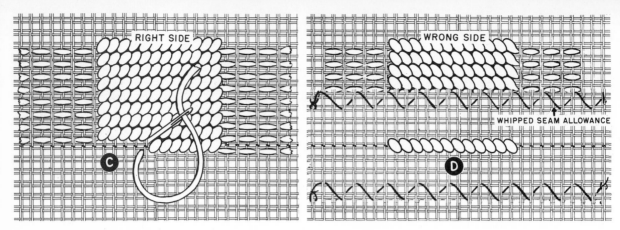

of the seamline as one row of meshes when working over it.

Start working from edge of original needlepoint on front of canvas, continue working until the backstitched row is reached. While working the rows near the seamline, take care not to catch seam allowance on the wrong side. Hold edges out of the way while working until the pieced row is reached.

When reaching the pieced row use the "frame method" to make this row of stitches. Insert needle downward from front, as in **Diagram C,** going through one seam allow-ance, then insert needle upward from underside through other seam allowance.

Diagram D shows the back of pieced canvas with the single row of stitches that has been worked through the seam allowance. When working rows immediately below seamline, do not work through seam allowance.

Vertical Piecing on Single-Thread Canvas

When adding width to a piece of this type canvas, do it in the same way as for horizontal piecing.

Enlarging with Fabric

USE THIS METHOD when you prefer not to become involved in piecing the canvas, and when converting old chair covers to new chairs.

Because the atmosphere changes the yarn colors through the years, it would be almost impossible to match the original pieces. A good upholstery fabric that blends or contrasts with the needlepoint background will add beauty to the finished object when it is properly attached to the canvas.

After determining placement of needlepoint piece on object to be covered, mark correct placement on upholstery fabric. Then mark ⅜ inch or ½ inch inside first outline for seam allowance. For a square opening cut out center and clip corners, as in **A**. If fabric is not very firm, make tailored corners. Turn fabric edges under, as at **B**, and pin right side up over needlepoint. Slip-baste turned edge to needlepoint. Backstitch along seamline from wrong side of fabric, as at **C**.

If a round or oval edge is used over needlepoint, cut paper pattern in desired shape and mark upholstery fabric accordingly. Cut ½ inch inside marked outline. Finish with fitted facing, as in **D**, and clip seam allowance. Turn facing to wrong side and press. Lay right side up over right side of needlepoint and slip-stitch edge, as in **E**.

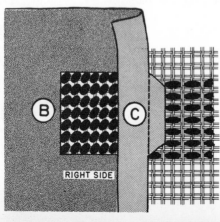

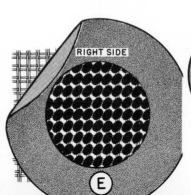

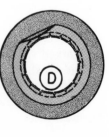

Left-Handed?
No Problem!

You CAN ENJOY DOING THE CANVAS STITCHES just as much as those individuals who use their right hand to make the stitches.

Seven basic stitches are shown in this chapter, and we hope that you will try all of them on canvas.

If you wish to do any of the additional stitches included in this book, do as follows:

Turn each diagram upside down, and then follow the reference letters even though they will be upside down on the illustration. As you read the instructions just transpose the directions. For example: top becomes bottom, right becomes left, and so on.

Never again should you have difficulty in doing any needlepoint stitches, and your stitches will always slant correctly.

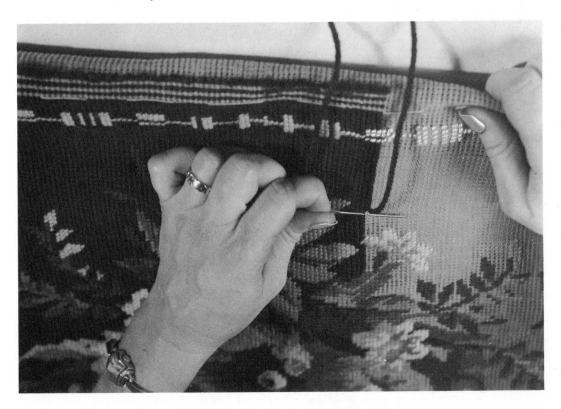

Left-Hand Continental Stitch

MANY NEEDLEPOINTERS PREFER THIS STITCH. It can be used on both single- and double-thread canvas. Always work from left to right. Refer to page 28 for instructions on starting and ending stitch. All the stitch illustrations show the running stitch outside of the outlined area.

Double-thread canvas: Work through large meshes, over double threads as illustrated below right. *Single-thread canvas* is shown underneath.

1st Row—Start on front of canvas at the lower left corner, outside the outlined area, with running stitches. See **A** in diagram. Draw needle to front of canvas in first mesh of area to be worked. Insert needle one mesh to left in row below, and with one motion bring point

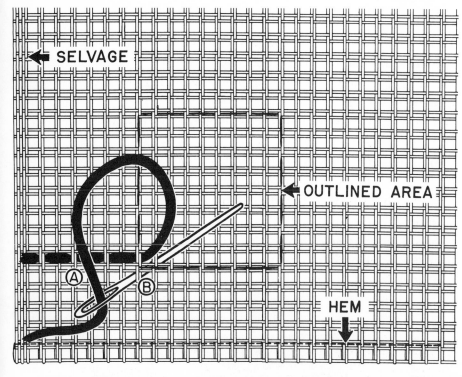

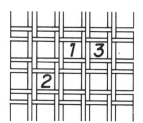

Double-thread canvas

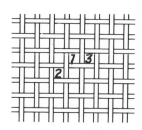

Single-thread canvas

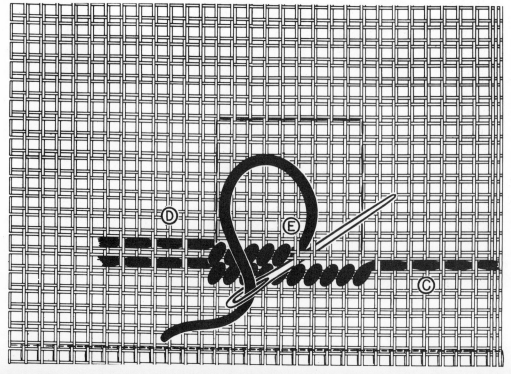

of needle up in mesh directly right of first mesh where yarn is drawn to front. See **B**. Continue across row, repeating the stitch to end of outlined area, ending with needle on front of canvas. End row with running stitches as in **C**. Cut yarn.

2nd Row—Start on front of canvas with running stitches as for first row. See **D**. Draw

needle to front of canvas in first mesh of area to be worked. Insert needle one mesh to left in row below (in same mesh as stitch in previous row). Repeat same as for first row. See **E**. End row with running stitches. Cut yarn.

Continue working each row in the same manner until the entire outlined area is filled in. Refer to page 30 for *Filling in Around Design.*

Left-Hand Petit Point Stitch

PETIT POINT REFERS TO THE SIZE of the stitch to be worked on the canvas. The number of meshes per inch determines whether the stitch is petit or gros point. Most experts consider it a petit point stitch when worked on canvas 20 meshes to the inch or finer.

The petit point stitch is worked exactly the same as the continental stitch opposite, except that each stitch is worked over single, not double threads.

Either single- or double-thread canvas can be used for this stitch. See comparison below.

Double-thread canvas: **Diagram A** shows how the threads are separated in double-thread canvas while in work.

Single-thread canvas: **Diagram B** shows how petit point stitch is worked exactly the same as the continental stitch.

Refer to page 23 for instructions on *Separating Yarn.* This is necessary when doing finer stitches.

Filling in and Around a Petit Point Design— with Petit Point Stitches. Because petit point meshes are very fine and close, we recommend that stitches close to the design be worked with distinct up-and-down movements rather than drawing the needle through with one motion. This is the same method used when working needlepoint on a frame. See page 93.

With Gros Point Background on Double-Mesh Canvas. Work the continental stitch as close to the outer edge of the petit point design as possible. Also fill in the open areas (large mesh) in the design with the continental stitch. Whenever a full gros point stitch cannot be made next to the petit point design, work petit point stitches in the background color to fill the area. This creates a three-dimensional effect.

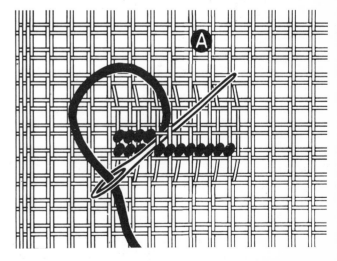

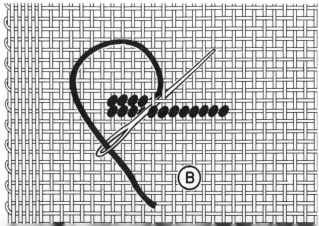

Left-Hand Basket Weave Stitch

ANOTHER NAME FOR THIS STITCH is *bias tent*. Authorities who do ecclesiastical needlepoint prefer this stitch. It can be worked on both single- and double-thread canvas. For starting yarn, see *Waste Knot* on page 28.

Double-thread canvas: Work through large meshes, over double threads. *Single-thread canvas:* Work over single threads in same way.

Diagram A—Draw the needle to front of canvas in first mesh to be worked in lower left corner of outlined area. Insert needle one mesh to left in row below, draw needle to front of canvas in mesh 2 directly right of top of stitch 1. Holding needle vertically, insert needle one mesh to left in row below, and draw needle through at mesh 3.

Diagram B—To complete third stitch, insert needle one mesh to left in row below, draw needle to front in mesh 4.

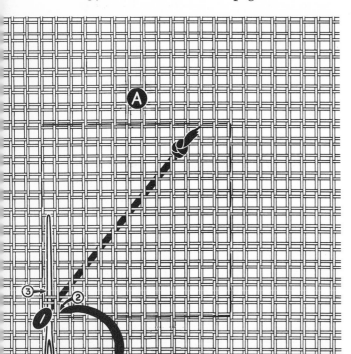

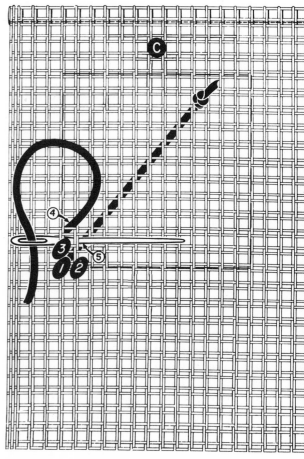

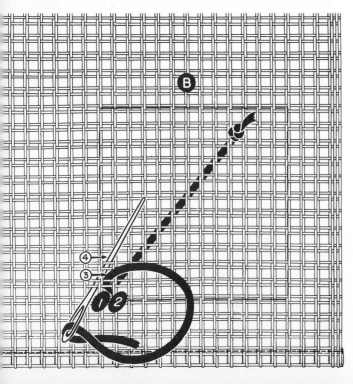

Diagram C—Holding needle horizontally, insert needle one mesh to left in row below, draw needle to front in mesh 5. Continue down row with needle in horizontal position.

Diagram D—After stitch 6 is completed in bottom row, draw needle to front in mesh 7. Holding needle in vertical position, insert needle one mesh to left in row below and work up canvas.

Proceed up canvas as shown in **Diagram E.**

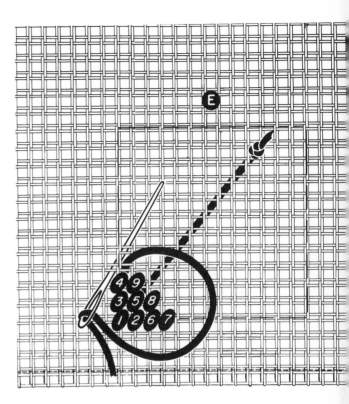

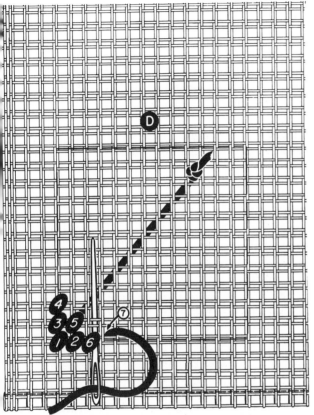

Diagram F—The secret of maintaining the count for this stitch is to *always make two stitches next to each other horizontally* as at 1–2, and two stitches *one above the other vertically* as at 3–4.

The needle is held vertically when working up the canvas and horizontally when working down. Always alternate an *up row* with a *down row*. Repeat this procedure until outlined area is completed.

Ending a length of yarn. It is safer to stop work at the middle of a diagonal row rather than to stop at the bottom or top of the outlined area. Then you will always know in which direction you are going. Always continue stitches from where you leave off. Do not go to another part of the background.

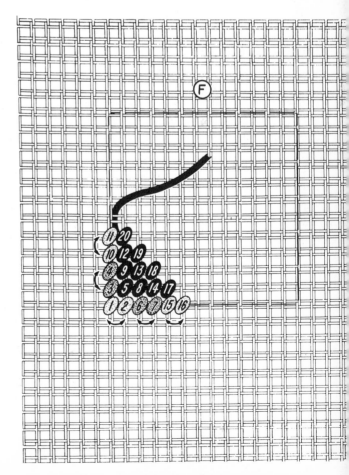

Left-Hand Diagonal Stitch

THIS STITCH CAN BE USED on both double- and single-thread canvas. See page 67 for variations of this stitch which is excellent for covering entire canvas.

Double-thread: Work through large meshes, over double threads. Start on the front of the canvas above the outlined area in the upper left corner with running stitches as shown.

Diagram A—Draw the needle to the front of the canvas in the first mesh of the area to be worked (see 1). Insert point of needle one mesh to left in row below (see 2), and with one motion bring needle out at 3. Insert point of needle down in 4, up at 5.

Diagram B—Continue diagonally until the bottom right corner of outlined area is reached. Finish with running stitches, and cut yarn.

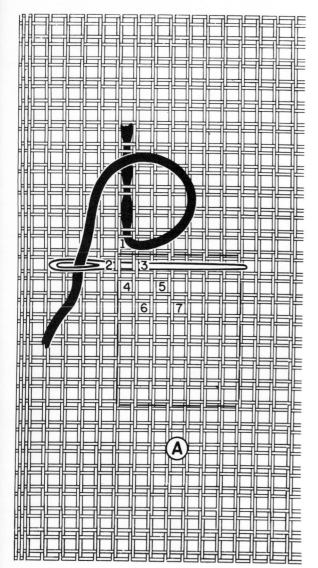

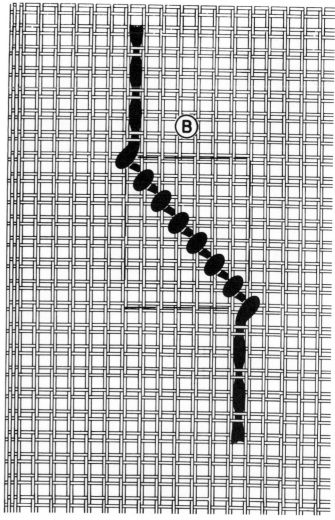

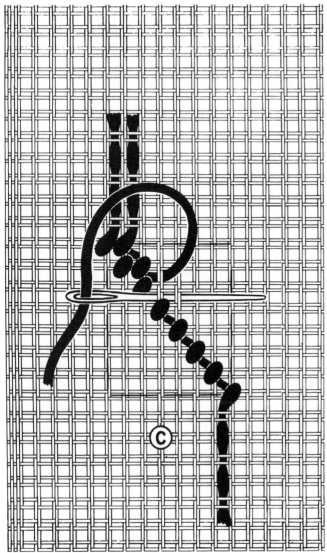

Diagram C—Start each row from upper left corner in same manner as first row. Always begin each new row to the right of the previously completed row.

Diagram D—Continue working until entire right outlined area is completely filled in. Reverse your canvas so the top is at the bottom. Turn **Diagram D** upside down to see how upper half appears finished. Follow directions from beginning to end exactly as for first half of canvas.

It is recommended that you *work one way only* so as to obtain both unusual and consistent design patterns.

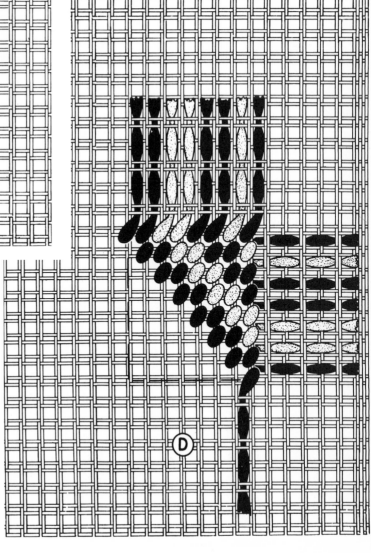

Left-Hand Half-Cross Stitches

THESE THREE STITCHES are grouped together because of their similarities: regular half-cross, simplified half-cross, and elongated simplified half-cross.

Regular Half-Cross

This stitch can be used on both single- and double-thread canvas.

Double-thread canvas: Work through large meshes, over double threads.

Diagram A—Start in the upper left corner of canvas with running stitches outside outlined area as shown. Draw needle to front of canvas at 1; with one motion, insert point of needle in at 2, draw out at 3. Continue across canvas in same manner (needle down in 4, up in 5, down in 6, up in 7, and so on). Finish with running stitches as at start. Cut yarn.

Diagram B—Make each succeeding row by returning to left side of canvas and working each row exactly the same as first row, inserting needle one mesh to right and above in same mesh as stitch in previous row.

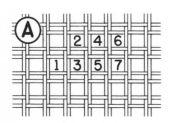

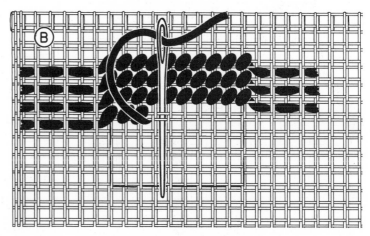

Simplified Half-Cross

This stitch has been adopted by many in place of the regular half-cross because it allows a more comfortable position for the hand and tends to let the yarn fall in a natural untwisted loop below the hand while working. This helps to retain the original fluffy quality of the yarn.

When the simplified half-cross is worked in one direction, as recommended, it is easier to block and more uniform in appearance. In addition it is a stitch that works up quickly. Use only on *double-thread canvas.* Work through large meshes over double threads.

Start on front of canvas with running stitches above outlined area.

Diagram A—Draw needle to front of canvas in first mesh of area to be worked.

1st Row—Insert point of needle one mesh to left in row below, and with one motion draw

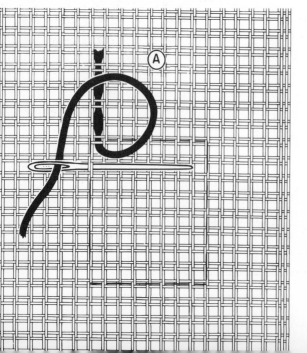

84

needle through mesh to the right. Work with needle in horizontal position so that you make a slanting stitch on front of canvas and a straight stitch on back. Continue this stitch to bottom of outlined area. Draw needle to front of canvas and end with running stitches.

Diagram B—Make running stitches directly right of first row. Draw needle to front in first mesh of area to be worked.

2nd Row—Insert needle one mesh to left in row below (in same mesh as the stitch in previous row). Draw needle through mesh directly to the right. Continue to bottom of outlined area, and end as for first row. Refer to page 31 for *Working in and around Design*.

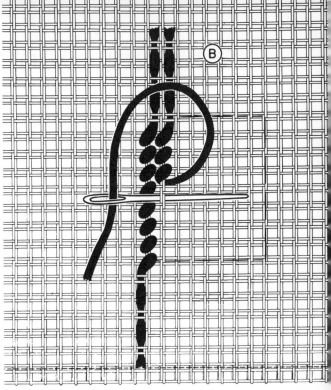

Elongated Simplified Half-Cross

This is a variation of the preceding stitch developed so it could be worked on single-thread canvas. It is worked in exactly the same way except that the horizontal needle is inserted under *two* threads instead of a set of double threads.

Diagram A (below)—Start with running stitches and draw needle to front of canvas in first mesh of area to be worked.

1st Row—Insert needle *two* meshes to left in row below and bring point of needle up in second mesh directly to the right. Continue this stitch to bottom of design area. Finish with running stitches. Cut yarn.

Diagram B (below)—On front of canvas, skipping one mesh to right of first row, make running stitches in line with first row. Draw needle to front of canvas.

2nd Row—Insert needle two meshes to left in row below (in same mesh as stitch in previous row). Draw needle through second mesh directly to the right. Continue to bottom and end as for first row.

This stitch is both easy and interesting to work. See the effect obtained in the photograph used for the jacket of this book. A black and white reproduction is shown on page 47.

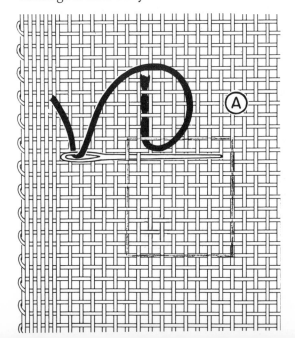

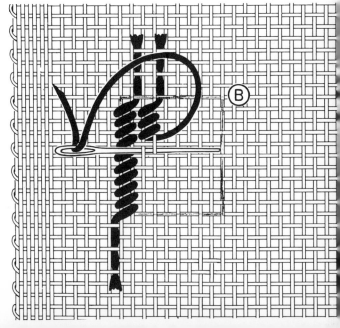

Blocking · Mounting · Finishing

THE CORRECT METHOD and the care with which needlepoint is blocked and mounted will be important factors in the appearance of the finished item.

Materials for blocking are listed on page 26.

Never cut the canvas before blocking. Use the selvages and/or hems or bias binding as support for the tacks when blocking.

If you do not have the time, patience, or experience, be sure to employ a skilled craftsman to do your blocking. Take your needlepoint to a shop which specializes in this type of professional work.

Professional blocking is recommended for very large pieces of needlepoint such as rugs, screens, panels, and intricate furniture coverings. Handbags and luggage should be entrusted to a bag maker for blocking and mounting of the needlepoint.

Considering the hours of work expended in making your needlepoint and the years of use and pleasure derived, the cost of professional blocking and mounting is not high.

The measured size of the needlepoint can be marked directly on the muslin cover of the board, but as various sizes are marked in the future, the overlapped markings will become confusing. Therefore, we recommend that you tack a piece of wrapping paper to the board, over the muslin, for marking the outlines of the area to be worked. Once you have finished the blocking, the paper can be discarded. The vertical and horizontal center lines are basic guides, and these should be marked on the muslin as instructed below.

While a minimum of stretching may be required on some needlepoint, on others a great deal of effort will be needed to stretch them into shape. The greater the amount of stretching needed, the greater will be the amount of water used.

Aluminum push-pins are shown in use for minimum blocking because they are sufficiently strong, are easy to insert and remove.

When stretching needlepoint which needs maximum blocking, use strong, rustproof, long-pointed thumbtacks. Once these tacks are hammered into the board after the needlepoint is adjusted, they will not pull out while the canvas is shrinking during the drying period.

Blocking boards can be made from drawing boards or from ½-inch plywood. Marine plywood is preferable because it is waterproof.

Drawing boards come in sizes from 12 by 17 to 24 by 36 inches. Plywood can be cut to any size. A 2-by-3- or 3-by-4-foot board should be large enough for blocking anything at home, such as chair seats, panels, or large pictures.

Cover the board with heavyweight muslin or drill cloth. Smooth the cloth over the board and down over the edges to the underside, fastening it with thumbtacks closely spaced. Cut away some of the excess fabric at the corners to lessen bulk on the underside. Using a wet sponge, dampen the muslin cover so that it will be taut and smooth over the board. Allow to dry thoroughly.

Mark the center of the muslin in both directions, using a triangle at the center to be sure that the lines are at right angles to each other. Draw the lines, using a ruler and a dry marker or a laundry-marking pen, extending the lines from edge to edge on the board.

Cut and mark paper. Cut a piece of wrapping paper larger than the canvas to be blocked. Center the paper over the muslin and thumbtack the edges to the board, spacing the tacks far apart. Draw the vertical and horizontal lines across the paper. (When you outlined the area to be worked, we recommended that you make a note of the size, and we suggested that you extend the lines to the edge of the canvas at all corners.) Measure and mark the size of the outline on the paper, extending the lines beyond the corners.

Trademarks that Bleed. Before you start to block, check the canvas for any name stampings or marks which might bleed when wet. Lay the stamped area over paper towels, and with a very wet sponge, rub over the area to remove as much of the ink as possible.

Minimum Stretching. Lay needlepoint, right side down, on the paper, lining up the pencil lines at the four corners. Place an aluminum push-pin or a thumbtack at each of the top corners, inserting the point in the canvas close to the worked areas. See **A.**

Stretch firmly but carefully to align the two lower corners, placing each tack close to corner. Add more moisture if necessary to make all corners square. Insert tacks in the canvas along one side of the piece just outside the worked area, following the guidelines and placing tacks a scant 1 inch apart. From the opposite side stretch carefully, inserting tacks in the selvage, hem, or bound edge directly opposite the first row in order to keep the canvas threads straight. Remove the tacks, one by one, on the first side and insert them closer to edge of canvas. See **B**.

Insert tacks in the two remaining edges, working from the center of each side toward the corners. Remove the tacks at the corners of the design. Allow to dry for at least twenty-four hours. Be sure that it is completely dry before removing it from the board.

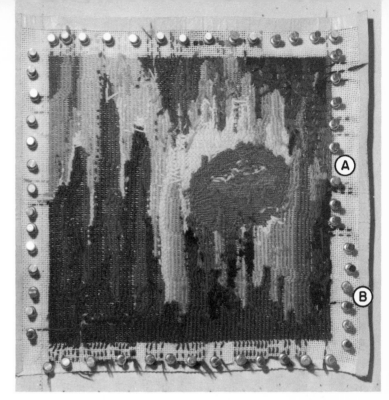

Maximum Stretching. Wet the needlepoint thoroughly and roll it in a Turkish towel to remove the excess moisture. Do not wring it; just squeeze it on a flat surface and remove from towel.

Lay needlepoint, right side down, over the board, following the same procedure as outlined above under minimum stretching, using thumbtacks to hold in place. After all threads are even in both directions, hammer tacks securely into board. More moisture is not needed; you can pat the piece with a towel to remove any excess moisture still remaining.

The needlepoint should remain on the board until it is thoroughly dry, even for a week if necessary. While the needlepoint is drying, keep the board in a horizontal position to avoid having the edges spot or having water streaks form from uneven drying.

Sizing or Stiffening. Panels, rugs, and pieces that are not mounted, as well as handbags, luggage, and items which will be handled, should be sized in order for them to keep their shape.

Before removing tacks after blocking and drying, apply a very thin coating of sizing to the back of the worked area.

Dry glue can be purchased from hardware and artist supply stores. Mix according to directions on the package, making only enough for immediate use as this type of glue will not keep. Spread with a knife or with a stiff brush. Cover completely but do not work glue into the surface. Remove any excess and let dry.

Scotchgard Fabric Protector. When the needlepoint is dry, remove it from the board and turn it right side up. Follow the directions given on the can of Scotchgard, applying it to the needlepoint in the same way as for any upholstery fabric.

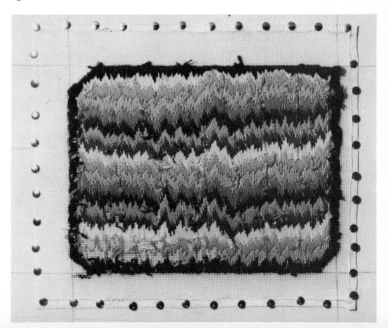

Mounting

THE TERM "MOUNTING" is used to describe the various ways in which needlepoint is applied to an item as a decoration or the ways in which it is to be used.

The selvages and hems should be left on the canvas while it is being mounted unless they interfere with the mounting procedure.

Canvas Fraying. When it is necessary to cut the canvas in order to mount the needlepoint, fraying can be prevented by using one of the following methods:

Machine stitching. Use a long stitch (eight to the inch) and make two or three rows of stitching close to the outlined area, or stitch over the outside row of needlepoint stitches. Do not stitch over the edge of the needlepoint unless it is to be turned under.

Glue. A line of quick-drying glue can be squeezed directly from the tube just outside the worked area. This method should be used on all small needlepoint items. Once the glue has dried, the canvas threads cannot ravel. Refer to *Adhesives* on page 206.

Cushions, Pillows, Bolsters. These can be made entirely of needlepoint, or they can be combined with fabrics as suggested on page 99. Follow the instructions in any sewing book for making covers to fit over foam rubber or stuffed shapes.

Doorstops should be heavy enough to serve their purpose. A brick (from a building supply company), a lead block (from a plumbing supply company), are excellent materials to use for doorstops. See designs on page 154.

After working the design, trim away the excess canvas, fold it around the block, and hand sew or glue one edge over the other. Needlepoint can be used to re-cover doorstops already in use.

Furniture is usually upholstered in needlepoint so that part of the frame is visible. The way in which needlepoint is applied depends on the style of the frame. See page 96 for stools that are completely covered with needlepoint.

If needlepoint is replacing upholstery fabric on a chair or stool, remove the original fabric carefully so that you can use it as a guide in shaping and applying the new cover.

Slip-seats are removable, so the seat is covered and then put back into place. See instructions on page 105.

Permanent seat. There are several ways to cover a permanent seat, depending on the style.

Entire seat covered. The cover is brought down over the frame to the underside of the seat and fitted around the legs or shaped at the corners. Turn under the edges where it is fitted around leg and baste under to back of needlepoint. Tack other edges to underside of frame. Tack lining over raw edges as instructed for slip-seat on page 105.

Nail or braid finish can be handled in two or three ways. Upholstery nails come in various finishes and colors; upholsterer's braid or gimp is available in a wide range of colors. If used with the nails, the braid should be the same width as the heads of the nails.

Stretch the needlepoint over the seat, fitting it around legs, arms, and back. Place a row of medium-sized carpet tacks, widely spaced, ¼ inch above the line where the needlepoint is to end. Trim canvas to exact finish line of frame, cutting very carefully. Apply a thin line of glue to the unfinished wood under the cut edge and press the edge against it.

Braid and nail finish. Apply braid over raw edge with glue. Let it set; then hammer the ornamental nails, side by side, all the way around. See examples of this finish on pages 96, 97, 104.

Braid can also be glued on without using nails. Apply glue to the braid an inch or two at a time, tacking in place with small wire brads. The Victorian chair on page 97 shows this type of finish.

Wall Hangings. Panels of needlepoint that are to be used as wall hangings should first be sized. See page 87. Turn under the canvas edges, mitering the corners. Hem, using long stitches. Line with a heavy sateen to give body and to protect the needlepoint. Make a casing at top of lining for inserting a rod for hanging, or attach small rings at intervals across the top edge and run the rod through them.

The illustration above shows the original design used on the book jacket. Claire Valentine combined four stitches to develop this design. The geometric design on the last page of the insert was worked in two stitches.

The double spread which follows shows a color chart done in wool yarn on single-thread canvas. See page 52 for color information.

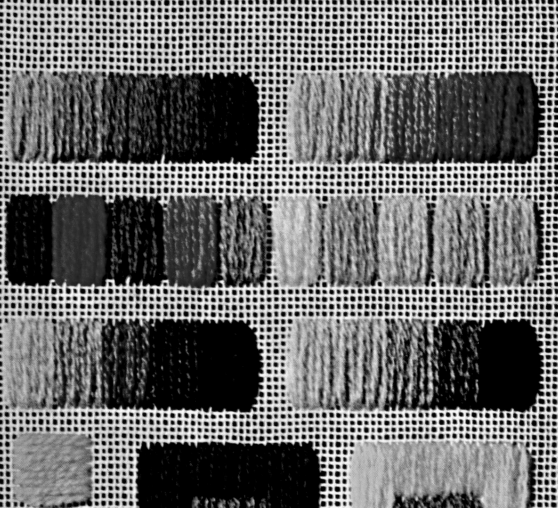

Pictures. Small pictures are smoothed over cardboard, but for medium- and large-sized pictures use ¼-inch plywood. Most needlepoint pictures are framed without a mat. See page 24 for measuring.

Cut cardboard or plywood ⅛ inch smaller than the frame all around. The worked area should be the same size as the backing so that only plain canvas turns over the edge toward the back to eliminate bulk.

Line up the picture from the right side, placing pins or push-pins through the canvas into the edge of the board at the corners and at intervals around the edges to hold the needlepoint straight. Turn over, right side down, and fold canvas over edges. Measure 1½ inches from the edge and trim away excess canvas all around. Miter the corners and hand whip folds at each corner. Steam press seam at each corner on the back only.

With carpet thread and a long needle, lace the edges together from side to side and from top to bottom. Remove pins and tacks. Insert in frame and finish as for any picture.

Matting a picture. Outline inside edge of mat on the cardboard. Line up needlepoint squarely and tape it flat before laying mat over the needlepoint and inserting in frame.

A new nonglaring, nonreflecting glass is available to cover framed needlepoint.

Rugs. In most cases, rugs should be blocked and finished professionally. However, if the rug is small, or if it has been made in sections, (see below) you may wish to finish it yourself.

After blocking, a rug should be sized. See page 87. Turn the raw edges to wrong side and hem, using long stitches. Use rug binding to cover the canvas margins; then line rug.

Design worked in sections. It is sometimes more convenient to work a design in sections rather than on a single piece of canvas. See the rug on page 5. Use the same type of canvas for all pieces. Block each piece separately. Lap canvas as instructed under *Piecing* on page 74 and work the needlepoint stitches over the double layers of canvas.

Wastebaskets can be covered in a number of ways, depending on their shape. If leather-trimmed, or if the basket has a complicated shape, it should be mounted professionally.

Mounting with Glue. Needlepoint, finished in suitable shapes, can be applied with glue to cover or to decorate accessories.

Note: The solvents and vapors in fast-drying adhesives will mar finished surfaces on contact. Working surfaces should be protected with plywood, glass, or several layers of heavy cardboard while mounting.

Flush application. Work the needlepoint in the exact size of the area to be covered so that it is flush with the edges. The glove box on page 106 is an example.

A framed effect is obtained by making the needlepoint smaller than the area on which it will be glued. The memo pad on page 106 shows a piece of needlepoint centered on its cover.

The *gluing method* permits the purchase of plain, less expensive items to which you can add the beauty of needlepoint. An imitation leather desk set, composed of a blotter, a mail holder, and a pencil container, can have the two holders and the corners of the blotter covered with needlepoint.

When needlepoint is to be glued on an accessory, the manner in which the canvas edges are finished depends on the item to be covered. The instructions given below for the wastebasket and the mail holder are two more ways of mounting with glue.

A wastebasket with a pansy design is shown on page 101. The needlepoint covers the basket and was glued in place as the final step. This basket could be covered as described below because it has an oval shape with straight sides from top to bottom.

Measure the height and circumference of the wastebasket, using these measurements to mark the area to be worked on canvas. Finish needlepoint from top to bottom to within three rows of canvas meshes at both ends. Block the piece.

When it is dry, place around basket, overlapping the end meshes. Mark the fit exactly and remove from basket. Relap the ends and baste so that meshes are overlapped evenly from edge to edge. Continue the needlepoint stitches, working through the two layers as instructed under *Overlap Piecing* on page 74.

Draw the needlepoint over wastebasket, centering the design on one side. The top and bottom edges can be turned back against canvas and glued to basket at both edges, or the needlepoint can be turned over the top edge and glued to the inside. The lower edge is turned under and glued on the bottom. After the glue has dried, cover the bottom of the basket with felt cut ¼ inch smaller than the bottom. Use a linen self-stick tape to cover the top edge on the inside of the basket. See *Miscellaneous Edge Finishes* on page 199.

Mail Holder. While only the outside of the two upright sections will be covered with needlepoint, it is necessary to mark the canvas to include the bottom section between the two uprights as shown in the photograph at right.

Use a tape measure so that you can measure around the edges for thickness. Add ⅝ inch to the width and thickness on both edges for turn-under.

For length, measure the outside, starting at the front top edge, and carry the tape underneath to the back top edge. Add ½ inch for turn-under at both ends.

Place canvas around holder to check the fit. Tape the top edges to front and back crosswise edges. Fold side edges over holder edges. Lap corners on crosswise edge over corners on lengthwise edges. Mark edge of overlap. In order to prevent excessive bulk, do not needlepoint the four side corners.

The two crosswise lines in the center indicate where the canvas folds for the bottom section.

(*Mail Holder—continued on page 114*)

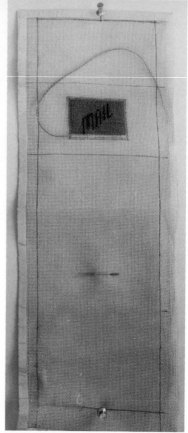

Cushion Weights. Two bands, weighted on the bottom ends, will hold a cushion in place against the back of a small upholstered chair.

Make the bands of the same upholstery fabric used to back the needlepoint cushion. Cut two strips about 2 inches longer than the height of the cushion and about 4 to 4½ inches wide. Fold in half lengthwise, wrong side out; stitch the lengthwise edges and stitch twice across bottom end, making ½-inch seams. Trim corners and turn right side out. Press.

Buy four large metal drapery weights. Drop two weights into each band and pin open ends to back edge of cushion.

Place cushion on chair as illustrated below left. Adjust placement of bands so that the cushion is properly balanced. See below right. Check to see if there is enough weight to hold cushion in place; if not, add more weights.

Remove from chair. Insert raw ends of bands into seam of cushion and hand sew securely.

The cushion below was worked in the uneven bargello stitch on quick-point canvas.

Sewing instructions for finishing a variety of items start on page 98.

Rehabilitation and Recreational Therapy

NEEDLEPOINT CAN BE BENEFICIAL for the development of dexterity and coordination, for mental relaxation, for perceptual training, or for one-handed training.

If a physical condition affects your hands, arms, or eyes, or if you have been under a nervous strain that requires much adaptation or adjustment opposition, consult your physician or therapist before starting to do needlepoint or any similar activity as a therapeutic process.

The recreational value of needlepoint for patients who have long days of confinement should not be overlooked. Needlepoint requires little equipment, is not messy, takes up relatively small space, and can be done with one hand. It can be done easily by a patient in bed or in a chair. The appropriate techniques described in other sections of this book can be used. No specific directions are needed here. For the person doing needlepoint for the first time we suggest a small project such as an eyeglass case, wallet, picture, or pillow. The canvas should be a large mesh, ten meshes to the inch or more. The stitching should be simple with only a few changes of color, and the design should be uncomplicated.

At the bottom of this page are examples of needlepoint pieces created by patients with the temporary use of only one hand. The photographs at the bottom of the opposite page show a cushion made by a patient, and used on the back of a chair.

It is usually easier to work needlepoint without a frame so that it can be carried with you when desired. Often, however, a person having a limited use of one or both hands can do needlepoint only when the canvas is in a taut position. In cases such as this we recommend the use of a frame.

Before buying or making a frame take time to determine the type best suited to your particular need. Most art supply shops carry a frame composed of interlocking strips used for stretching artists' canvas. These strips can be joined to make a frame to hold your needlepoint. The strips come in a variety of lengths, 8 to 36 inches long, and 1⅝ inches wide. They are collapsible, inexpensive, and easy to store.

For example—two 8-inch, and two 12-inch strips will make an oblong that is a practical size to use in making any small item. Also, by shifting the canvas as you work, this size can be used for needlepoint pieces larger than the actual frame. See illustrations on following page.

Above right: Zippered case worked in Parisian stitch. *Left:* Uneven Bargello.

Far right: Cushion in Parisian stitch. Eyeglass case in simplified half-cross stitch.

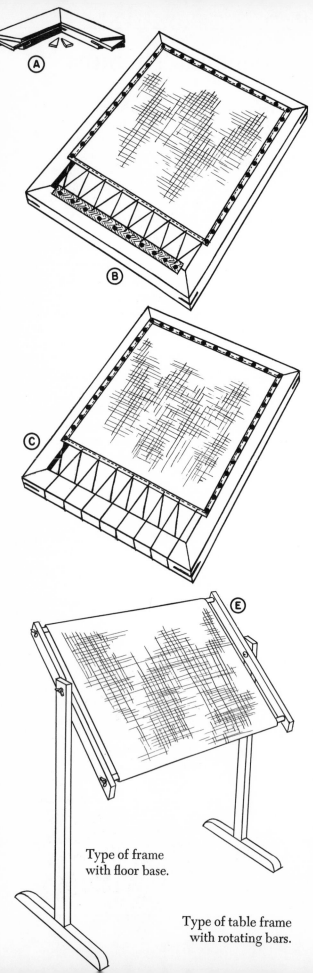

A—Interlocking strips joined at one corner.

Attaching Needlepoint Canvas to Frame.
When using the *plain wooden frame*, thumbtack canvas directly to frame, inserting tacks through the binding. Keep the canvas threads straight in both directions. If canvas is square or smaller than frame, attach on two or three sides with thumbtacks through binding, and then lace the free edge to frame. The lacing can be done in either of the following ways:

B—Tack a length of twilled tape to the empty edge of frame. With a heavy needle and carpet thread take a stitch first in the canvas binding, then in the edge of the tape. Zigzag from edge to edge across open area, and then draw lacing thread taut so that canvas is stretched smooth. Fasten thread securely.

C—The bound edge is laced directly to frame. With needle and carpet thread take a stitch in the bound edge, then carry thread under and over frame and back to canvas. Zigzag back and forth across open area. Draw thread taut to stretch canvas. Fasten thread securely.

When canvas is longer than frame, shift canvas as you work and roll end over edge of frame. See illustration at bottom of opposite page.

This type of frame can be propped against a book or other object while in use to enable you to work the stitches comfortably and freely.

Frames. All types and sizes can be found at various sources. Instructions for using a frame are included with the purchase.

The table or lap frame illustrated (**D**) is one type with rotating crossbars. Your canvas would be basted to the twilled tape which is shown stapled to the crossbars. Larger frames can be obtained with back stand for use on a table, or with a floor base similar to illustration (**E**). A larger frame can be acquired and used when your progress makes it advisable, particularly if you are working on a large chair cover or a needlepoint rug.

Type of frame with floor base.

Type of table frame with rotating bars.

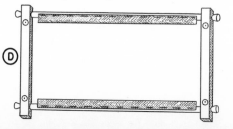

92

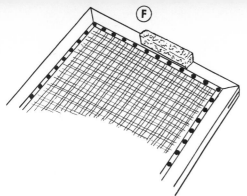

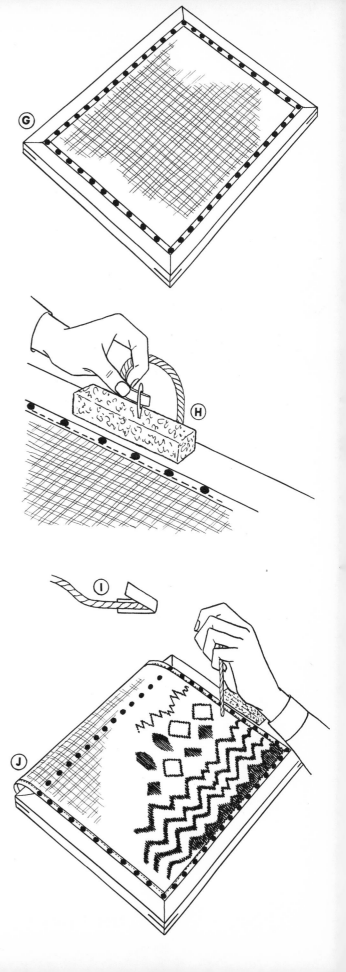

Working with a Frame. If you can use only one hand, glue Styrofoam to one side of the frame to hold point of needle for threading. Cut the piece of foam about 3 inches by 1½ to 2 inches deep, and about one half the frame's width (**F**).

Needlepoint canvas thumbtacked to frame. Insert rustproof tacks through binding, hems, or selvage along outside edge of canvas (**G**).

Threading the needle with one hand is possible when the needle is held steady by inserting the point into the Styrofoam (**H**).

Needle threader (**I**): Cut a piece of bondweight paper about 1 inch long, and wide enough to slide easily into the eye of the needle. Fold the paper in half. Insert the end of yarn into the folded strip. Grasp paper firmly over yarn and insert folded edge of paper into the eye of the needle.

Keep a supply of folded paper threaders handy by cutting a few at a time and storing the extras in an envelope that can be tacked to a corner of the frame.

J. If you have the use of only one hand, insert the needle from underneath the frame (wrong side of canvas), pushing part of the needle's eye through to the upper part of the canvas so that it will stay lightly anchored in the mesh until you can pull it up without difficulty from the top. If you do not do this, the needle will keep falling out of the canvas before you can draw it up. The eye of the needle holds in the canvas because it is wider than the shaft. It takes a little practice to master this technique, but it is well worth the effort.

After you have drawn the needle and yarn through to the right side, then insert the needle downward into next mesh to be worked.

Two distinct motions are required for each stitch—this is known as the *frame stitch method.*

LA BANQUE CONTINENTALE, *New York City*

This bank, located on Fifth Avenue at 60th Street in New York City,
is a most unusual one. It is living proof that a business
establishment can be as gracious as a home.
The exquisite pair of French chairs with needlepoint
backs, seats, and arm rests, are both convenient and elegant.

94

Interior Design

THE ELEGANCE OF NEEDLEPOINT IS AT HOME ANYWHERE. Leading decorators are using these colorful heirloom accents in contemporary room settings as well as with antiques.

A visit to your local museums or restorations will increase your knowledge of the use of needlepoint through the ages, and serve as an inspiration for your own designs. Colonial Williamsburg, for example, contains a varied and interesting group of needlepoint furnishings. For those of you who have an opportunity to go abroad, a visit to various castles throughout the world will expose you to magnificent examples of needlepoint.

You can indulge any taste. Your room can reflect the era you desire, be it Louis XIV, English or French traditional, Early American or contemporary. As your interest in needlepoint grows, you will find more uses for it and additional ideas will crop up.

Neophytes generally start with chair seats, stools, pillows, and pictures, and as their interest and skill develop, branch out to projects such as room dividers, wall hangings, and screens. Needlepoint rugs grow in popularity each year, adding a special touch to almost any room.

Once your particular needlepoint project has been decided on, take the time to select the right design and colors to suit your particular purpose or room. Design and the choice of colors are the factors which lend variety to heirloom pieces. Choose those background colors which harmonize with or complement the room in which you plan to use your finished needlepoint.

Remember that even though the initial cost of your needlepoint material may be high, the result is worth it. Not only will you get gratification from a satisfying hobby, but also you will have created an heirloom to last many generations. Few upholstery fabrics have the durability of needlepoint.

Benches—Chairs—Stools

NEEDLEPOINT CAN BE USED on all sizes, shapes, and styles of furniture, as these pages illustrate. Mounting directions are given on page 88.

The bench, above left, shows a blotch floral design, mounted with decorative brass tacks. A braid trim could be combined with the tacks as a finish. On the right, the traditional design is worked on a light background, then framed in a darker color wool. The contemporary piano bench has a slip-seat covered in a traditional allover design.

The antique settee is worthy of a needlepoint cover. The colorful yarns against the dark frame make it an attractive piece.

Many homes have one or more stools that can be placed conveniently for conversation or for watching TV. Nine separate pieces of canvas are used for the single stool at lower right. Roses cover the seat, rosebuds decorate each leg, and thorny stems twine around the rungs.

The octagonal dot design also has nine pieces. It would appeal to most men and costs about the same as the rose design. Both stools are sturdy and long-lasting, and of special interest because the design covers the entire stool.

Above left: One of the most popular single chairs, it has a slip-seat which is easy to finish and mount at home. See page 105. *Right:* The antique armchair is covered with a contemporary floral design. One flower decorates the chair back, its stem leading to the leaves and stems on the seat.

Below left: The Victorian chair is a period piece that can be used with almost any type of furniture. On this occasional chair the needlepoint is carefully rounded over the corners and finished with decorative braid. *Right:* This comfortable, graceful chair is suitable for a formal room. The muted colors of the floral design give the chair a feminine air. The needlepoint is applied to the frame with upholstery tacks.

Cushions Unlimited

It is almost impossible to name a subject or type of design that has not been needlepointed at one time or another for a cushion or pillow. The design possibilities are endless. Turn your imagination loose, and see how original you can be.

Russell Lynes did just that for the cushion on the left. After cutting a piece of canvas to the desired size, he started in the center and worked outward as his mood directed. The patchwork and geometrics show a few more of Mr. Lynes's pillow designs.

Bold mod designs, such as the zebra stripe and mammoth beetle, are fun to make on rug canvas with the larger yarns. They work up quickly and give one a change of pace.

Three examples of the many traditional designs readily available are illustrated by the allover floral, peasant and rose cushions at the top of the opposite page.

Shaped or fitted cushions can be made for any furniture piece, as the cane-bottomed settee on the left shows.

Such a cushion can be made with or without a boxing strip in the background color.

98

On the right below, the pot of gloxinia glows in rich reds, purples, and greens against a beige background. Velvet in a dark beige was used for the back of this knife-edged cushion.

The designs of most needlepoint cushions are so colorful that it is best to finish them with plain or corded seams or a simple fringe.

Upholstery fabric can be used for the backings of pillows and cushions and for piecing needlepoint (see page 76). Select the fabric carefully for texture and color so that it does not detract from your needlepoint design. Velvet, velveteen, and other napped or piled fabrics combine with needlepoint most attractively.

Leather or leather-like material can be used similarly to the upholstery fabrics. The anemone floral has suede leather boxing; imitation leather is used for the back and for the boxing of the paisley design. The boxing strip can be seamed at the corners, but be sure that the nap runs only in one direction on all the strips.

Needlepoint fabric is manufactured to look like plain needlepoint. It comes in beautiful decorator colors, and it can be used to supplement handmade needlepoint if you prefer not to make large areas of solid-colored stitches. When a needlepoint design is used for the back, seat, and arms of an upholstered chair, the sides and back can be covered with plain fabric.

The Personal Touch

MANY PEOPLE like to have "something special" throughout their homes. Needlepoint can serve this purpose, whether it be a small piece, a chair, a rug, or a magnificent hanging.

The photograph above shows some designs available for telephone book covers. You might enjoy designing your own with odds and ends of yarn worked into a way-out design.

All the items shown on this page and across the top of the opposite page are a combination of needlepoint and real or imitation leather. For best results these should be mounted by a professional unless you are an experienced hand.

Address books and memo pads decorated with needlepoint make welcome Christmas and birthday presents as well as gifts for special occasions. The cover design can be a name or monogram worked into a background color that will harmonize or contrast with the room in which it will be used. Refer to page 136 for instructions on developing words and monograms.

In addition to the items mentioned previously, jewel boxes, magazine holders, stationery boxes, writing cases, and anything else having an appropriate shape can be covered or decorated with needlepoint.

Bell pulls are seldom needed as they were formerly, but old needlepoint pulls can be used as a decorative feature in a foyer, or you can hang one on each side of a mirror. An unusual cornice trim can be made by placing the pulls horizontally.

Luggage racks can be useful as well as decorative. See page 12 showing the use of a luggage rack in Blair House. A large tray, placed across a rack, makes a convenient TV table. After the tray is removed, the rack is easy to fold and store. The straps for luggage racks come in two types: in individual pieces or in a continuous piece which is cut into strips of the desired length. Allow 2 inches at each end of strap for tacking to the rack. See below.

Card table covers in needlepoint make an ideal surface for playing, but they should be functional, not elaborate. Select a cover with a border design and a plain center or a plain cover which can be personalized with a monogram in the center. See page 137 for monograms. Keep the colors muted so as not to conflict with the cards.

A holder for decks of playing cards can be decorated with needlepoint which shows a matching monogram but smaller in scale.

Rugs

THE MAKING OF A NEEDLEPOINT RUG presents a real challenge even to the expert needle-pointer. The rug should be designed to fit a specific area or room. One of the most popular sizes is 4 feet by 5 feet which makes a perfect accent rug for under a coffee table, in front of a fireplace, or in a foyer. Most rugs are worked in either the continental or basket weave stitch.

A needlepoint rug is one project which should be blocked professionally. Apart from the large size, the canvas is usually heavy, large meshed, and worked in a thick, heavy wool. Rug wool is specially designed to withstand constant pulling through coarse canvas.

Most rugs have a tendency to become out of shape as they are worked, and it takes skill, as well as great physical strength, to pull them back into shape when they are blocked. We consulted expert rug makers and professional blockers, and they were unanimous in stressing the importance of having the blocking, backing, and finishing done professionally.

A needlepoint rug will involve a substantial investment of your time and money. Before you undertake a project of this magnitude, we recommend that you find out the cost of the basic materials and where and how much it will cost to have it finished professionally.

Designs for rugs come from many sources in nature, art, and abstract design, as well as from old world oriental rugs. Rug patterns can be bought with the design already worked, leaving only the background to be filled in.

A fine example of trompe l'oeil (visual deception) design. The lemons and apples look natural enough to pick up from the needlepointed floor.

The three designs at the top of the opposite page are examples of patterns that have to be completely worked. The center rug has tasseled corners; the one at right has fringed ends. Instructions for making fringes and tassels can be found in most sewing books.

The other four rugs have designs which were custom-made for individual clients. If your talents run in this direction, you can do this work yourself as instructed on page 33.

Above: The butterfly design exemplifies a highly individual taste. You can imagine the brilliant colors which were used. The second rug shows unusual handling of oriental motifs.

Below: Large-sized round rugs are rare. This beautiful one has a floral design suitable for traditional surroundings.

This panel screen shows a typical Vertès design. The full-length figures show exceptional verve and beauty. See pages 164 and 165 for more examples of this artist's work.

Screens—Panels—Pictures

A LOVELY SCREEN has always been a cherished possession whether it was a fireplace screen, used as protection against sparks, or a folding panel screen used as protection against drafts. In today's heated homes, screens are used mostly as decorative pieces, frequently mounted on a wall.

If a screen taller than the available canvas designs should be needed, add canvas to the bottom of the panels to gain the extra height. The additional canvas can be joined by piecing as described on page 74.

Screens should be framed or mounted by a professional. *Panels* are usually lined and hung as wall hangings; *pictures* are stretched and framed. You will find many ideas suitable for framed needlepoint throughout this book.

The French fireplace screen has a traditional floral design; the black lacquer frames a design with oriental overtones.

104

Mounting Slip-seat Chairs

Block needlepoint as instructed on page 86. Remove the seat from chair frame and check the padding. Place needlepoint on top of seat, using the vertical and horizontal center lines on canvas to position the design correctly. Place a pin at each corner and a few along the sides to prevent slipping.

Turn the seat over. Fold the two sides over the edges, placing a tack at each corner through the canvas selvage or binding into the wood. Add tacks every 1 or 2 inches along both sides, checking to see that the canvas is being pulled evenly along the edges of the seat.

Fold the front edge over and tack. Make neat square corners and ease edge of canvas between tacks so that needlepoint is smooth on the edge of seat.

The back edge of the seat is done last. If it is curved, lay small darts or pleats in the canvas edge so the tacks will keep the folds flat, as shown in the first photograph.

The second photograph shows how lining is placed over the bottom of seat to give a neat finish. Turn under edge of lining and tack in place with small carpet tacks.

Yarn Storage. Place some leftover yarn under the needlepoint or backing so that it will be available for repairs in case of damage, especially if it is on furniture.

The photograph on the right shows yarn ends folded back on a corner of the lining. On a cushion, spread the yarn lengths smoothly under the backing. A few lengths of all the design colors may be stored, but the background color is the one most often needed.

Reinforcing a Cut Area. If canvas has been cut or torn accidentally, baste a canvas patch, ½ inch larger than the damaged area, under the weak spot on the wrong side. Align the meshes and work the stitches through both layers. Trim away all canvas threads that show through.

Noncolorfast Wool. If it becomes necessary to reblock old needlepoint, check the colorfastness of the wool.

Wet a corner and blot with a dry cloth to

see if the color runs. If it is not colorfast, sprinkle the right side generously with salt and wet the wool with cold water until saturated. Allow needlepoint to dry. If it is out of shape, reblock and dry again.

Refurbishing Needlepoint. Once or twice a year freshen and brighten needlepoint that is in daily use by cleaning it with a shampoo type of cleaner. Select a cleaner recommended for fine upholstery fabrics, and follow the instructions given on the label.

After the needlepoint is thoroughly dry, hold a steam iron 4 or 5 inches above the surface, allowing the steam to restore the loftiness of the wool.

Above: The book cover with handles was worked in the uneven bargello with a few rows of petit point stitches added for a change of texture.

The covers of the memo pad and glove box are decorated in brilliant colors with the uneven bargello stitch. The needle case was made with the chevron stitch, and the slip-case for the compact was made with the brick stitch.

The accessories shown in the photograph below were worked in the continental stitch, and they show sparkling designs that are in tune with current fashion trends.

Fashion Accessories

IF YOUR MENTAL IMAGE OF NEEDLEPOINT is based solely on the Victorian precepts of subdued colors and simple, even stitches, forget it!

The needlepoint yarn of today is available in an array of colors, shades, and tints that staggers the imagination. Using these brilliant colors in stitches which give textured effects can make your fashion accessories as modern as tomorrow. However, a word of caution is advisable in the category of wearable needlepoint; don't overdo a good thing. Designs should be distinctive, yet basic and of a style which can be worn with a variety of seasonal fashions. Needlepoint accessories should enhance the look of the entire outfit; they should not be glaringly obvious.

Styling for men is constantly in a state of change, but you must bear in mind that not every man will wear a needlepointed item just because you made it for him. Keep the likes and dislikes of the man in mind, the colors as well as the design, when you are selecting an item to be worked for him.

There are many fashion accessories on which needlepoint can be used effectively:

Handbags in all sizes and shapes

For use in handbags: cosmetic case, compact holder, comb case, change purse, eyeglass case, wallet, address book, credit card or business card holder, memo pad cover, rain hat holder

For traveling: plastic-lined cosmetic case, jewel case, stocking case, shoebag cover

Wearing apparel: hat, belt, slippers, vest, waistcoat, cummerbund

Closet accessories: cases or box covers to hold gloves, scarves, jewels, stockings, or handkerchiefs

Miscellaneous: brief case, typewriter cover, dog coat and collar

A paper or muslin pattern can be made from any ready-made item to use as a guide for developing needlepoint designs. See pages 112 and 198 for instructions on making some of the accessories mentioned above.

Bags—Daytime, Evening, Travel

UNTIL QUITE RECENTLY, the most popular of all needlepoint fashion accessories was the handbag. For centuries these bags were usually done in petit point. Most were small, having delicate designs, and they were used for formal affairs. Now, however, needlepointers are making bags in all sizes and shapes for all occasions, including luggage for travel.

The cost of blocking, framing, and mounting will depend on the type of frame, the quantity of leather required, and whether the bag is to be lined with leather or fabric. A price of $35 for a small clutch bag is about average, but for the larger, more detailed bags, prices will range sharply upward. Make sure that your cost will include blocking your needlepoint, a step which *you* should not attempt to do if you want a perfect result.

The importance of entrusting your work to a specialist, capable of high-quality work, cannot be overemphasized. Before you select the bag maker for your work, look at samples of finished work of as many makers as you can.

Select a frame for your handbag of a style and durability which will suit the usage you

(*Bags—continued on page 115*)

Below are shown a clutch bag, four styles of handbags with handles, and a simple tote bag. Shoulder-strap bags are shown on page 106 and a monogramed bag on page 137.

Opposite page, far right, shows an attractive combination of needlepoint on a wicker bag. See page 114 for instructions.

Luggage. Bags, such as those illustrated, have original needlepoint designs made up into tote bags. The prices for bags of this type, excluding the needlepoint, range from $65 upward, depending on size, frame, type of mounting, lining, and fittings.

The two large bags have two pockets on each side of the lining, two heavy-duty zippers, a change purse, and a mirror. Each zipper opens three-quarters of the way down each side, making it easy to pack a wide range of items.

The oblong bag with the dark background has a washable plastic lining, fitted with cosmetic bottles. The jars and bottles must be supplied to the mounter in the desired shapes and sizes for custom fitting.

Wearing Apparel

Waistcoats (weskits) and vests are practical garments which appeal to many men. Men who do needlepoint frequently design and make their own. See page 160 for an outstanding vest design.

The waistcoat, shown at top left, was worked with cotton yarn in blue and rust, using the bargello stitch. It was lined and bound in navy. White, deep gold, blue, and black were used for the abstract design of the vest. Black satin was used for the back and for the lining.

Cummerbund. The family crest above decorates a man's needlepoint sash, which hooks in center back.

Feminine versions of the above items would make excellent accessories for a suit or for an evening outfit.

Slippers done in needlepoint are popular with both men and women. Scuffs and sandals can be made from strips of needlepoint. See opposite page. Before you start a slipper project, be sure you know where they can be finished and mounted, as this is a highly specialized craft.

Many needlework specialty shops include the cost of mounting in the cost of the canvas, design, and yarn. The price will depend on the style you choose.

The row of men's slippers shows a variety of geometric designs; the pair sports a decorative beetle. See also the tiger slipper on page 166 and the woman's mule on page 106.

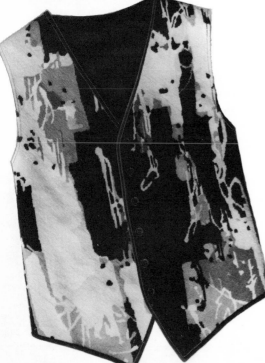

Hats should be made on fine or medium canvas. Shown are two styles of pillboxes. The squared one is made of two pieces: a band cut to the measurement of the head and a flat top section. The unworked painted canvas pieces are shown in the background. The other style is a shaped pillbox. Before you start to make this hat, consult your needlework shop for directions. The pillbox must be steamed and shaped on a milliner's block by a professional.

Small personal accessories that can be made in needlepoint include a wide range of attractive items. A few are shown below and on page 106. Two cosmetic bags and an eyeglass case are shown on page 91.

Belts. Practically any band or border design can be made into a belt. A metal buckle is attached to the ends of the first, while the ends of the second have hooks and eyes.

Eyeglass cases can be made for one or two pairs of glasses as shown at the right.

Sets of two or three items can be made in a matching design. A wallet and an eyeglass case set are illustrated.

Scissors holders should be made to fit a specific pair of scissors, and they should come to a tapered point at the closed end.

111

Personal Accessories

The items shown here include accessories that can be carried with you as well as some that would be used in the home. See *Mounting with Glue* on page 90.

Brief case. The zipper in a brief case should be in the boxing strip or sewn into the case. The case shown has a zipper across its top. Select a brief case which has corded edges so that the edges of the needlepoint will be protected when the case is in use.

Apply needlepoint to one side only. If the brief case has flexible sides, fill it with books or magazines before applying needlepoint.

Make a paper pattern of the side to be covered, rounding the corners carefully. Trim ¼ inch all around, lay the pattern on canvas, and mark the outline.

The design shown was worked in an uneven bargello, to within three meshes of the outline. Block and dry thoroughly.

Trim away canvas ½ inch outside the outline. Turn canvas edge to wrong side along outline, mitering the corners or clipping the canvas at ½-inch intervals for rounded corners. Baste.

Continue needlepoint around the edge, taking stitches through the two layers of canvas. Use a yarn color that will frame the design. Trim away any excess canvas.

Spread glue on the side of brief case and on the back of the needlepoint. Lay the needlepoint over the case, smoothing out the panel from the center. Add glue around the edges and press firmly into place. Lay a piece of paper over the needlepoint and place heavy books on top to apply pressure while the glue is drying. See *Adhesives* on page 206.

A wicker handbag having a top closure should be selected so that the needlepoint can be glued to the side panel without interfering with the opening and closing of the bag. The raised edge frames the needlepoint attractively. See instructions for mounting on page 114.

Accessory boxes for gloves, handkerchiefs, scarves, and stockings can be decorated with needlepoint panels. On page 106 the glove box has a panel applied flush with the edge of the cover. The uneven bargello was worked in a diagonal effect, and a plain border frames the piece.

Memo Pads—Address Books. The memo pad on page 106 has a panel worked in a design similar to the box cover but without a worked border. It was framed by mounting the needlepoint within an imprinted border on the cover.

At top of opposite page are two more memo pad panels. On the left the outline of the area to be worked is marked on the canvas. You must finish the title as shown here, before you fill in the background. In the center, the title was worked on the diagonal with an uneven bargello stitch worked in the same direction.

The edges of the canvas are turned to the wrong side, one mesh outside the edge of the design. Cut away excess canvas diagonally at the corners so that the edges lap about ¼ inch at each corner.

A long backstitch was worked through the two layers of canvas for a simple framing effect. Use a matching or contrasting wool for this step.

Two stitches were used to work the address book cover. The title and upper section are in the continental stitch. The lower section is worked in the diagonal stitch.

The mounting of this cover will depend on the type of book it is. The same general instructions used for the memo pads can be followed. If the needlepoint is to be combined with leather, it should be done professionally.

The accessories described previously were mounted with glue; those described below are finished by lining and sewing. See instructions beginning on page 198.

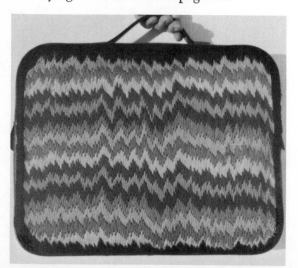

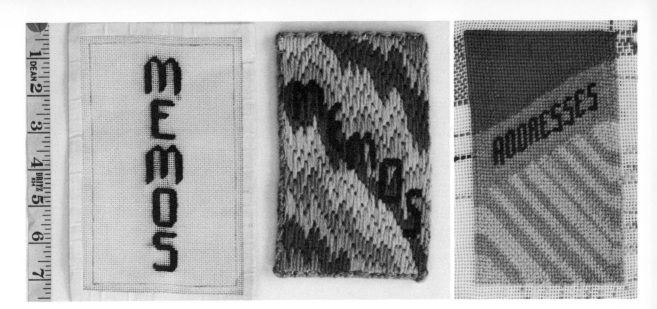

Eyeglass cases are one of the most popular of the small accessories made in needlepoint. The cases can be stiff and shaped, or they can be soft and flat. The stiff ones should be mounted professionally. The soft cases can be made in a variety of ways.

On page 111 are shown a few designs of the many commercially available, and on page 91 is an illustration of an eyeglass case made on large-mesh canvas.

Book covers can be made to fit a specific book, like the missal cover shown at right, or a cover can be made to fit a group of books. Divide the groups into paperbacks, regular size and larger size books.

Make a cover in a snug fit if it is for a specific book, but if it is to fit a number of books it should be made roomy enough to allow for the differences in size of the books it will cover.

The book cover shown on page 106 was made from the three pieces of needlepoint in the photographs below.

(*continued on following page*)

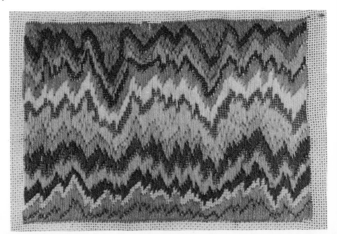

Compact Slip-case. This type of case can be made for a favorite compact or for several. The case shown on page 106 was made with square corners so that it could be used to hold compacts of various shapes. A square case is easier to needlepoint, sew together, and line.

Needle Book. See the illustration on page 106. This holder is called a book because it has layers of fabric fastened to the center of a needlepoint cover like the leaves in a book. Needles are inserted into the fabric for storage and protection. It is a practical case to use for your needlepoint needles.

Rain Hat Holder. Instructions for making a shaped needlepoint case to hold a folded rain hat are given on page 199.

(Mail Holder—continued from page 90)
The title is worked first. See detail on page 129. A block of contrasting color is worked around the title; then the remainder of the background is worked.

Block the needlepoint. Trim canvas along the sides, three meshes from edge of needlepoint, cutting evenly from top to bottom. Trim top and bottom edges six meshes from needlepoint.

Squeeze a line of glue directly from the tube onto the bottom of holder about 1 inch from all edges.

Center the bottom of holder on the wrong side of canvas in the space marked for it. Press against canvas for a few minutes until glue has set. Fold top end of canvas strip over top edge of front section. Use masking tape to hold in place. Fold bottom end of canvas strip over top of back section; tape to hold in place. Check to see that holder is centered on the width; adjust if necessary.

Fold side edges of canvas over edges of holder, making a small pleat in canvas at each bottom corner if necessary for a smooth fit. Overlap top corners, cutting away excess canvas but still overlapping canvas edges by two or three meshes.

Spread glue on side edges of canvas and

squeeze a line of glue on the inside of holder. Press together and hold until glue has set. Glue the two top edges in the same way. Let dry thoroughly. A piece of matching felt can be glued to the bottom of holder over the canvas.

Self-adhesive paper in a suitable color and texture can be applied to inside of holder to cover raw edges of canvas to give a finished look.

Mounting Needlepoint on Wicker Handbag

(Illustrated on page 109)

SELECT A BASKET BAG CAREFULLY; there is a great variation in quality, and many of them are not true in shape. Make sure that the sides to which the needlepoint is to be glued are as smooth as possible. Make a paper pattern for each side so that any variation in shape can be transferred to canvas. Trim off ¼ inch on all edges of pattern.

Lay the pattern on canvas, and accurately mark the area to be worked. Work the design.

Before blocking, machine stitch (eight stitches per inch) three or four times around the edge, stitching over the two outside rows of needlepoint stitches. Block the canvas. When completely dry, trim the canvas from ⅛ inch to ¼ inch outside of the machine stitching.

Apply glue directly from tube or bottle to the entire back of canvas, covering the edges heavily. Apply canvas to basket. Press hard only on the edges; do not press on middle of canvas or it will take on the unevenness of the basket weave. If basket has a very coarse weave, place a layer of cotton padding under the needlepoint. Make the padding ½ inch smaller all around so that the canvas edges will adhere directly to the straw. Continue to press only the edges of the canvas.

After the canvas is glued in place, apply the braid. Start braid end at one of the bottom corners, adding glue to braid several inches at a time and finger pressing over the cut edge of canvas. If a small speck of glue shows after the glue has dried, it can be picked out with a pin.

(Bags—continued from page 108)

have planned for the bag. Once you have made your choice, place a deposit with the shop so that your frame will be there when you are ready to have the bag mounted. Many bag makers will furnish a pattern to guide you for the size of the frame you have selected. Whatever charge is made for the pattern usually will be deducted from the mounting cost if you have the bag finished at the same shop.

Regardless of the care you use in the choice of the bag maker to finish your needlepoint bag, there is no guarantee that you will have chosen correctly. A satisfied customer is the strongest recommendation, so see if any of your friends have used a source with which they are satisfied. However, if you must find a source strictly on your own initiative, there are a few guidelines which may be of help.

There should be a good selection of frames, leathers, and linings on hand from which to choose. Samples of finished work, modern in design and perfectly mounted, should be available for your inspection. The bag maker should be able to offer constructive suggestions.

Do *not* shop around for a low price for the mounting and finishing. Be guided rather by what you are going to get for your money than by how much you will spend.

Selecting Materials

Know the size, shape, and usage for the bag.

Select canvas of the proper size of mesh (see sizes on page 18). Petit point canvas is used for small and/or delicate designs. Larger bags and tailored bags are usually worked on canvas having 10 and 12 meshes to the inch.

Buy sufficient yarn to complete the bag.

Marking and Working the Design

Mark the area to be worked, adding approximately 1 inch outside the outline of the design. This is especially important at the top of the piece so that the frame will **not** overlap, cutting off the top of design.

Gusset: If the bag requires a gusset, measure it carefully. The width of the gusset determines whether or not the bag will open wide enough for you to get your hand in and out easily. Use a nonstretch tape measure.

The outside edge of the gusset is measured by placing end of tape at one corner (bottom edge of frame) and carrying tape around bottom of bag to the opposite corner. See diagram **A**.

To measure the top of **Y**, open the frame three-quarters of the way and measure as shown in diagram **B**.

Diagram **C** shows how to make the pattern for the gusset using the measurement you have taken. In most cases the best length for the **Y** section is 4 or 5 inches. If it is made too long, it will not fold into place properly, and the bag will not open wide enough.

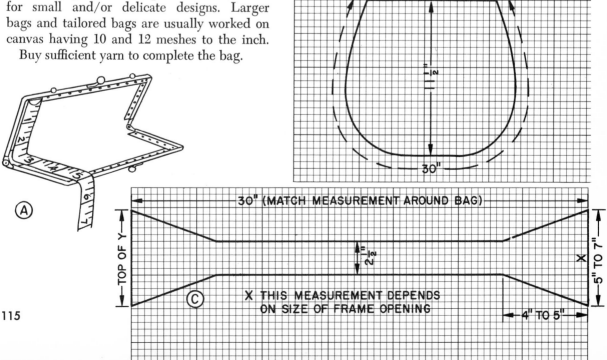

This beautiful hanging (5 feet by 8 feet)
was developed as a family record.
It was designed by Rosetta Larson
for the late Mrs. Henry Pomeroy
Davison of Locust Valley, New York.
Mrs. Davison did the needlepoint,
which was hung in her Long Island home.

In the foreground "Appledore" shows
a lovely brick house
with a cutting garden
and swimming pool on one side.
In back of this is Athabasca Ranch,
her Canadian summer home.
Mountains and
a river make the background.
Note the various animals—
dogs, horses, donkeys, and bears—
incorporated in the design.

The border is composed of
apple blossoms on the right
and bottom edges, with evergreen
and pine cones on the left and top
edges. The family coat of arms
is at top center.

Mrs. Davison's grandson
and his wife brought the hanging
back to Rosetta Larson of Madison
Avenue, New York City,
to be cleaned and relined, and this
gave us the opportunity
of photographing this outstanding
piece of needlepoint.

House and Home

House and Home

To EVERY PERSON "house" and "home" have special meanings. Aside from work, our living activities are widely varied.

What activities are connected with your home or everyday living? Does the family love cookouts or picnics? Swimming pool, tennis court, putting green? Flower or vegetable garden, greenhouse, or aquarium? Is a sailboat or yacht a part-time home? Or a cabin in the woods for hunting and fishing?

Have you another idea? It is not necessary to depict your home with a building. After examining the various pictures in this chapter you might decide on what new approach you can take in this area of needlepoint. Imagination, sentiment, and perseverance will all help to make a piece of needlepoint belong expressly to an individual or a family.

You can make an all-inclusive record as shown by the hanging on pages 116–117, or depict some special interest such as a house, garden, or swimming pool, as illustrated on the following pages.

A needlepoint of a house can be used as a picture or as a chair back, pillow top, or wall hanging. We have seen a house and garden done in needlepoint for a desk top, held in place with braid and tacks as would be done on a chair.

One man took a picture of his boyhood farm home, then needlepointed the house, the well with its bucket, and the hollyhocks at the door. He showed it in summer, the colors delightfully bright. See *The Four Seasons* on page 123.

Above: This house of modern design featuring a sloping flat roof, a carport, and a massive chimney shows how attractive the contemporary style can be when worked in needlepoint. This illustration was used for the cover of a book on decorating published by a carpet company. It is a good example of how to accent dark areas with bright highlights in order to achieve interesting tonal effects.

Needlepainting means just what the word implies: the making of a needlepoint picture in the same way that an artist works. Make a pencil outline of the scene or subject on the canvas, and use the needle and yarn to bring out details. Interesting results may be obtained by varying the stitches for different areas of the picture.

As you progress with the needlepoint, the effect in an area may not satisfy you. Just take out the stitches of the color which displeases and replace them with stitches of the correct color.

Ripping should be done very carefully so as not to damage the canvas. Cut only those stitches which you wish to remove. See the directions for removing stitches on page 73.

Left: This is a copy of the rough pencil drawing developed from snapshots of the Lowell Thomas home in Pawling, New York. More details were added before it was transferred to single-mesh canvas.

The house is built in the Colonial tradition of handmade brick with a slate roof. The window trim is white.

Because the canvas is only 18 by 24 inches, the details of the large trees and the foliage are simple so as not to overshadow the house. The lake is just suggested in the foreground.

The soft red of the brick, the fine nuances of the sixty colors used by Mrs. Thomas to do this painting in needlepoint, make this a treasured heirloom.

The three needlepoint designs shown here were inspired by views of an estate in Bristol, Rhode Island, named Windhill.

The swimming pool with diving board and adjacent bath houses have a real photographic quality. Appropriate and colorful plantings do their part in adding to the beauty of the picture, which is mounted for use as a fire screen.

Opposite page, lower right:

Behind the family sailboat, sailing on Narragansett Bay, is a mininature view of the home on the hill.

A flower garden with its profusion of blooms was carefully copied, then mounted for a pole screen. Note how the frame follows the needlepointed columns and arch.

All these pieces were designed and worked by Martha F. Sayles Nicholson. Mrs. Nicholson drew the designs on canvas and dyed her own needlepoint wool.

Although Russell Lynes worked with the graphic arts continuously, he preferred to record his homes in needlepoint rather than to have them in drawings or photographs.

At the right is the view of a garden in back of his town house, designed as a cushion cover. Mr. Lynes worked this out as a whimsical Garden of Eden scene, from sketch to finished needlepoint.

Below, his country home as he drew it and executed it in needlepoint. The white house, red window frames and shutters, green grass, and darker trees give a color

ensemble that is decidedly handsome and pleasing to all who see it.

Other examples of Mr. Lynes's work appear elsewhere in this book.

Fishing, Boating, Skiing. Take a snapshot of your country home or other retreat, preferably in color, enlarge it, and transfer it to canvas.

You can add a personal touch by including things such as a boat, fishermen, skiers, hunters, or whatever is appropriate to the locale. Such an addition lends a feeling of motion to an otherwise static landscape. Mr. Lynes's picture of his country house on the preceding page illustrates this point.

The Four Seasons. Do you enjoy the changes of the seasons? The same scenes will vary just as greatly in needlepoint because of the colors used to portray spring, summer, fall, and winter.

The colors of spring are delicate pastels—dogwood, forsythia, pale green leaves.

Summer colors are light but brilliant—rich green, gold, red, and blue.

Deep rich, vibrant colors for fall—rust, orange, and browns.

A winter snow scene can make a beautiful needlepoint piece with the white expanse of snow highlighted by blue and gray shadows contrasting with the bare trees and varied hues of the evergreens.

Those who see the wedding sampler above usually want to make
one or more themselves. Reva DeBerry of Portsmouth, Virginia,
designed and made this one. She has made many similar ones
as wedding gifts, for friends, for her own family.

Mrs. DeBerry makes two kinds. The one illustrated is done in
gros point with only the faces in petit point. The second type is
a smaller size worked in petit point on single-thread canvas.
Instructions for developing a similar sampler for yourself
are given on page 128.

Samplers · Mottoes · Monograms

AMERICAN SAMPLERS WERE INFLUENCED principally by three European countries—England, Holland, and Germany.

As household linens increased in use, it was necessary to identify individual pieces with monograms. The alphabetical samplers were used for reference in preparing these.

Originally samplers were narrow strips of linen because looms were narrow. The early English types were chiefly practice pieces.

An entire name might be used or just initials. The initials were most likely the forerunners of monograms which can be either simple or quite elaborate.

Many of the illustrations in this chapter show complete names, initials, or monograms. A date is usually combined with the name or initials to show who did the work and when, a highly desirable practice.

Mottoes in embroidery developed from the original samplers. The letters of the alphabet were still made, but in groups forming words. Usually some decorative motifs were combined with the mottoes to add interest and color.

The samplers of today are usually pictures, and in most instances they also record information about an individual or a family.

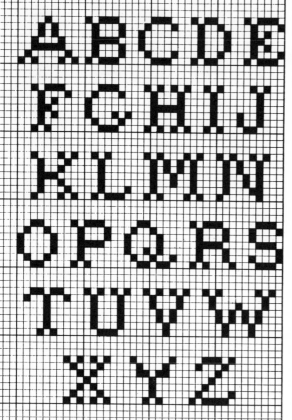

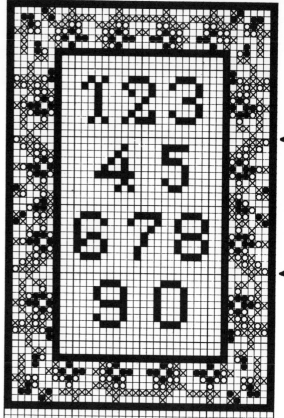

Alphabets. Two styles of alphabets are most often found in period samplers and in those made prior to our century. The first, block letters with serifs, is used most often as capital letters with numerals. See above. The second, script letters, is used in both capitals and lower case. See opposite page.

Above: Block letters with serifs can be made in a wide variety of weights. Use a single line of stitches for the lightweight and smaller sizes. Each letter illustrated is seven squares high, but the width varies. The numerals are seven squares high and five squares wide with the exception of 1. A large block letter alpha-

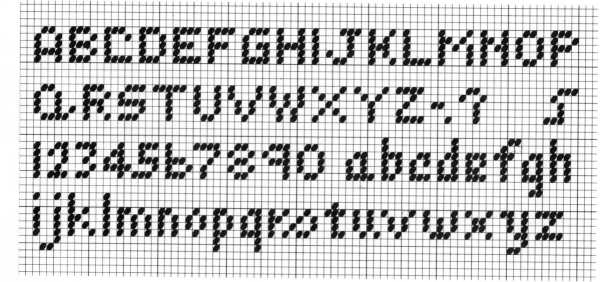

bet showing 3½-inch diagrams is referred to in the bibliography on page 203.

The decorative border around the numerals could be adapted to various sizes by separating the four corners and adding motifs similar to those between the arrows at the side.

Opposite page, bottom: This block letter alphabet is simplified and is much less trouble to develop in designs. To make it easier to see how each letter will look when it is made in needlepoint stitches, ovals (representing the slanted stitches) are used in each square of the graph paper instead of filled-in squares.

The letters in this alphabet are made with as few stitches as possible, although a couple of the capitals could be further condensed if it were necessary. The numerals are five squares high to match the capitals. Most of the lower-case letters are four squares high, but the ascender and dotted letters (b, d, f, h, i, j, k, l, t) and the descender letters (g, j, p, q, y) vary in height. The wedding sampler

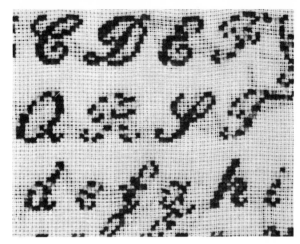

on page 124 and the birth sampler on page 129 were made with simplified letters.

Below: The American 19th century sampler shows a fine script alphabet that can be used for today's needlepoint by blocking out the alphabet on graph paper. The enlargement above shows a few letters in detail.

Family Record Samplers

Mrs. DeBerry, designer of the wedding sampler shown on the left and on page 124, has a few words of caution for the person starting to work such a sampler.

Neither side border should be worked until the side having the longest name is blocked in. Then block in the name for the opposite side. Notice how nicely the names are balanced here. Each full name is centered between the top and bottom borders. A little less space can be allowed between the names and middle initial if the name is one or two letters longer.

For an extra long name add a couple of rows of stitches at the bottom below the hill on which the church is set. Additional rows at the top above the birds will also not detract from the overall design.

In the bottom section of the border any date will fit. Spell out short-named months, abbreviate the longer ones.

Another suggestion is to use bright, clear colors. Mrs. DeBerry uses several shades of green, some black, brown, red, and bright blue. The background is a light cream with a hint of clear yellow.

You can draw your own tree, your own figures, choose your own colors. Use care in the proportions and you will have a sampler to please yourself and to delight those for whom you make it.

For gros point, start with a piece of double-mesh canvas (10 meshes to the inch was used here) 15 by 20 inches or 22 to 24 inches when the names are longer than shown.

Family Tree. A family record of this kind is easy to do in gros point. Draw a tree, placing the blossoms and leaves to suit. Use the favorite color of each person to make the flower nearest his name. Outline a space large enough for each name. Names may be boxed in as shown, or the outside lines can be omitted.

The names should be worked first because the tree branches can be adjusted more easily than the letters. If the names are to be in boxes, work the outlines next.

The word "mail," right, shows how the stitches fill in around the word to form a block, just as you would around each name on the

sampler. The background color outlines the block.

Wedding and Birth Samplers. The two samplers above could be used as a pair, framed separately. The first has a bride and groom, with sufficient space within the border to work names and marriage date. The second shows a stork carrying a baby, and below the word "born" the baby's full name and birth date would be worked.

The elaborate birth sampler records more information than the example above. The mother's maiden name and the father's full name are included along with the son's name, date and place of birth. The initials of the needlepointer and the date it was made appear in the lower left-hand corner.

Block letters with serifs were used to identify the contents of this antique document case. See page 191 for details of the complete case.

129

Opposite page, top: "Finished in February 1878 by B" is all the information we have about this interesting sampler of motifs and initials. The design in the four corners is the only one repeated; it helps to unify the piece.

There was a period during the late 18th century and throughout the 19th century when decorative cards were distributed by thread and drug companies as a form of advertising. It is very likely that these cards inspired much of the needlepoint design of this period. The variety of subject matter in this sampler could have developed from such cards.

Opposite page, bottom: All these motifs are done in very fine embroidery. The flowers in the upper left- and upper right-hand corners are needlepoint. The detailed flowers and shapes are in direct contrast to the simple motifs in the sampler above.

Top of column: A contemporary sampler with a serifed alphabet. The bands of geometric designs between the lines of letters show how attractive simple groupings of stitches can be. Developing similar bands is good practice for originating your own designs.

Although the two 19th century samplers in this column are similar, both having many motifs, they also differ greatly.

In the top one all the motifs are very carefully balanced, and it is framed by an attractive border.

All the motifs in the bottom sampler, except the alphabets at the top, are crowded together although the individual designs are interesting.

Mottoes

THE OLD RELIABLE "God Bless Our Home" is still one of the most popular mottoes sold. When blocking your own letters, you can make a motto in one, two or more lines, and fit it into any desired shape. Depending on which direction you are working, the best stitches to use for words and sentences are the continental and half cross.

A modified Old English typeface was used to develop the motto on the left. A word is shown in detail on graph paper. The size of the letters is determined by the size of the canvas.

The amusing Pennsylvania Dutch saying appeals to many people. It uses block lettering with decorative serifs.

The motto at the bottom of the page is exceptionally well designed to suit the subject matter. Roses can replace the houses, or a simpler border can enclose only the words. This motto is a universal favorite because of its humorous touch. A monotone color combination can be used overall, or the houses can be made in a variety of colors for a very gay effect. The words are in condensed block lettering with heavy top and bottom serifs. See detail on graph paper.

Marking Canvas for Lettering. Generally, any transfer method can be used. See pages 44 and 134.

Baste marking can be used on the darker canvas to outline the letters. It is a practical way of marking very thin letters or letters done in white or very delicate colors.

Diagram **A** at the top of opposite page shows how the thread is worked into the canvas. Carry the basting thread from letter to letter on the wrong side.

The horizontal bastings mark the height of

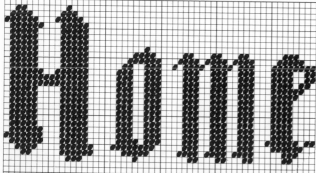

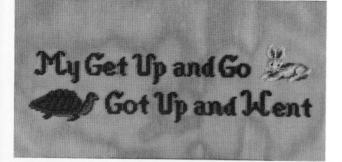

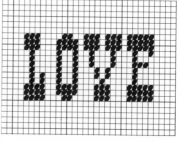

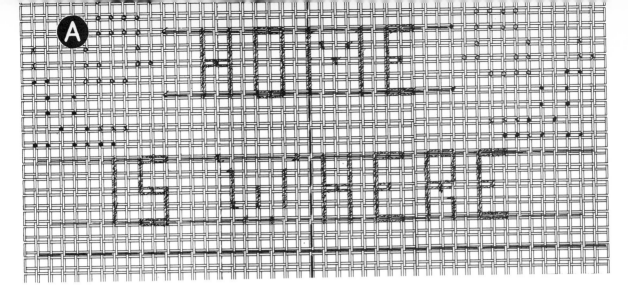

each line of words and help you keep all the letters even. Remove these bastings after the letters are needlepointed.

The silhouette sampler, below left, is typical of the late 19th and early 20th centuries. A sampler such as this could be developed into a family project, each family member working a section of it.

When each line is centered, lay out carefully on graph paper to make it easier to work the letters on canvas. Certain letters of the alphabet are more difficult to make because of their shape or width. Study the various examples on these pages as a guide for grouping letters.

The time-honored children's prayer below is another very popular wall decoration. This prayer could be made without the design motifs, and enclosed in a simple border.

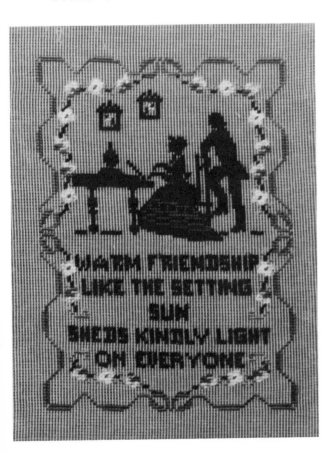

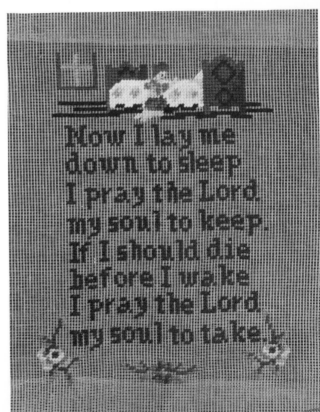

Transferring a Name to Canvas. A girl's name, complete with her year of graduation, is blocked in on the graph paper (above) as a chair seat design. The date under the name indicates the year in which the piece was worked.

Pin the paper strip under the canvas in the correct position. The left end of the name shows the letters outlined in pencil. After all the letters are transferred to the canvas, pin the paper above the marked line as shown. It is a good guide for working the names. In this case the continental stitch was used because it covers the canvas better when only a single line of stitches is used, as in these letters. The half-cross can be used by those who prefer it to the continental stitch.

The needlepoint slip-seat cover above was used on a chair like the one photographed at left. These chairs are used in the dining room of a private school for girls, each seat containing the name of one of the graduates.

Computer numerals can be used for dates. Use your bank checks or charge account numbers for a guide to the individual numerals. The sketch shows how these numerals can be used to form an allover design.

134

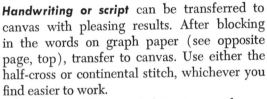

Handwriting or script can be transferred to canvas with pleasing results. After blocking in the words on graph paper (see opposite page, top), transfer to canvas. Use either the half-cross or continental stitch, whichever you find easier to work.

Because this type of lettering works up quickly in needlepoint, it can be used as a greeting for various occasions. The background need not be filled in.

The photograph shows a piece of canvas used as a birthday card, bound with bias binding of an appropriate color. If time permits, add a flower or a decorative border. Use your imagination, and have fun.

Highlighting a Design or Adding Detail. The detailing is done either with embroidery cotton or silk floss. After a needlepoint design has been completed, some important detail may be lacking. This can be added by backstitching over the wool, as was done in the upright sections of the clock (right).

Letters or Numerals Made with Backstitches

Very fine backstitches are used to outline the letters or numerals over the completed needlepoint stitches. This procedure is necessary when the lettering is very compact or uneven as shown in "Liberty Bell." The clock numerals had to be added over the wool stitches because each numeral is set at a different angle. See page 173 for complete designs of the bell and the clock.

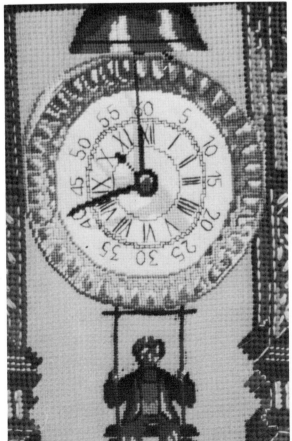

135

Monograms

Designing a prominent monogram, such as the one used on the handbag opposite, will take some creative talent. It is a simpler task to design a monogram as a secondary part of the design. Bold block letters are best suited to the masculine taste while a woman's initials can be more fanciful, or even combined with a flower spray or other delicate device. The colors used for the monogram are determined by the design and whom it is made for.

Monograms can be designed in all shapes and sizes. The initial of the surname should predominate. However, if all the initials are of the same height, place the initials in their proper sequence, first, middle, and last. If the last initial is to be larger, place it in the center, between the first and middle initials.

The style of lettering used for a monogram is often determined by the initials themselves. Rough out a given group of initials in several styles of lettering and in various shapes—horizontal, vertical, diagonal, circular, or square—before doing the final design. In this way the most pleasing effect will be achieved before it is transferred to canvas.

Each letter of a monogram should be clearly recognizable, not twisted and intertwined so that it is undecipherable.

During the 19th and 20th centuries some fine books were printed which showed alphabets, monograms, and other design details suitable for all styles of embroidery. If you are interested in this phase of needlepoint, check your library or old bookstores for such books.

Certain combinations of letters lend themselves to unusual arrangements. See monograms "V. A." and "P. H." below.

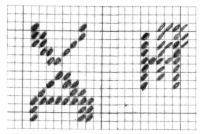

Depth and importance are added to a monogram if the letters are shadowed. This usually shows to better advantage with the heavier letters.

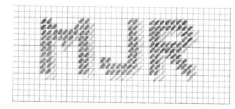

Below center shows how canvas looks when a stencil is used for marking. The center monogram shows how the stitches were worked over the open areas left by the stencil.

In the stenciled monogram on the right, space was left between the strokes of the letters because oriental scripts are formed in this way. The monogram on the far left was used on a holder for a rain hat. Petit point frames the initials, and an irregular bargello makes the colorful background.

The upright script letters shown may be

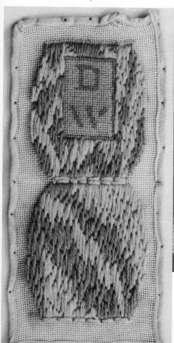

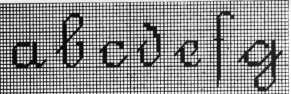

easier for you to group together than the usual slanting scripts such as those in the sampler on page 127.

If a letter is difficult to recognize when it is separated from the rest of the alphabet, modify the letter to make it more legible. The lower-case "d" here could be similar in shape to the "a" with the ascender added. Compare these letters with the hand script at the top of page 135.

The block letter monograms were translated into needlepoint stitches from early 19th century embroidery designs.

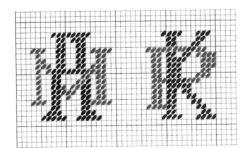

Old English or block letters can be grouped together in several ways. Try them on various sizes of canvas.

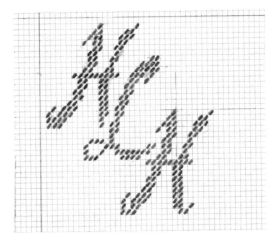

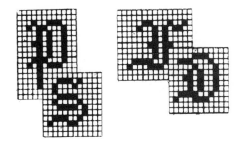

The monogram above was centered on a card table cover. The monogram was 6 or 7 inches high, worked in cocoa beige against a hunter green background.

The attractive handbag below has a paisley motif design on one side and the monogram shown on the opposite side. A fine line of white highlights the deep color of the letters.

TRINITY CHURCH
New York, N.Y.

The spire of Trinity Church is like
an ascending beacon among the massive
office buildings in the Wall Street area
of the city. Many New Yorkers take
real pride in this distinguished church.
Visitors come from all over
to see it, attend services there,
and pay their respects to a church
that has stood the test of years
of community service.

Devotionals

While we were aware that needlepoint was represented in many churches and synagogues, we had no idea of its widespread use until we had researched the subject.

Our purpose in showing you beautiful examples from four churches and three synagogues is twofold. We want you to enjoy the variety of designs illustrated in this chapter, but also we want to build up your enthusiasm so that you will join or form a committee to create similar beauty in your own house of worship. Suggestions for forming such a committee are outlined in detail on page 149.

Three of the churches represented used traditional designs in keeping with their edifices; the fourth church is contemporary in its architecture, and the kneelers are of corresponding design.

The outstanding Ark curtains in two of the synagogues contribute greatly to the beauty of their contemporary architecture. The wall hanging, "The Voice in the Wilderness," smaller in size and of more simple design, is used in the rabbi's study in the third synagogue.

Wool needlepoint is a wise choice for religious decoration because it endures for ages, retains its color, and can be cleaned, all important considerations.

For those interested in symbolism, explanation of the designs is given beginning on page 200.

Opposite: Our pictures show the needlepoint kneelers in front of the altar in All Saints Chapel. The Bishop's chair and kneelers are at the right of the altar.

The chair cushion and kneeler at the lower left are so perfectly done that they look like paintings. Their church-red background brings color and beauty to the dark wood of the chair and the substantial marble of the floor.

WASHINGTON CATHEDRAL • *Washington, D.C.*
The Cathedral Church of Saint Peter and Saint Paul

This magnificent edifice belongs to the people of the United States. It is a landmark—praised, prized, and pictured for the world to see.

Funerals of great statesmen have been held here. Visiting dignitaries attend services here. Half a million visitors a year come from all

over to see it and kneel in reverence.

Perhaps no church anywhere has as much unusual needlepoint as can be seen in this National Cathedral. Nearly one thousand pieces were done in about eleven years, including rugs, kneelers, cushions, and a wall hanging. In each of the eight chapels and at the high altar there are kneelers designed on a different theme.

It is estimated that the needlepoint in the cathedral will last at least two hundred years. In order to ensure this, the Altar Guild takes extra pains to care for it.

two pieces and joined so perfectly that it seems to be one, is an ambitious piece of work valued at $10,000.

Two other pieces on either side are called the Gospel and Epistle rugs. These rugs were designed by four sisters, the Misses Tebbetts. The beauty of their designs could hardly be surpassed and their love of church and people is obvious in all their work. Twenty-two individuals worked on the rugs.

It would take some time for one to grasp the significance of all the elements of this complex design.

Opposite:

This beautifully designed high altar rug has the feeling of an old and rare tapestry with its jewel-like colors of rose, blue, and gold against an ivory background, bordered in rich green. It is, without doubt, one of the handsomest pieces of needlepoint to be found anywhere in the United States. The rug, made of twenty-

Below:

The same colors used in the rugs are also used for the high altar kneelers. Deep blue is the background color with the symbols worked in ivory, rose, and green.

Top cushion: The three long kneelers at the 30-foot communion rail have this design.

Center and bottom cushions: Some of the designs used for the smaller kneelers were developed from symbols featured throughout the cathedral in wood and stone carving and marble inlay.

(*continued on the next two pages*)

Above: North Transept, West Wall. Each of the different religious symbols is centered on a blue shield with background worked in two shades of red.

Where necessary, the cushions are made to fit the uneven stonework of the wall. Even the boxing on the cushions has an interesting border, which adds to the unifying effect.

Center: In 1955 Dean Sayre asked all bishops of the Episcopal Dioceses to send a diagram of their diocesan seal with color instructions to the needlepoint committee.

Each seal is centered on a choir cushion. The colors of the diocesan seals stand out brilliantly on the beige background, which complements the carved-oak choir stalls.

Bottom: Opposite side of North Transept.

These cushions portray various cathedral workers. The foot-tall figures are worked in shades of gray and taupe against a red background.

The design of these cushions is entirely different in effect from most of the pieces of needlepoint in the cathedral.

Below: In St. John's Chapel there are 175 kneelers memorializing renowned Americans.

The inspiration for these kneelers came from Chelsea Old Church, Chelsea, England. When restoring this historic English landmark, which was completely destroyed by bombs during the Second World War, needlepoint kneelers were designed to commemorate many of the church's former parishioners.

For the American chapel, a list of outstanding historical characters in the United States was drawn up by three authorities from the Smithsonian Institution. The first list had over 400 names, and it was very difficult to whittle it down to 175, which is the number of chairs the chapel can hold.

Each historic kneeler has tantalizing allusions. The designs are all different, but a unifying factor is the bright red background used throughout, worked in the diagonal stitch.

Detailed descriptions are given on pages 200–202.

Two cushions can be seen in detail.
O ye Lightnings and Clouds (white, orange)
O ye holy and humble Men of heart
    (blues, orange, white)

ST. THOMAS' CHURCH *in the Fields*
Gibsonia, Pennsylvania

Many women of St. Thomas Parish and interested women of other parishes and denominations worked on the kneelers shown here. These Communion kneelers demonstrate how well enthusiastic and dedicated women can work together.

The memorial kneelers are unique in two ways. First, each of the contemporary designs represents a line of the "Benedicte, Omnia Opera Domini," one of the oldest hymns sung in the Episcopal service. Second, over twenty different stitches were used in the designs instead of the one, two, or three stitches usually used for church needlepoint.

A tongue of flame or fire in reds and orange is used on each kneeler as a unifying design feature. The deep-gold wool used for the background on all kneelers is the other unifying feature. The sixteen kneelers average 48 inches by 16 inches by 2 inches in size. They are used on three sides of the Communion rail.

The initials of each craftsman are on the lower right-hand corner, in the boxing of each kneeler.

The line of the hymn depicted by the design on each cushion is given below or near each photograph.

O ye Ice and Snow
(white)

O ye Winter and Summer (brown, yellow, red, white)

O ye Beasts and Cattle (yellow, orange, brown, white, black)

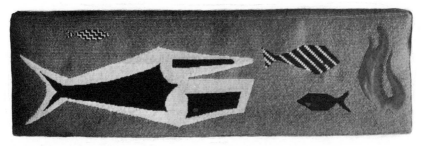

O ye Whales, and all that move in the waters (black and white)

O ye Servants of the Lord (gold, orange, blue, red, white)

GRACE CHURCH ● *Providence, Rhode Island*

The symbols of the four Evangelists decorate the kneeler cushion
shown below. This kneeler was done about 1957 by a daughter
in memory of her father, a former vestryman of the church.

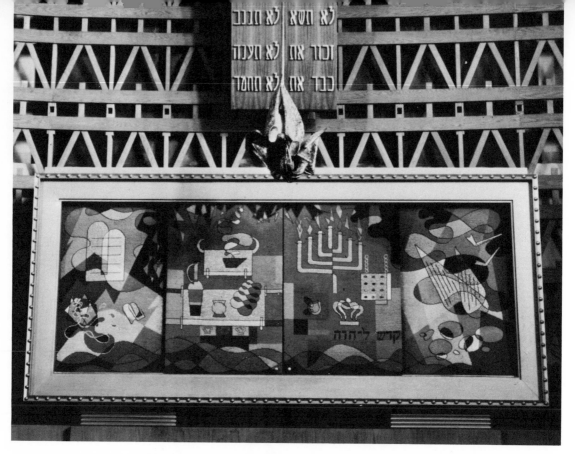

BALTIMORE HEBREW CONGREGATION   •   *Baltimore, Maryland*

The use of a needlepoint curtain for the Ark was suggested to Mrs. Randolph Rothschild by an architect. After considerable research she developed the design for the needlepoint which is titled, "Forty Years—A Symphony in Needlepoint."

The design is divided into four sections, each mounted on a wood panel. While the two end panels are stationary, the two center panels are the doors of the Ark which separate and slide in front of the end panels.

TEMPLE
RODEF SHALOM
•
Pittsburgh, Pennsylvania

Continental, Florentine, and Gobelin stitches were used for this wall panel, one of a pair made for the rabbi's study. It is titled, "A Voice in the Wilderness."

146

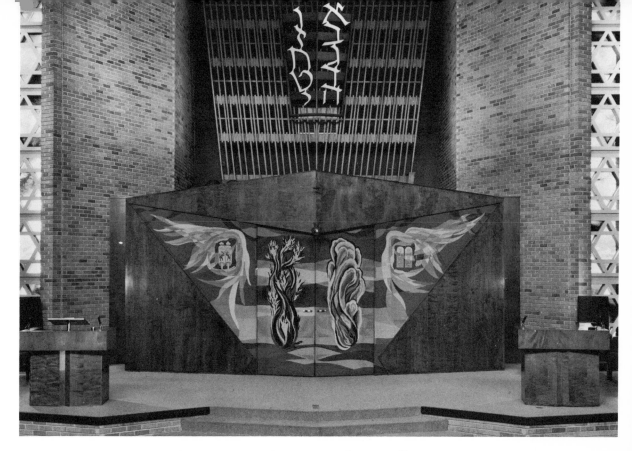

TEMPLE BETH AM ● *Chicago, Illinois*

This impressive Ark cover was designed by artist Harold Haydon. The theme was suggested by Exodus 13:21 and the stained-glass windows of the sanctuary were the inspiration for the color scheme. The curtain is large, 22 feet wide by 9 feet high, and was hooked in heavy wool on warp cloth. Although it is not canvas embroidery, we are showing it here because of its exceptional design, which could be done in needlepoint as well.

Many Jewish and Christian religious symbols are either the same or similar, but those representing specific feast days or holidays are different, of course. Space permits our showing only a few here. The reader interested in the religious symbolism can refer to page 200 and the bibliography on page 203.

Prayer Book Cover. This cover is decorated with Hebrew symbols and lettering done in the petit point stitch with a contrasting stitch used for the background of the front and back covers. On the left of the backbone is the Gobelin stitch; on the right is the brick stitch. The use of petit point for the backbone is an effective way to join the two sections.

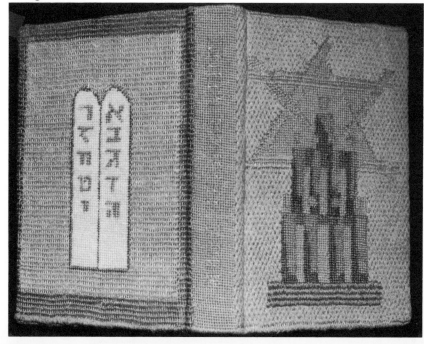

Devotionals in the Home

THE LORD'S SUPPER has always been a highly favored subject for needlepoint. It is made in various sizes, suitable for the home or for church, and it is a project usually worked by one person. The example shown here was created by working over a tramé piece. Page 72 shows how tramé is developed and worked over.

Madonnas and the Madonna and Child are perhaps the second most popular choice in religious subjects. The design for the Madonna here is also a tramé piece. A Madonna and Child, developed from a design chart is shown on page 49. Similar religious subjects are available either in tramé or painted on canvas. In either case, the purchase price usually includes the yarn in all the colors needed to work the piece.

Religious mottoes are appreciated by devout people the world over. See the motto on page 157 and other suggestions in *Samplers, Mottoes, Monograms*, beginning on page 125.

148

A NEEDLEPOINT PROJECT not only will beautify and give a "we care" feeling to your house of worship, but it will also generate a feeling of comradeship among the workers.

Select a willing and able committee headed by:

Chairman
Executive Secretary
Treasurer
Workmanship Chairman
Upholstering Chairman
Maintenance Chairman

Requirements

Finances: Obtain the initial working capital, then determine how further financing will be handled.

Invite the parishioners to take part in the program, many willingly contribute money as well as time to this permanent gift to their church or synagogue. Many women who may not contribute money are pleased at the opportunity of doing the work.

Designers and Artists.

Each section of your church or synagogue should have a design created specifically for the area. The photographs of Washington Cathedral show how the designs differ from area to area.

Requirements for kneelers and/or cushions for each section:

1. A master plan of the design theme.

2. Priority list of areas to be completed.

3. Selection of designs to blend with setting.

4. Uniform background color for each area.

5. Uniform thickness of padding to be used.

6. Correct size to fit specific area by making templates. (See instructions on page 44.)

7. Agreement on the basic background stitch to be used for pieces. Our research shows that the preferred stitch is the basket weave (bias tent) on page 56 or the diagonal on page 66. Consistency is all-important. In a few cases a wider range of stitches has been used on church kneelers. On pages 144 and 145 are shown contemporary kneelers that have as many as twenty different needlepoint stitches on a single piece. If you are interested in stitches other than the ones we have illustrated, see the references on page 203.

Workmanship Committee and Workers

Select proficient needlepointers as judges to insure that all workmanship meets high standards. It is important to get people who have done needlepoint. In the interest of perfection and uniformity, samples of all individual work should be submitted in the stitches chosen by the committee.

Qualified teachers should be available to train willing hands and to supervise initial efforts until the stitches meet the standards set by the committee. After a person has begun a project, an expert should check the work at regular intervals to avoid mistakes that would necessitate ripping.

Required Basic Materials

1. Special designs for each location.

2. First-quality, mothproof needlepoint wool. Sufficient yarn to complete an entire group of pieces should be purchased at one time. Extra yarn should be stored as suggested on page 105.

3. French canvas—usually single mesh. At the Washington Cathedral about one thousand pieces have been finished over the past eleven years. In most instances #14 single-mesh canvas was used, but because the Diocesan seals have petit point designs with gros point backgrounds, #14 Penelope double-mesh canvas was used for them.

4. Needles. Size is determined by the number of strands or the thickness of the yarn to be used as well as the size of the canvas meshes.

The cathedral workers used a #19 needle for the #14 single-mesh canvas and a #21 needle for the petit point stitch on the #14 double-mesh canvas.

Blocking and Upholstery Committee

If there are professional upholsterers among the parishioners, this would be the committee for them.

In many instances cushions are designed to fit into and around columns or unusual corners as shown in the illustration on page 142. This perfection of fit is difficult to accomplish without the use of highly skilled people.

If there aren't any expert upholsterers available for this committee, it will be necessary to establish reserve funds early in the planning to insure that the finished needlepoint pieces will be properly mounted by a professional.

An expert needlepoint blocker is also essential to the project. Shop around well in advance to find the most expert blocker available.

Record of Donors and Workers

Additional enthusiasm can be generated for the needlepoint project by planning to display a permanent record of the names of all donors and workers. The manner in which the National Cathedral in Washington displays its record is an excellent example.

The names of all who participate in the needlepoint project are inscribed on parchment sheets bound into an exquisite morocco-covered book, hand-tooled in gold. This permanent record is displayed in a beautiful carved oak case in Kellog Bay at the cathedral.

Maintenance Committee

The constant use to which needlepoint is subjected in a house of worship necessitates consistent care and attention. Maintenance of finished needlepoint pieces is an absolute must, and as such it becomes a vital part of the overall needlepoint project.

The responsibility for keeping kneelers, cushions, etc., clean and in good repair should be entrusted to a specific group of people with a well-organized plan to care for the needlepoint pieces.

Recommendations for the Care and Upkeep of Needlepoint

For seat cushions or kneelers a very soft brush (similar to a silver polishing brush) is effective. A clean cotton dustcloth can be used to flick off dust and dirt.

A low-powered vacuum cleaner or a good carpet sweeper can be used to clean needlepoint rugs.

If an accident should occur, resulting in damage, needlepoint repairs should be undertaken immediately by the most skilled needlepointer in the group before the damaged area spreads with additional usage. Prompt repairs should be undertaken in the event that the needlepoint begins to wear thin so that it does not reach a point where it is beyond repair.

Actual size—
petit point
bouquet
worked on
silk scrim.
On pages
182 and 191
are two other
examples of
pieces worked
on silk scrim.

Teaching

GROUPS THAT MIGHT BE INTERESTED in forming a class are religious organizations, adult education classes, women's clubs, Girl Scouts, and Brownies. See index for page references.

Suggested Curriculum

I. Introduction:
   A. What is needlepoint?
   B. Difference between needlepoint and tapestry.

II. Basic materials used in needlepoint:
   A. *Canvas*—the number of meshes per inch determines size and type of canvas. Have canvas, needles, and yarn on hand so each student can have a swatch on which to practice.
   B. *Yarn*—Difference between needlepoint yarn and other types of yarn.
   C. *Needles*—The size depends on the thickness as well as the number of strands of yarn used and the size of the canvas mesh. Explain the introduction of metal needles.
   D. See page 26 for other materials required.

III. Explanation of various stitches. Right-handed; left-handed.

IV. Practicing stitches:
   A. Proper method for threading needle.
   B. Suggested yarn lengths.
   C. Twisted yarn.
   D. How to begin and end a row of stitches.
   E. How to work in and around a design.
      1. Around gros point design.
      2. Around petit point.
   F. Demonstrate the various stitches for right-handed and left-handed.
   G. If canvas shows through worked areas, check for the following:
      1. Are strands of yarn too long?
      2. Is the yarn pulled too taut?
      3. Is the correct type of yarn being used?
      4. Are you using the required number of strands to cover canvas on which you are working?

V. Design:
   A. How to select a suitable design.
   B. How to measure the area to be worked.

VI. Presentation of various objects decorated with needlepoint, such as pictures, pillows, footstools, chair seats, fire screens, and rugs, as well as accessories like wallets, eyeglass cases, purses, luggage, etc. If needlepoint pieces are not available, use the pictures in this book.

VII. Color—Suggestions for choosing colors for designs and backgrounds.
   A. Background color.
   B. Color Combinations.
   C. Colors that harmonize or contrast with the finished design.
   D. How to select colors that will blend with the total decor of a room.

VIII. Blocking needlepoint.

IX. Mounting.

X. Piecing.

XI. Miscellaneous:
   A. Create your own design.
   B. Where to have designs painted on canvas.
   C. How to put designs on canvas with tramé.
   D. How to work over tramé.

Special Note to Teachers: Ask each member of your class to select a different type of needlepoint for a first project. Then, as problems arise in the various items being worked, each student can learn how to solve them from your classroom demonstrations on each problem.

The picture above was done in wools
on canvas by Mary Wright
of Newport, Rhode Island, about 1754.

It is in the mood of one of
Sir Joshua Reynolds' portraits of children.

The 18th-century influence
can be seen in the fitted dress,
the flower-trimmed bonnet, and the
velvet ribbon tied under the chin.
This is possibly a self-portrait.

For Children

NEEDLEPOINT CAN BE DONE BY AND FOR CHILDREN. Both types of design are illustrated on the opposite page.

Often a gift of needlepoint may be the first step to interest a child in working a piece. If children are taught to do needlepoint, they learn muscular coordination. They learn to use a needle and to protect themselves from it. They learn the advantages of a thimble. They learn about design and colors.

One of the things we learned at the Menninger Clinic was that people to be truly happy must learn to share with others. No children are too young to begin to think of sharing. They can make attractive gifts such as an eyeglass case, a pin cushion, or a picture for Mother, a book cover, bookmark, or doorstop for grandparents. They have the fun of learning, of "showing off" their work, and of gift giving.

Any subject that is of interest to a boy or girl can be transposed to canvas, be it a baseball player, skin diver, a space ship or the appealing likeness of a favorite pet. If a specific design is not readily available, it can be made to order. See page 14. On the following pages are shown a few designs that have appeal for children.

Opposite page: At the lower left is a portrait of a boy, designed and executed in 1930 by his mother. She wisely marked it with the boy's name and the date. To achieve a likeness in a needlepoint portrait requires real skill in handling the yarns. The background colors must be selected with great care so as not to overshadow the portrait.

Gretchen's grandmother, whose pet name is Boppy, needlepointed the pert little kitten and then had it framed. It will always serve as a symbol of affection and will be a treasured possession.

A kitten design made into a small pillow adds the right touch to a child's room. Children like the feel of wool, and as pillows these are decidedly cuddly.

"Children at Prayer" is an appealing example of the type of design available in kits. Such a kit often has a pair of subjects, with yarn to work, and frames to use when the needlepoint is finished. See *Needlepoint Kits* on page 15.

Clowns have such varied characteristics that they always seem to be in favor. Depending upon your needlepoint work habits, you can find clowns already worked with only the background to complete. Sometimes these are done in tramé, or just painted on canvas.

The deer and sailboat at the bottom of the page are examples of painted canvas designs.

Doorstops. As you can see from the few illustrated, doorstops come in great variety. Available are mottoes combined with simple motifs, geometrics, flowers, houses, etc. Or let your imagination go and make a design to suit the spot where the doorstop is to be used. Select a design that will complement the area it will decorate.

The humorous motto designs will be fine at

154

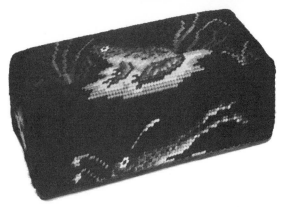

the foot of a door to a den, game room, or family room.

For a child's room use a frog, a poodle, or a needlepainting of a favorite pet.

The geometric doorstop worked in complementary colors will suit an Early American room, while the rose design is more formal in feeling.

A doorstop makes an ideal gift. If you put a brick inside for weight and wrap it gaily for a birthday or Christmas gift, the recipient can have fun guessing what it is.

These are good items to learn on; they do not require too many stitches. Initials, as we show them, will allow you to personalize a gift.

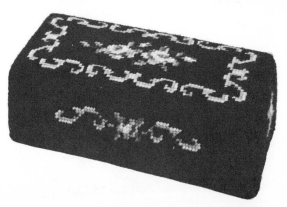

155

The floral, done by nine-year-old Gretchen Greener, was originally planned for a pin cushion but considered such an achievement that it was framed instead. The photograph shows the canvas bound with bias binding. With the art training many children get in school today, they can easily draw a simple motif such as this and apply it to canvas with colored crayon in readiness for working.

For a small but attractive gift the 3-inch square pin cushion is easy to make. Add initials of both the recipient and the maker to personalize the gift.

A cushion about 14 inches square can portray a favorite fish, horse, cat, dog, or flower. It is easy to transfer the design to canvas, to color, and to work. This pillow was worked by an eleven-year-old girl. It has a velvet back and is edged with a cord covered in velvet.

The last design would certainly please the budding ballerina. Notice how the mat gives added importance to the picture.

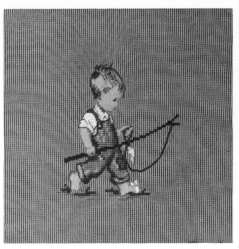

Wyatt Earp

Here are two pictures to thrill the cowboy-and-Indian fan. Or would "Gone Fishing" interest him more?

The Scandinavian Christmas greeting makes a most unusual card. Fringe edges the needlepoint. When finished the piece is glued to a folded piece of heavy paper or a greeting card so that the signature can be written inside.

For a very personal birthday card, bind the edge of a 4-by-6-inch piece of white, single-mesh canvas, using bias binding or ribbon in a favorite color to edge trim your card. See instructions on page 134 for blocking out words and finishing them in needlepoint.

"The Lord is my Shepherd" is a favorite motto around the world. Many of the simplest of homes have this. It may be the only framed picture or decorative cushion in the house. We understand it is available in a minimum of twenty languages, including Russian and Chinese.

If you wish to make your own version of this motto, refer to the simplified block alphabet on page 126. A silhouette to fit your idea can be easily blocked out on graph paper. See page 43.

Garrison Burdett Arey, sea captain on the *Duke of Newcastle,* used his free time to do needlepoint. We show a beautiful bird, one of two birds of paradise that he did. Mr. Arey worked on the birds from 1865 to 1869, often when his ship was becalmed. When finished, the two framed pieces were used to decorate his cabin. One can imagine his landing in a port, especially in China or Europe, and dashing off to find the beautiful yarns necessary for such exquisite color work.

These marvels of design were donated by Captain Arey's daughters to the Historical Society of Old Newbury, Newburyport, Massachusetts. See them if you are ever near enough. They are beautiful beyond words.

Left: A painting of Captain Arey's clipper ship, *Duke of Newcastle.*

158

Men and Needlepoint

ALTHOUGH MOST PEOPLE THINK OF NEEDLEPOINT AS STRICTLY FEMININE, we have found the contrary to be true. The Duke of Windsor has enjoyed doing needlepoint for years. He learned the art from his mother, Queen Mary. He has found needlepoint relaxing and frequently has a piece in work. Most men create their own designs and are highly individual in the techniques they use to develop them.

Not only are many of the outstanding needlepoint designers men, but also the industry is almost entirely controlled by them. The leading needlepoint manufacturing firms are owned and run by men. Usually one of the top executives in each firm travels all over the world seeking new designs and also arranging for needleworkers to be trained to exacting standards. Many of the hundreds of art needlework shops throughout the United States are owned by men. Men run three of the shops on Madison Avenue, New York City, that were very cooperative when we were compiling information for this book.

Alice Maynard, one of the oldest needlework shops, dates back to 1864. William B. Quaintance, an importer, acquired this shop in 1904. Today, son Charles and grandson Linsley handle its operation. Linsley Quaintance has a flair for designing and has created many exciting patterns. The development of the tiger motif in great variety is one of his successes.

Robert Mazaltov & Son is also owned and run by men. For over fifty years Mr. Mazaltov, Sr., headed this well-known New York needlework shop. Today his son is continuing the tradition of fine needlepoint. They have designed for the great and near great.

Inman Cook and Daren Pierce, interior decorators by profession, established the Woolworks, Inc., on Madison Avenue in New York City, where the most unusual in designs can be found. Both of these men are expert needlepointers, and they enjoy the craft as well as the shop.

Russell Lynes, writer and former managing editor of _Harper's Magazine,_ is an avid needle-pointer and has been for over fifteen years. During this time he estimates he has done "millions upon millions of stitches." Mr. Lynes usually works on a canvas that takes about 100 stitches to the square inch. He turned to needlepointing when ordered by his doctor to find something to relieve the tension under which he worked.

Mr. Lynes's approach to this art is unorthodox because practically every piece is developed in a different way. Several of his techniques are shown here and in other sections of this book.

Trompe l'oeil means visual deception developed in some art form. This term applies to any design in which objects are done in such fine detail that one gets the illusion of being able to pick up and handle them. The two needlepoint illusions opposite illustrate this term beautifully. The books, mouse, cup, and scissors above form a cover for one section of a hi-fi, which blends right in with the books on the shelf.

The vest is a single piece of needlepoint, but you feel you can lift any of the items from the pockets.

Opposite page right: A copy of a picture by Ben Shahn, illustrator and painter. Although it is developed in rather muted color tones, it has a great deal of movement and depth.

Another needlepoint technique developed by Mr. Lynes is seen in the pointillism picture above, which was originally drawn by Bernard Perlin in colored crayons. It gives a shimmering effect that well portrays the iridescent quality of the peacock. Pointillism is the neo-Impressionist method of achieving luminosity by placing in immediate juxtaposition spots of varying pure color, which are then blended by the eye. Yellow beside blue will give the impression of green, for example. The drawing was about 18 inches square; it was photostated up to 30 inches square, then transferred to canvas.

James De Weese of Kansas City, Missouri, formerly a marine steam engineer, took up needlepoint as a hobby after he retired. He started with children's picture books, tracing the pictures for patterns. Now he uses a pantagraph to enlarge or reduce the subject he wants to transfer to canvas.

Landscapes are his favorite subject, copied from such famous western painters as Frederic Remington or Thomas Hart Benton. When working from a black-and-white reproduction, Mr. De Weese does his own color separation. We show here only a few of his many interesting pictures.

For variety, Mr. De Weese did the silhouette profile of his niece shown above and has made banners for the Scottish Rite, of which he is a member. He has won several awards for the needlepoint he enjoys so much.

The needlepoint picture on the left was copied from a newspaper photograph titled "Lasso."

Michelangelo's statue of *David* was inspired
by the original in Florence, Italy.
It is done in very fine petit point.
See page 42 for other details.

Louis J. Gartner, Jr., special project and
creative crafts editor of *House & Garden*
magazine, used to be a frustrated artist. He
loves working with color and design but it was
not until he started needlepainting that he
found the medium for self-expression.

When Mr. Gartner first decided to do
needlepoint, the commercial designs available
did not appeal to his aesthetic taste so he

decided to transpose his ideas to canvas himself. The wide range of design illustrated here
and in other chapters of this book shows how
he gains inspiration from various sources.

A personal favorite is the goat's head, which
was developed from a German engraving and
is on one of his dining room chairs. Each chair
has a different needlepoint design.

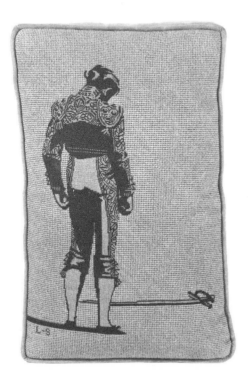

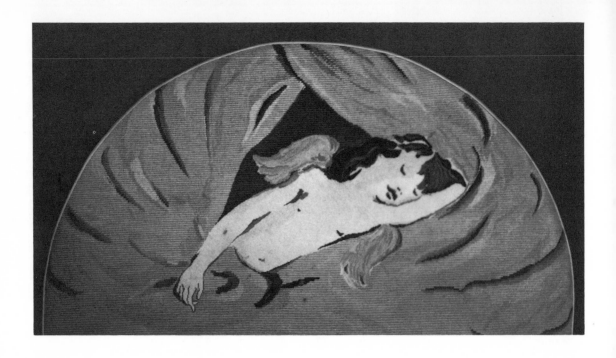

Marcel Vertès, Hungarian by birth, spent his boyhood in Budapest and his later years in Paris and New York. He was a painter, illustrator, and designer of stage settings and costumes. His work hangs in many museums throughout France and the United States.

Needlepoint was just another outlet for his great talent. He was urged to try designing for this field by Carmel Snow, the late famous fashion editor of *Harper's Bazaar.* His wife Dora helped him by working many of his designs, guided by Vertès' exquisite feeling for color.

His needlepainting designs were done exclusively for the manufacturer "Heirloom," and one is fortunate indeed to own a Vertès original. This artist brought sophistication to a traditional medium and won, in his lifetime, very real acclaim including the Academy Award Oscar as color coordinator for the film *Moulin Rouge.*

The delicacy of this artist's designs is easily seen in the four examples shown here, owned by Mrs. Vertès, who lives in New York City.

The headboard above shows how outstanding needlepoint can be used in such a manner. The full-length figure with the dogs makes an effective fire screen or wall panel.

On the opposite page are pieces suitable for a cushion or shaped chair seat.

A beautiful three-panel screen designed by Mr. Vertès is shown on page 104.

For centuries the big cats—lions, tigers, leopards, etc.—have been
of interest to man, and in the last two centuries
to the big-game hunter.
Princeton University took the tiger as a symbol for its football team.
Then along came Esso to urge all to "Put a tiger in your tank."
This gave the tiger a vigorous position in advertising,
and he, along with
other members of the cat family,
is used in a wide variety
of advertising media.

The Hobbyist
and the Collector

With the electronic age giving us more and more free time, we find ourselves developing new interests to fill our leisure hours.

A hobby, pursued for relaxation and pleasure, can be either active or placid depending upon the personal taste of the individual.

In our age of affluence and leisure, more and more people are indulging in the joys of collecting. Antique cars, stamps, coins, miniature soldiers, guns, and Indian relics are but a few of the things that interest collectors from a historic point of view as well as for the sheer joy of possession. These also make excellent subjects for needlepoint. Some of them are shown on the following pages. Needlepoint can be a hobby on its own or be an adjunct to a collection. These subjects worked on canvas will please the recipient because they are constant reminders of a favorite pastime. They can solve the problem of gift giving in a most satisfying way.

Designers of needlepoint have found the big cats to be most adaptable, as they could use either the whole animal, or just the head. Needlepoint inspired by these animals has been used for rugs, cushions, pictures, headboards, slippers, and traveling bags.

Birds and domestic animals have become popular subjects for needlepoint design because they have almost universal appeal.

Samoyed dogs are native to Siberia. The pair above, Kheta and Alba, were family pets for many years on an estate in Rhode Island. It would be difficult to paint a more realistic picture than the one shown, which captures even the confident expressions of the two dogs.

Speaking of expressions, surely Lucky, the cocker spaniel, knew he was being pictured for this fire screen. He shows both boredom and patience.

If someone you know has a treasured dog, take a snapshot of the dog in an attractive pose and work it into a design for a picture, a cushion, or a back rest for a car seat.

A hunter would appreciate a photo of his own pointer or retriever in action, recorded for posterity via needlepoint. The poodle is one of the favorites of the many breeds of dogs available on canvas.

168

The flying ducks would make a welcome gift for many sportsmen. The background color can be a tone to harmonize with a den or family room.

Many people love horses whether or not they own, ride, or race them. You can have a photograph of a valued horse transferred to canvas and needlepoint the entire picture, or you can buy a canvas with the horse already worked, with just the background remaining to be filled in.

The individual taste of an ornithologist or an amateur bird watcher might be successfully satisfied with one of the three designs on this page: birds in flight silhouetted against a grille-like background, colorful birds in a natural looking habitat, or a highly stylized bird, combined with flowers and leaves.

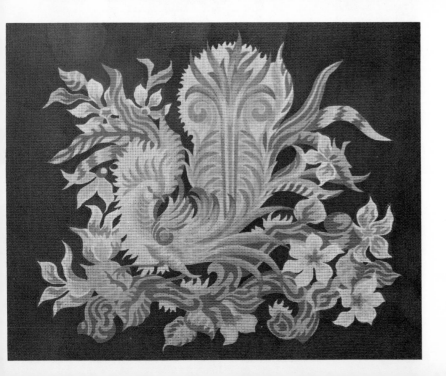

These designs will be of interest to those of us who have been fascinated by the ever-changing sea, whether on board a boat or just walking along the shore.

Only two highly decorative shells are used on the pillow on the right. Perspective is gained by adding the simple two-tone border effect.

An entirely different feeling is obtained in the next picture. A background of brilliant colors—deep coral, red, and green against royal blue—outline the pastel-colored shells and flowerlike motifs.

Which young fish fancier would not like the simply framed picture below? He might even do the needlepoint himself by copying some of the fish in his aquarium.

Create a personal design for a fisherman by using a picture of the prize fish he has caught.

The design on the bottom shows a "fish that never was" against a wavy background. It is suitable for framing or for use as a cushion cover.

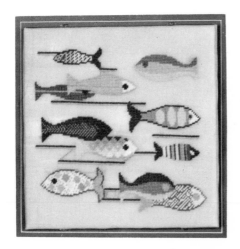

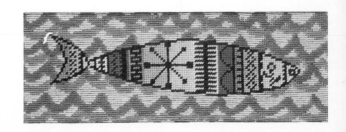

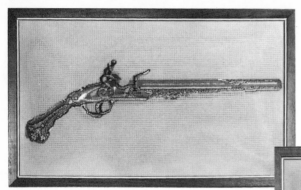

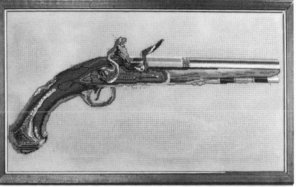

The unusual mural-like hanging used across the top of these two pages was created for an American living in France who wanted to have some of America's western heritage in his home. The encampment of the forty-niners, the stage coaches, the riders, all have been executed beautifully in this panel, which is 16 inches high and 24 feet long. A needlepoint hanging which pictures French points of interest is used to decorate this same man's home in the United States.

One collector of guns had a screen made with nine of his favorite firearms shown in needlepoint. The two pistols shown on the opposite page are flintlocks.

The uniforms and accouterments of historic soldiery are of great interest to many collectors. One of the very famous collections is that of James A. Linen, Jr., former president of *Life* magazine. Three Colonial American soldiers are shown. If you are interested in military figures, you might delve further in costume books of the various eras.

The Liberty Bell would interest a collector of Americana or a collector of bells.

The clock design was developed at the request of a man who had a fine collection of clocks.

Packard Limousine 1902

Chevrolet Roadster 1912

Ford Touring Car 1911

You don't have to be a collector of antique automobiles in order to appreciate these interesting old-timers.

The wood-burning steam locomotives pictured below were in use by the railroads before the Civil War.

A series of either subject would make unusual cushions for a sofa or day bed or would be very decorative as a wall grouping.

Mary Martin, the famous actress, is an avid needlepointer.

The design for the rug on the right was adapted from a room-sized rug that Mary Martin made for her own home. As can be seen from the theatrical masks and clasped hands, each motif represents a cherished event or memory in Mary Martin's life.

Musical instruments or symbols can be combined with colorful flowers to make a needlepoint piece to please the music enthusiast. The designs shown would be decorative when used in a number of ways.

Anyone for tennis? Here are two suggestions for tennis racket covers. The male mouse can be teamed with a female mouse—a must for mixed doubles.

175

Historic America is portrayed in these four interesting reconstructions
of a few of the most important events in our history.

A specialty shop can develop designs based on incidents of personal interest to you, or you can do your own research and put your own "moment of history" on canvas.

Travel the world by recording some of your favorite places in needlepoint. Use a map of a hemisphere and highlight the sections of the globe that you have visited.

Does native or ancient costume appeal to you? A series of needlepoint figures in colorful national dress could be the start of an individual and outstanding collection.

HENRY CLAY, 1777–1852. *"The Great Pacificator"*
The needlepoint picture above was based on a painting that now
hangs in the House of Representatives wing of the United States Capitol.
It is reported that a number of these needlepoint pictures
were made and used for publicity in Mr. Clay's political campaign
when he was a candidate for the Presidency.
His interest in agriculture is symbolized by the plow and the cow
in the background, but his gesture toward the globe and flag
indicates his concern with world affairs.

Advertising & Publicity

VIA NEEDLEPOINT

FOR CENTURIES NEEDLEPOINT HAS BEEN USED IN THE HOME, for religious themes, and for dress accessories. The examples shown on the next few pages illustrate how needlepoint has kept pace with the times. It is a live art used for advertising by some leading business organizations. See pages 180–181.

The familiar Chase Manhattan Bank symbol was developed in needlepoint to advertise one phase of its services.

The magazine and book covers are good examples of needlepoint designed and used for a specific purpose.

A long-time favorite of needlepoint as decoration is on the box of Whitman's candy, the "Sampler."

A needlepoint distributor had needlepoint made for the interior of his car to advertise his business. It was put in at the factory in place of the regular upholstery. Beautiful it is and highly prized by the owner.

As you can see, needlepoint is both modern and adaptable. It may be used for practical as well as decorative or sentimental purpose.

Above: Most of us have had the pleasure of listening to the great Mormon Tabernacle choir. This Columbia record cover, reproduced in 1965 from a needlepoint design, shows how a variety of lettering can be combined to fit a given space. The simplified house and tree motifs illustrate the title of the album.

Left:
The shading in the Chase Manhattan Bank emblem is obtained by the use of four colors. You could develop a similar border as a frame for one of your needlepoint efforts. For example, "Mom and Dad" with wedding date. See alphabets on page 126.

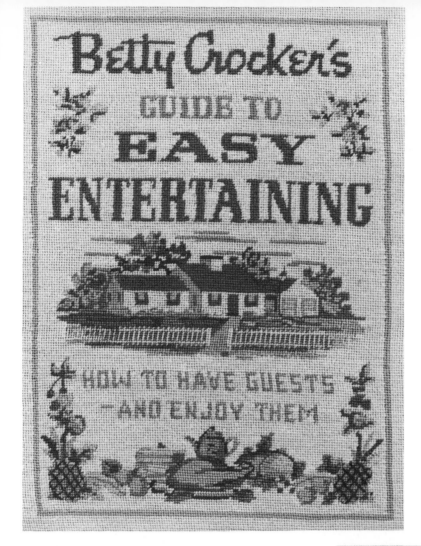

Left:
The Betty Crocker cover shows
how several styles of lettering
can be combined attractively.
This design might inspire you
to make an interesting sampler
for your own use.

Combine a picture of your home
with a motto of your selection,
such as
"Home Is Where the Heart Is,"
or "My Home, My Castle."
A decorative border
can be used to unify the whole.

Right: The *Coronet* cover design illustrates
how attractively a seasonal subject can be
developed in needlepoint. Santa Claus
and pack are surrounded by a border
of holly leaves and berries.

The *Coronet* design is beautifully detailed,
and you will recognize that it was done
by a fine artist. You can develop
a similar but simpler design to mark any
occasion, such as birthday, anniversary,
Easter, or Thanksgiving. Have fun choosing
your own colors. Make it as bright and
gay as the good wishes
that will accompany the giving.

The wall pocket above was used for letters and memoranda.
It is made of embossed leather with a petit point picture,
silk on scrim, inserted in the center of the front section.

AMERICAN—
19th Century

The story of this hanging is that the needlepoint
was made by a girl, seven years old, who failed to curtsey when
she entered a room where there were guests.
She was required to do this piece of petit point
to remind her forever after to remember her manners.

Museum Treasures

A GREAT NUMBER OF THE LARGE AND SMALL MUSEUMS IN THE UNITED STATES include needlepoint among their holdings. After referring to the *World Almanac* we wrote to those that listed needlework as part of their acquisitions. Replies were received from most, and we appreciate their generous cooperation.

Inquire about the heirlooms of needlepoint that a museum in your town or nearby metropolis might have. In many cases no appropriations are available for mounting, but embroidery, even when it is not on display, can usually be seen on request. This cross section of the needlepoint in our museums has been carefully selected as typical of what can be seen. We hope that our sampling will help you to explore further, not only to find inspiration but also to encourage you to continue the art and tradition of needlepoint.

One treasure that turned up unexpectedly during our travels is the Henry Clay hanging shown on page 178. It was found in the Division of Political History, Smithsonian Institution.

Most of the needlepoint items shown are of either English or American origin. This is easily understood because of our original ties with England. French, Spanish, and Flemish works in American museums are also represented with one item from each. Only the last four illustrations are from a foreign museum.

As you will have noticed, some of the illustrations in the preceding chapters are also museum pieces.

AMERICAN—18th Century

Mahogany side chair (left), showing
Queen Anne influence, is upholstered in
petit point. See an identical chair, except
for the needlepoint design, on page 7.

AMERICAN—
Early 18th Century

Needlepoint chair-back detail.
Shepherd and flock
with prancing deer.

AMERICAN—18th Century

This is an unusual design for
a seat cover. Two primitive
figures are combined with an
allover floral effect.
The figures are identified
by the names Abel and Cain
above their heads.

184

FRENCH—18th Century

This armchair (right)
of the Louis XV period
is upholstered in petit point
with carved antique frame.

ENGLISH—
Late 18th Century

A beautiful Adam-Hepplewhite
armchair (below).
The needlepoint seat is held in place
with tacks and decorative braid.

ENGLISH—Early 18th Century

Stool with walnut cabriole legs.
The upholstery is wool needlepoint, which is
brought to the underside and tacked in place.
A lining conceals all raw edges.

SPANISH—Late 16th to Early 17th Century

The hanging above is an example of storytelling via needlepoint.
The title, "Galceran de Pinos Disembarks at Salona Near Tarragona
and Stops the Sending of the Ransom," helps one envision adventure
even though we do not know the story portrayed here.
On the right, outside the walled town can be seen a shore line
with several ships anchored among highly stylized waves.

ENGLISH—
16th Century

Needlepoint first came
into favor during
the Elizabethan period.
Above is a section of a
satin hanging with very detailed
flowers and fruits
worked in petit point.
Note other design interest—
the butterflies, caterpillars,
and moths.
Top row: bluett,
crab apple, morning glory;
bottom row: jasmine,
sweet pea, grape.
Below is an
enlargement of the grape design.

The Bible was the main source of inspiration in developing
needlepoint designs for most hangings,
just as it was for sculpture and painting.
The Meeting of Jephthah and his daughter is based on
an Old Testament story recorded in Judges 11:30–40.
The picture above looks like a happy meeting, but
in reality it was a sad one.

ENGLISH—
17th Century

ENGLISH—
17th Century

The Finding of Moses
was a happy event
recorded in the Bible.
Pictured is the
Egyptian princess
being shown the baby
in a cradle among
the reeds.

The garments worn by
the princess and her
attendants are
seventeenth-century
dress rather than
early Egyptian.

188

FLEMISH—
Early 17th Century

We show one section of a narrow, horizontal panel that is composed of a series of Biblical scenes.

The close-up shows Mary and Joseph with the baby Jesus fleeing into Egypt.

ENGLISH—
Early 17th Century

The three strips from an altar frontal were worked in silk petit point and joined with braid.

A frontal is a decorative covering used in front of an altar. It is usually removable so that it can be changed with the seasons of the church year.

The titles at the top edge indicate that all the scenes have a religious significance. The titles for only three scenes can be deciphered. Because of the Elizabethan costumes it is hard to judge what each scene means.

See page 202 for titles and Biblical references.

ENGLISH—17th Century

Early books were so prized that
some were bound
with a needlepoint cover.
The petit point book cover shown is
for *Reliquae Sacre Carolinae*.
Today, most
books are bound very simply,
but we can make a slipcover of
needlepoint to
add a personal touch.
See page 113.

ENGLISH—17th Century

This chest, covered in white
satin and decorated with
petit point, seed pearls, and
coral, was where milady kept
essentials such as smelling
salts, handkerchief, possibly
a little snuff and more
often "make-up" as we know it.
Such chests were made as wedding
gifts, from mother to daughter.
After the pieces of petit point
were applied to the chest the
edges were finished with ribbon,
braid, or velvet bands.
It is recorded that many a
needlepoint-covered hat box or
personal box, as it was sometimes
called, went to the American West
by stage coach held on the lap
of the lady.

AMERICAN—18th Century

This pocketbook is done in Hungarian
point, a type of flame stitch. The
bag is bound and lined in leather,
with an antique silver clasp.
Leather, especially suede, makes
a happy complement to needlepoint.

190

AMERICAN—
Early 19th Century

Hand screens or coquettes'
fans were a fashion
favored during this
period. Those illustrated
are petit point done on
silk scrim. These fans
have long gilt handles.
Such fans had jewels sewn
into the petit point
and were used when
attending the theater.

AMERICAN—
Early 20th Century

Document cases were used to protect valuable papers.
The outside of the case shown is of suede with a
needlepoint panel.
The case is lined in moiré and has a panel in needlepoint
to indicate the contents. When folded, ribbon ties hold
the case together so that the contents are protected.

The words are
composed of capital
block letters
as shown in the
alphabet on page 126.

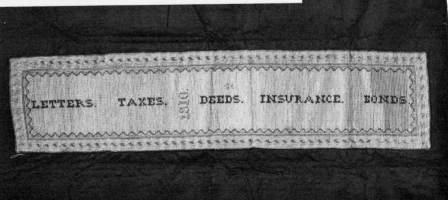

LETTERS.   TAXES.   DEEDS.   INSURANCE.   BONDS

ENGLISH—Early 18th Century

An attractive picture
well illustrating
its title, *Harvesting*.

AMERICAN—18th Century

A lovely rural scene, typical of this period,
with figures at leisure, children, and pets among colorful
trees and flowers. It is signed "Sarah Warren 1748."

PRISCILLA A ALLEN DAVGHTER TO MR BENIAMIN ALLEN AND MR ELISBETH ALLEN BOSTON IVLY THE 20 1746

AMERICAN—
18th Century

A stylized picture showing the forest surrounding an estate.
Compare the many design effects similar to those seen
in the pictures on page 194. The designs
may have come from the same source. The legend reads,
"Priscilla A. Allen daughter to Mr. Benjamin Allen
and Mrs. Elisbeth Allen Boston July the 20 1746."

193

This primitive picture shows everything—the land owners, the house, domestic and wild animals, birds, trees, and flowers. The house is typical of the architecture of Pennsylvania and the period.

AMERICAN—
18th Century

AMERICAN—
Mid-18th Century

Another picture with everything—house, barn, windmill, and family, also a wide variety of animals and birds. Likenesses of individuals were obviously striven for, as can be seen by the lady in the foreground.

AMERICAN—
Mid-19th Century

A pictorial sampler done in cross-stitch with worsted yarns on canvas. This is an example of a needlepoint picture without a filled-in background. Worked in 1840 at Patterson, New Jersey (now spelled "Paterson"), by Mary Louisa McCully, age nine years.

AMERICAN—
Late 19th Century

A floral picture worked in gros point, using wool on perforated cardboard. Some people believed that it was easier to mark the design on cardboard than on canvas. But it took almost twice the time to work because two motions had to be made for every stitch, one down and one up. Cardboard will crack if bent.

195

The Birthday

REPUBLIC OF SOUTH AFRICA
20th Century—1960

The preceding photographs in this chapter
are of needlepoint that can be seen in some of
the great museums in the United States.
On these two pages are four photographs of needlepoint
from a foreign museum, the subject matter of which
is akin to our own early history. At first glance
it would appear that the hangings portray American
covered wagons going West. Actually they depict
the "Great Trek" to the sea in South Africa in 1832.

Across the Orange River

196

Retief's Departure

The panels, fifteen in number, hang in the museum
of the Voortrekker Monument in Pretoria, South Africa.
This monument pays homage to the heroic deeds
and endurance of those who took part in the Great Trek northward.
One of the panels is 9 feet long, ten are 5 feet,
four are 6 feet in length. Their height throughout is 32 inches.
One hundred thirty different colors of wool were used,
and it has been reported that approximately
3½ million stitches went into the canvases to make these
astonishingly beautiful pieces of needlepoint.

Prayers

Cutting and Sewing Fashion Accessories

See page 26 for list of sewing essentials.

Fold-Under Finish. When coarse canvas is folded over at the edge of the needlepoint design, a white line becomes apparent. We suggest adding two rows of half-cross or continental stitches outside the finished edge of all accessories made on coarse canvas. These stitches are to be turned under and pressed before the lining is applied.

An alternate method is to overhand the edges with matching wool yarn so the canvas edge is covered.

Lining. Because canvas is very flexible, use lightweight, firmly woven fabric for all linings. They can be silk, cotton, or synthetic. Lightweight felt is also suitable; it can be purchased in packaged squares of assorted colors. Satin should be avoided because it is difficult to control.

Add ¼ inch to all lining fabrics on all edges for the turnunder except for felt which should be cut to the exact size or slightly smaller than the size of the needlepoint.

Cut all lining pieces on the straight grain of the fabric.

Block and stretch needlepoint as instructed beginning on page 89.

Pressing with steam iron. The starch in the canvas causes it to stick to the iron and to ironing board covers. Use paper or cloth over the board and under the iron at all times.

Mitered corner or hem. The heavier the canvas, the more difficult it is to square the corners.

After edges of canvas are turned to the wrong side along edges of needlepoint, square corners of canvas and crease, making as flat as possible. Steam press, using a press cloth.

Open corner and fold point of canvas back diagonally close to point of needlepoint (**A**). Crease sharply. Open corner and squeeze a line of glue ⅛ inch outside diagonal fold. When the glue is

dry, trim away point ⅛ inch outside line of glue.

Fold one side of corner back to position with diagonal edge flat (**B**). Fold opposite edge along diagonal crease and fold over flat edge, (**C**) keeping point of corner smooth and square. Sew securely.

Compact Slip-case. See illustration on page 106.

Finished size—4½ inches by 8½ inches.

Cut lining—5 inches by 9 inches.

Fold canvas along edge of needlepoint. Pin the corners as square and as flat as possible. Steam press, using press cloth. Open folds and trim canvas in the row of meshes *outside* the line of glue: trim corners as instructed under mitered corner. Refold and baste canvas edge to wrong side of needlepoint, being careful not to sew through to the right side.

Prepare lining. Fold raw edges to wrong side and press. Lay wrong side of lining over back of needlepoint so that all canvas is covered. Pin folded edges together, seeing that all corners are square. Use overhand stitch to sew the edges together.

Fold in half, needlepoint side out, and sew side edges together. You can whip the edges together with mercerized thread or with matching wool yarn.

Eyeglass Case. The size of the case will depend on the size and weight of the eyeglass frame. The average case measures 3 inches wide by 6 inches long. Cut a brown paper pattern in a 6-inch by 6-inch square. Fold in half and tape side and one end together.

Slip eyeglasses inside. The fit should not be tight because the canvas is heavy and the lining will add bulk.

Prepare the needlepoint in the same way as for the compact slip-case. The lining can be sewn as instructed above, or felt can be cut ¼ inch smaller and used for the lining.

Center lining over back of needlepoint and pin around edge. Hem edge of felt into place. Fold needlepoint in half and whip edges together along the side and bottom end.

Needle Book. On page 70, the needlepoint used for the cover of this case is shown actual size.

After the needlepoint has been blocked, trim canvas to ⅜ inch on all edges. Turn raw edges to underside, easing needlepoint back from fold so that no canvas is visible from the right side. Finish

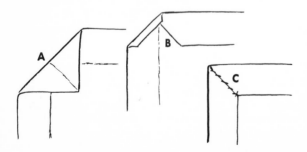

corners as instructed under mitered corner. Baste or hem edge of canvas to back of needlepoint, taking care that no stitches go through to the right side.

Cut felt lining slightly smaller than the needlepoint. Lay felt on wrong side of needlepoint. Smooth out felt and pin so that there are no excess wrinkles when cover is folded in half.

Cut two layers of wool or cotton flannel slightly smaller than the cover, and pink edges. Fold two layers in half; pin fold in center of cover. Backstitch the two layers to the felt down the center fold. If the ends of fabric layers show when cover is closed, trim off edges with pinking shears.

Clutch Bag. See illustrations on page 91.

Zipper—neckline type is the size needed for the opening, matching or contrasting with the needlepoint colors.

Lining—felt or cotton in the same or in a similar color as the zipper. Felt is cut to the same size as the needlepoint. Fabrics have a ¼-inch turn-under on four sides.

Fold canvas along edge of needlepoint; pin corners square and flat and steam press. Open folds, trim canvas about ¾-inch from edge of needlepoint. Finish corners as instructed under *Mitered Corner.* Baste canvas edges to back of needlepoint. Lay lining over needlepoint, wrong sides together, and slip-stitch edges together.

Fold in half, needlepoint side out, to form bag. Open zipper and pin each top edge over the tapes, starting at the closed end so that the edges will be even. Sew needlepoint to zipper tape, either by hand or by machine, cutting off ends of tape if necessary. Slip-stitch end of case together, then finish by overhanding with wool yarn.

Book Cover with Carrying Handles. See illustrations on pages 106 and 113. The size will depend on the size of the books to be carried. Make the handles ¾ inch to 1 inch wide and 12 to 14 inches long.

Fold canvas along edge of needlepoint; fold corners flat and steam press. Open folds, trim canvas about ¾-inch from edge of needlepoint. Finish corners as instructed under *Mitered Corner.* Baste canvas edges to back of needlepoint.

On the handles fold canvas along both sides and press. Open folds and trim canvas from ½-inch to ¾-inch from edge of needlepoint, depending on the width of handle. Cut edges of canvas should overlap and be basted together to give added strength for carrying. Line both handles.

Pin ends of one handle to one top edge of cover, right side of handle to wrong side of needlepoint. Pin second handle in the same way to op-

posite edge. Hold in hand to see if the handles are comfortable; adjust if necessary and tack all handle ends to the back of canvas.

Cut lining ¾ inch larger than needlepoint. Cut two extra pieces to form a pocket at each end of cover. Make them 3 to 4 inches deep and as wide as the lining. If you are using fabric, cut each end double and fold in half. The fold will become the finished edge of the pocket. Pin pockets to right side of lining, folds facing toward center. Machine stitch the three layers together.

Turn under raw edges of lining. Pin wrong side down over back of canvas. (Ends of handles are between edges.) Whip edges together on all four sides. Reinforce handles by taking extra stitches at these points.

Rain Hat Holder. The shaped needlepoint case below was made for a folded rain hat. See page 136 for instructions on making the initials. Line and finish the holder in the same manner as the compact slip-case.

Grosgrain ribbon, available in many widths and colors, makes an attractive edge finish for needlepoint accessories.

Mount the needlepoint with two or three rows of unworked meshes along the edge to be bound. Fold ribbon in half, lengthwise; steam press the crease. Spread a line of glue along the unworked canvas and on the inside of the covered item. Lay the ribbon on the canvas side so that the edge abuts against the first row of needlepoint stitches. Smooth carefully; then bring the ribbon over the edge of the item and down on the inside.

Self-Adhesive Edge Trimmings. Some of these new braids and bindings are worth considering as edge finishes on your needlepoint accessories.

Symbolism

138.   TOP—
Bishop's throne on right: Back cushion—Seal of the Diocese of New York
   intertwined with passion flowers and vines.
Seat cushion—Passion flower and vines.

BOTTOM—
Sedalia seat cushion—Columbine, symbolic of the Holy Ghost.
Pre-dieu—Medallion in center with a cross in each corner.

141.   High Altar Kneelers:
TOP CUSHION—All symbols relate to the Passion.
Crown of Glory—Mark of royalty superimposed on Crown of Thorns,
   symbolic of the Passion of Our Lord on Good Friday.
Cross and Monogram—Jesus Christ, Victor.
   Wheat—Bread of Eucharist. Grapes—Blood of Christ.
   Combined they represent the elements of Holy Communion.
   Laurel—Triumph, fame, eternity, purity.
Lance—One symbol of the Passion.

CENTER (left to right)—
Dove—The Holy Spirit. Grape vine—Christ, the true vine.
Keys—St. Peter, Guardian of the Gate of Heaven.
Book and sword—St. Paul. Book represents his epistles; the sword, his
   beheading.

BOTTOM (left to right)—
Tongues of Flame—Pentecost. Grapes and leaves—Christ, the true vine.
Lamb carrying banner—"Behold the Lamb of God."
Red Rose—Symbol of martyrdom. White rose—Purity.

142.   TOP—
North Transept—West wall. Seat cushions.
Open book—Alpha and Omega shown on ends of bookmarks are an at-
   tribute of Christ, symbolizing the Word of God.
Alpha and Omega—Christ the beginning, Christ the end, the all in all.
   Revelation, 1:8.
Palm—Victory, spiritual triumph, martyrdom.
Scallop shell with drops of water—Baptism.
Pomegranate—Resurrection, immortality, the Church, because of the inner
   unity of countless seeds in one fruit.

CENTER—
Diocean seals for Honolulu, Los Angeles, and Northern Indiana.

BOTTOM—
"The Workers" shows a kneeling figure, a stonemason, a gardener, a choir-
   master, a bell ringer, an acolyte with cross borne high.

143.   Kneelers:
TOP ROW—
   Daniel Boone
Bear and buffalo—Great hunter, led hunting parties.
Gun, powder horn, axe—Indian fighter.
Conestoga wagon—Blazed trail for wilderness road and led settlers
   through wilderness.

143. (*continued*)

Wilbur Wright

Glider with rudders—Flight at Kitty Hawk.

Engine—He and his brother built their own lightweight engine.

Kite—He flew a double box kite and learned many principles of flight.

Charles Evans Hughes

Governor of New York. Globe and gavel—World Court, The Hague.

Supreme Court Justice. Ballot Box—Worked for direct primary elections.

Burning books—Instrumental in repealing laws and effecting penal reforms.

Scales and sword—justice.

CENTER ROW—

Edna St. Vincent Millay

White Horse—Pegasus—lyricism.

Pulitzer '23 banner and harp—She won the poetry prize in '23 for "Harp Weaver."

Quill, paper, and seven volumes—her seven published books—the first in 1917 while still at Vassar, the last posthumously.

Albert Einstein

Nobel Prize Winner.

Center motif—energy released from the reaction of atoms.

Violin—Music and mathematics were his only hobbies.

Member of the Zionist Movement and deeply interested in World Peace.

Louisa May Alcott

Slate, etc.—School teacher. Quill—writer.

Rose and lilac—"an Old Fashioned Girl"; "Under the Lilacs."

Nurse—Nursed Union soldiers during the Civil War.

Pincushion and thimble—dressmaker.

Dustpan and brush—Worked as a domestic.

Henry Ford

Had great mechanical ability as a boy and repaired farm equipment and watches—first mass production of automobiles.

Laurel branch—Greatly interested in promoting peace.

Great interest in agriculture.

BOTTOM ROW—

Herbert Hoover

Farm house—his home in Iowa where he lived as an orphan farm boy.

Presidential Seal. Money bags—Wall Street crash.

Apple—sold on streets during Depression. Ship—Sent food to Europe.

Clasped hands—friendship—hands across the sea.

Winged wheel—He traveled around the world to feed the starving.

Humanitarianism—one of his greatest characteristics.

Alexander Hamilton

He wrote pamphlets for the Patriot cause early in his career.

Constitution of the U.S.—He worked hard for ratification and was one of the signers.

Scales of Justice—Practiced law in New York.

Seal of the Treasury—First Secretary.

Books—He wrote most of the Federalist papers.

Pistol—his fatal duel with Aaron Burr.

Abraham Lincoln

Log cabin—his birthplace. Top hat—his customary headgear.

Blue and gray hats—symbolic of Civil War.

Presidential Seal. Lincoln Memorial. "With charity for all."

(*continued*)

143.   (*continued*)
     Henry Clay
     Maine and Missouri—Missouri Compromise. Lectern—orator.
     Scales—Lawyer. Money—National Bank and High Tariff.
     Gavel—Speaker of the House of Representatives.
     Eagle and Motto—his famous slogan.

144.   INTERIOR, kneelers:
     1. Flashes of lightning and streaks of rain.
     2. Women sewing, carpenter, woman with child.

     BOTTOM
     1. Snowflake crystals.
     2. Tree in bloom; tree barren.

145.   1. Squirrel, acorn, animal footprints, turtle, rabbit, mouse, racoon.
     2. Various fish and a whale.
     3. Parachutist, machinist, painter, chemist.
     4. Symbols of the four evangelists.
        Winged man or angel—St. Matthew; Winged lion—St. Mark
        Winged ox—St. Luke; Eagle—St. John
     In the center of the kneeler the white roses represent purity, and the
     thistle is symbolic of earthly sorrow.

146.   TOP—Ark curtain—
     Panels one and four symbolize God, or the Spirit, and the givers of the
     Law. In panel one the light of truth and righteousness surrounds the Ten
     Commandments emerging from chaos. The broken tablets denote the
     weakness of man; the water gushing from the rock symbolizes God's
     power. In panel four the omnipresence of God is signified by several
     symbols, the cloud-covered mount, wings of the guiding angel, manna
     from heaven, the blowing of horns, and the shafts of light expressing
     exaltation.
        Panels two and three represent Man or the Earthly with the symbol of
     the Tabernacle in the wilderness. The Hebrew inscription, "Kodosh
     L'Adonoi," means "Holy to the Lord."
        The wavelike pattern across the bottom of the design denotes the
     wandering in the wilderness, and it is used to coordinate the four panels.

147.   TOP—Ark curtain—
     Left-hand door—Pillar of Cloud which contains twelve clouds represent-
     ing the twelve tribes of Israel. Right-hand door—Pillar of Fire having
     seven tongues of flame to suggest the menorah.
        The winged cherubim on the two triangular side panels give an im-
     pression of guarding the Ark. Four hands surround both the Tablets of
     the Law and the Torah scrolls which are held within the winged forms.
     The four hands, the symbol of Temple Beth Am, are of different sizes to
     indicate all ages.

     BOTTOM—Book cover—
     Tablets: Star of David above and behind a temple-like motif.

189.   BOTTOM—Altar frontal:
     Top left—Rebecca meeting Isaac—Genesis 24:1–67.
     Top right—Abigail meeting David—I Samuel 25:23–42.
     Bottom right—Solomon judging which woman is the mother of the child—
        I Kings 3:16–28. The other panels are unidentified.

Bibliography

Carrol, Alice. *The Good Housekeeping Needlecraft Encyclopedia.* Stamford House, New York, 1947.
> Alphabet of heavy block letters in design charts for canvas.
> A few simple design motifs. A needlepoint covered hassock in the shape of a child's A B C block.

de Dillmont, Therese. *Encyclopedia of Needlework.*
> D. M. C. Library, France (no date).
> Covers all types of needlework and was published in several languages. Reprinted many times and revised since World War II. Needlepoint stitches are shown under title "Tapestry."
> On page 137 we refer to a small book in D. M. C. Library series, titled *The Embroiderer's Alphabet.*

Ferguson, George. *Signs and Symbols in Christian Art.*
> Oxford University Press, New York, 1954.
> Illustrations in line drawings and photographs.

Freehof, Lillian S.; King, Bucky. *Embroideries and Fabrics for Synagogue and Home.* Hearthside Press, Inc., New York, 1966.
> 5,000 years of ornamental needlework. Hebrew religious symbols for all occasions. Hebrew script alphabet and how the letters are used.

Hanley, Hope. *Needlepoint.*
> Scribner's Sons, New York, 1964.
> Instructions and illustrations for more than fifty canvas stitches.

————.*New Methods in Needlepoint.*
> Charles Scribner's Sons, New York, 1966.
> Instructions for working and finishing a variety of accessories.

Harbeson, Georgiana Brown. *American Needlework.*
> Coward-McCann, Inc., New York, 1938.
> History from the late 16th century to the 20th century with interesting information about needlepoint.

Karasz, Mariska. *Adventures in Stitches.*
> Funk & Wagnalls Company, New York, 1949.
> Simplified design motifs that can inspire ideas for needlepoint.

Lane, Rose Wilder. *Woman's Day Book of American Needlework.*
> Color photographs of some historic needlepoint. Instructions for making the shell motif from Martha Washington's chair cushion.

McCall's Needlework Treasury.
> Random House, Inc., New York, 1964.
> Design chart for Under-the-Sea Rug which can be worked in sections or in one piece. Design chart for Siamese cats worked in quick point.

Martin, Mary. *Needlepoint.*
> William Morrow & Company, Inc., New York, 1969.
> Color photographs of a wide variety of items.
> Needlepoint rag-dolls. Cotton needlepoint.

Picken, Mary Brooks; White, Doris. *Needlepoint Made Easy.*
> Harper & Row, New York, 1955.
> Chapter on needlepoint as it relates to period furniture.

(continued)

(*continued*)

Sidney, Sylvia. *Needlepoint Book.*

Reinhold Book Corporation, New York, 1968.

Advanced techniques interestingly presented. Animals and birds shown in detail.

Libraries that have collections of illuminated manuscripts are:

New York Public Library, Fifth Avenue and 42nd Street, New York City.

Henry E. Huntington Library, San Marino, California.

Pierpont Morgan Library, 29 East 36 Street, New York City.

Reproductions of illuminated letters and pages are available from these libraries, some of which could be enlarged and transferred to canvas.

National Directory of Art Needlework Shops

Department Stores: Art Needlework Department
Visit your favorite store in your home town or a nearby town.

Specialty Needlework Shops

Arkansas
G. Brewster
601 West 35th Street
Pine Bluff, Arkansas 71607

Arizona
Camelback Knitting Shop
4812 N. 7th Avenue
Phoenix, Arizona 85014

The Yarn Tree
1016 West Fifth Avenue
Scottsdale, Arizona 85251

Yarn Carousel
18 No. Tucson Blvd.
Tucson, Arizona 85016

California
Jebba Needlepoint Design
9538 Santa Monica Boulevard
Beverly Hills, Cal. 90210

Nimble Needle
La Jolla, Cal.

Loretto Needlepoint Studio
150 S. Fairfax Avenue
(Farmer's Market)
Los Angeles, Cal. 90036

The Knittery
2040 Union Street
San Francisco, Cal. 94123

The Knittery Fox Plaza
105 Fox Plaza
San Francisco, Cal. 94102

The Yarn Depot, Inc.
545 Sutter Street
San Francisco, Cal. 94102

Mrs. Loretto B. Link
1228 State Street
Santa Barbara, Cal. 93104

Handcraft from Europe Importers
Sausalito, Cal. 94965

John R. Wallace
The Needlecraft Shop
13561 Ventura Blvd.
Sherman Oaks, Cal. 91402

Thumbelina Needlework Shop
1688 Copenhagen Drive
Solvang, Cal. 93436

Colorado
Edsu's Needlecraft
4421 W. 29th Avenue
Denver, Colorado 80212

Connecticut
The Handcraft Shoppe
Goodwives Shopping Plaza
Darien, Conn. 06820

Yarncraft Inc.
242 South Beach Avenue
Old Greenwich, Conn. 06970

Village Needlework Shop
293 Pequot Avenue
Southport, Conn. 06490

Freeman's Pickwick Yarns
Main Street
Stamford, Conn. 06901

Washington, D.C.
American Needlework Center, Inc.
2803 "M" Street, N. W.
Washington, D.C.

The Embroidery Shop
827-11th Street N.W.
Washington, D.C. 20001

Delaware
Colonial Yarn Shop
3830 Kennett Pike
Wilmington, Del. 19807

Florida
The Flying Needles
608 Indian Rocks Road
Belleair, Clearwater, Florida 33516

Bishop Woodside Yarns
633 N. Grandview Avenue
Daytona Beach, Florida 32018

Helen Hill
518 E. Atlantic Blvd.
Delray Beach, Florida 33444

Candle & Yarn Shop
6229 N. Federal Highway
Ft. Lauderdale, Florida 32748

Needlecrafts
2941 Corinthian Avenue
Jacksonville, Florida 32210

Knit & Needle
212 E. Orange
Lakeland, Florida 33801

Little River Knit Shop
8206 N. E. 2nd Avenue
Miami, Florida 33138

Smith Knudsen Inc.
Worth Avenue
Palm Beach, Florida 33480

Spinning Wheel Yarn Shop
1816 S. Osprey
Sarasota, Florida 33579

Needlecraft Studio
4241 El Prado
Tampa, Florida 33609

Ruthelmas Yarn Basket
1612 6th Street
Winter Haven, Florida 33880

Georgia
The Snails Pace
480 East Paces Ferry Road N.E.
Atlanta, Ga. 30305

Millwood Cottage
1846 Buena Vista Road
Columbus, Ga. 31906

The Yardstick
Medical Arts Shopping Center
Savannah, Ga. 31405

Illinois
Ball O Yarn
146 Merchant Street
Decatur, Ill. 62523

Lee Wards
840 North State Street
Elgin, Ill. 60120

Little Knit Shop
1322 Chicago Avenue
Evanston, Ill. 60201

Knit One Purl Too
657 Vernon Avenue
Glencoe, Ill. 60022

Lake Forest Sports Shop
265 Market Street
Lake Forest, Ill. 60045

Knit N Purl
Randhurst Shop Center
Mt. Prospect, Ill. 60056

Knit N Rip
1800 MacArthur Blvd.
Springfield, Ill.

Iowa
Hobbycraft Shop
801 Jefferson
Burlington, Iowa 52601

The Yarn Shop
122-2nd Street, N.E.
Cedar Rapids, Iowa 52401

Jane's Yarn Shop
3510 Cottage Grove
Des Moines, Iowa 50311

Steele's Yarn Shop
Plaza 20
Dubuque, Iowa 52001

Kansas
The Enchanted Cottage
513 N. Hillside
Wichita, Kansas 67214

Kentucky
Maud Hundley Studio
Box 264
Anchorage, Kentucky 40223

Louisiana
The Knit Shop
437 Heartstone
Baton Rouge, La. 70806

Angles Needlecrafts
602 East Morris Avenue
Hammond, La. 70401

Elber's Knitting Shop
837 Short Street
New Orleans, La. 70118

The Lusianne
127 Kings Highway
Shreveport, La. 71104

Maine
Knit-Nook
Columbia Street
Bangor, Maine 04401

Maryland
Baltimore Needlepoint Shop
2510 North Charles Street
Baltimore, Md. 21218

Massachusetts
Skein & Spool
714 Bliss Road
Long Meadow, Mass. 01106

Country Needle
Cushing Plaza
Route 3
Cohasset, Mass. 02025

Michigan
Berkley Knit Shop
3984 W. 12 Mile Road
Berkley, Mich. 48072

Yarncraft
Birmingham,
Michigan

Polachek Fabrics
411 E. Grand River
East Lansing, Mich. 48823

Yarncraft
341 Fisher Road
Grosse Pointe, Mich. 48236

Polachek Fabrics
109 W. Michigan Street
Jackson, Mich. 49201

Polachek Fabrics
305 S. Washington Street
Lansing, Mich. 48933

Mississippi
CELITA'S
Old Canton Road Plaza
Jackson, Miss. 39216

Montana
Shoppers Bazaar
Central Avenue
Great Falls, Montana 59401

New Mexico
Greer's Knit and Reweave
1711 San Pedro, N.E.
Albuquerque, N. Mex. 87110

New Jersey
Nassau's Inc.
235 E. Ridgewood Avenue
Ridgewood, N.J. 07450

Janet's Yarn Shop
Highway 35
Sea Girt, N.J. 08750

Stitch N' Knit Shop
420 Springfield Avenue
Summit, N.J. 07901

Nan Samons
589 Valley Road
West Orange, N.J.

New York
Carolyn Armbuter, Inc.
1235 First Avenue
New York, N.Y.

Bell Yarn Co.
75 Essex Street
New York N.Y. 10002

Fancy Work
1235 First Avenue
New York, N.Y.

Goldman Yarn Stores, Inc.
2540 Grand Concourse
Bronx, N.Y. 10458

Rosetta Larsen
22 East 69th Street
New York, N.Y. 10021

Alice Maynard
558 Madison Avenue
New York, N.Y. 10022

Robert Mazaltov and Son, Inc.
758 Madison Avenue
New York, N.Y. 10021

Museum ReCreations
220 East 57th Street
New York, N.Y.

Titillations
211 East 60th Street
New York, N.Y.

The Wool Gallery
141 East 62nd Street
New York, N.Y.

Woolworks, Inc.
783 Madison Avenue
New York, N.Y. 10021

Katherine Knox Yarn Shop
445 Plandome Road
Manhasset, N.Y. 11030

Millwork Needlework
Millbrook, N.Y.

The Knit Nook
324 S. Salina Street
Syracuse, N.Y. 13202

Hobby Yarns
217 Main Street
White Plains, N.Y. 10601

Morris Yarn Co.
188 Martine Avenue
White Plains, N.Y. 10601

Ohio
Madge Erf
16819 Chagrin Blvd.
Cleveland, Ohio 44120

Knit Knack Shop
2970 Far Hills Avenue
Dayton, Ohio 45419

Arlene's Knit Shop
5552 Secor Road
Toledo, Ohio 43623

Madge Erf
1804 Hause
Worthington, Ohio 43085

Oklahoma
Josie-Carter, Inc.
2422 N. Robinson
Oklahoma City, Okla. 73103

Su Hall Needlepoint
2068 Yorktown Alley (Box 4042)
Tulsa, Okla. 74120

Handcraft Shop
1405 E. 15th Street
Tulsa, Okla. 74120

Miljan Studios
1830 Utica Square
Tulsa, Okla. 74144

Pennsylvania

The Needle Eye
1720 Sanson Street
Philadelphia, Pennsylvania 19103

Rhode Island
Betty Schloss Handicraft Studio
187 Westminister Street
Providence, R.I. 02903

South Carolina
Porter's Gift Shop
130 S. Irby Street
Florence, S. Carolina 29501

Tennessee
The Yarn Barn
1301 Madison Avenue
Memphis, Tenn. 38104

Texas
House of Yarns
2730 Westhaven Village
Amarillo, Texas 79109

Lora's Knit Shop
202 W. 16th Avenue
Amarillo, Texas 79101

Gaye Weyand Needlecraft
358 Park Forest Center
Dallas, Texas 75229

The Knit Wit
6021 N. Berkshire Lane
Dallas, Texas 75225

Needlework Patio
6930 Snider Plaza
Dallas, Texas 75205

Circle Knit Shop
3465 Bluebonnet Circle
Ft. Worth, Texas 76109

Merribee
2904 West Lancaster
Ft. Worth, Texas 76107

Art Needlecraft Shop
62 Town and Country Village
Houston, Texas

Burrow Knit Shop
2150 Portsmouth
Houston, Texas 77006

The Knit Shop
3516 S. Shepherd
Houston, Texas 77006

Merribee
Montclair Shopping Center
Houston, Texas

Vernon Harris Knit Shop
1310 Avenue "Q"
Lubbock, Texas 79401

Robertson Knit Shop
1501 Jefferson Avenue
Marshall, Texas 75670

The Needle Art Shop
124 N. Jefferson Street
San Angelo, Texas 76901

The Knitting Bowl
7241 Blanco Road
San Antonio, Texas 78216

Janet Shook
P.O. Box 6002
San Antonio, Texas

Virginia
The Yarn Bazaar
Alexandria, Va.

Home Stitch Shop
4032 S. 28th Street
Shirlington Center
Arlington, Va. 22206

The Needlework Shop
Baaracks Road Shopping Center
Charlottesville, Va. 22203

The Knitting Corner
7 Corners Shopping Center
Falls Church, Va. 22044

The Knitting Shop
140 South Catoctin Circle
Leesburg, Va. 24571

Knit N Needle Shop
7552A Waros Corner
Shopping Center
Norfolk, Va.

Knit Kraft Shop
1809 High Street
Portsmouth, Va. 23704

Richmond Studio of Embroidery
318 Libbie Avenue
Richmond, Va. 23226

The Yarn Shop
1301 Maple Avenue
Roanoke, Va. 24016

Washington
World of Fabrics
Olympia, Wash. 98501

Yarn Barn
Paulsba, Wash.

Wisconsin
Ruhama's Yarn and Fabrics
420 E. Silver Springs Road
Milwaukee, Wisc. 53217

Wyoming
Georgette's
2304 Pioneer Street
Cheyenne, Wyoming 82001

Canada
Woolcraft, Ltd., Vancouver, B.C.

Woolcraft Limited
#4 Trading Company Building
Regina, Saskatchewan, Canada

Canvas
Canvas is available at the department stores and specialty shops listed above.

Mail Order Needlework Specialties:

Theodore E. Doelger
P.O. Box 126
Blauvelt, N.Y. 10913

D. M. C. Publications can be obtained from this company. Write for price list.

C. R. Messner Co., Inc.
22 East 29 Street
New York, N.Y. 10016

Paternayan Brothers, Inc.
312 East 95 Street
New York, N.Y. 10028

Adhesives
Elmer's Glue-All is excellent for use on canvas to prevent raveling and to join canvas to porous materials.

Scotch Super Strength Adhesive bonds canvas to nonporous materials as well as porous ones.

Dyeing Wool
Those interested in dyeing their own wool yarn can obtain an instruction leaflet and order form by writing to:

Creative Skills Resources
P.O. Box 326
Sea Cliff, N.Y. 11579

Needlepoint Bag Mounters
Artbag Creations, Inc.
735 Madison Avenue
New York, N.Y. 10021

Martha Klein
3785 Broadway
New York, N.Y. 10032

Modern Leather Goods
11 W. 32nd Street
New York, N.Y. 10001

L. Switkes and Sons
162 Madison Avenue
New York, N.Y. 10016

Christine's Custom Hand Bags
114 Madison Avenue
Detroit, Mich. 48226

Joel Beck
1259 Poplar Avenue
Memphis, Tenn. 38104

Acknowledgments

Our Heritage

2. Original idea suggested by Mrs. L. C. Levinson
   Developed and produced—Rosetta Larsen
   Design—Carl Lella © 1965
   Mounted—Gulio D'Angelis, New York, N.Y.
   Worked—Members of the Embroiderer's Guild in 1966 as listed below:
   Mrs. Howard L. Blum
   Mrs. Clinton Burnett
   Mrs. Fremont A. Chandler
   Mrs. Robert J. Davis
   Mrs. Howard M. Harris
   Mrs. Bernard Heineman
   Mrs. Leonard D. Henry
   Mrs. Edwin C. Jameson
   Mrs. William E. Lamb
   Mrs. L. C. Levinson
   Mrs. Jack Marquee
   Mrs. Grover O'Neill
   Mrs. Harry H. Schwartz
   Mrs. Lawrence W. Stern

4. *Top:* Old Sturbridge Village, Sturbridge, Mass.
   Bottom: The Mount Vernon Ladies Association, Mount Vernon, Va.

5. Boscobel Restoration, Inc., Garrison, N.Y.
   Photograph—Danny Wann

6, 7. Colonial Williamsburg, Williamsburg, Va.

Blair House

9. We wish to extend very special thanks to Sylvia Symington (Mrs. James), the wife of a former United States Chief of Protocol, who so kindly obtained permission for us to photograph the needlepoint in Blair House.
   Our deep appreciation to Mary Wilroy (Mrs. Farr) for her help and cooperation while photographing at Blair House.

8, 10, 11, 12. Photographs—Glen Leach, Rockville, Md.

10. Lowestoft china was named after the seaport town of the same name in England.

11. The lion statue is Bennington pottery, a prized stoneware made in Bennington, Vermont, from the late 18th century to the late 19th century.

Needlepoint Essentials

14, 15, 28, 29, 30, 32. Heirloom Needlework Guild, Inc.

16. John Dritz & Sons

17. *Top:* Woolworks, Inc.
    Bottom: Paragon Needlecraft

19, 23, 30, 31. Artist—Claire Valentine

20, 21. Chart Layout—Claire Valentine

20, 21, 24, 25. Photographs—Sherman Deutsch

Design and Color

35. *Top:* Designed, worked, owned—Mrs. Raymond E. Ostby
    Bottom: Designed, worked, owned—Mrs. E. H. Howard
    Photographs—Val's Photo Studio, Coventry, R.I.

38. *Top:* Woolworks, Inc.
    Bottom: Artist—Helen Disbrow

39. *Top left:* Artist—Claire Valentine
    Top right: Heirloom Needlework Guild, Inc.
    Rug—Paragon Needlecraft
    Cushion—John Dritz & Sons

40. Heirloom Needlework Guild, Inc.
    Artist—Claire Valentine

41. Heirloom Needlework Guild, Inc.
    Artist—Helen Disbrow

42. *Left:* Worked and owned—Louis J. Gartner, Jr.
    Right: Bernhard Ulmann Co.

43. Artists—Helen Disbrow, Claire Valentine

45. Heirloom Needlework Guild, Inc.

46, 47. Designed and worked—Claire Valentine
        Photographs—Sherman Deutsch

49. Fleetway Publications Ltd., London, England

50, 51. Charts—Claire Valentine

Canvas Stitches

53–85. Stitch designs and drawings—Claire Valentine
       Finished art—Charles Palmer

74–76. Samples worked—Doris White
       Photographs—Sherman Deutsch

Blocking—Mounting—Finishing

87. *Top:* Designed and worked—Claire Valentine
    Bottom: Designed and worked—Doris White

Rehabilitation and Recreational Therapy

90, 91. Photographs—Sherman Deutsch

92, 93. Drawings—Claire Valentine and Helen Disbrow

Interior Design

94. La Banque Continentale, New York, N.Y.

96. *Top left:* Woolworks, Inc.
    Left, second, and top right: Heirloom Needlework Guild, Inc.
    Left, third: Designed and worked—Mrs. Paul C. Nicholson
    Owned—Mrs. Stanley Livingston, Jr.
    Photograph—Val's Photo Studio, Coventry, R.I.

97. *Bottom (two):* Heirloom Needlework Guild, Inc.
    Top left: John Dritz & Sons
    Top right: Woolworks, Inc.
    Bottom left: Paragon Needlecraft
    Bottom right: Rosetta Larsen

98. *Top and left, second:* Russell Lynes
     Photograph—Richard Fraser
     Bottom (two): Woolworks, Inc.

99. *Top:* Heirloom Needlework Guild, Inc.
    Center: Woolworks, Inc.
    Bottom (two): Alice Maynard
       Photographs—Richard Fraser

100. *Top:* Alice Maynard
       Photographs—Richard Fraser
     Left center: R. Mazaltov
     Bottom (three): John Dritz & Sons

101. *Across top:* Woolworks, Inc.
     Bell pull—R. Mazaltov
     Wastebasket—Alice Maynard
     Luggage rack—Heirloom Needlework Guild, Inc.

102. *Top* (*two left*): Heirloom Needlework Guild, Inc.
     Top right: Woolworks, Inc.
     Bottom: Woolworks, Inc.
        Photograph—Marian Stephenson

103. *Top:* Designed and worked—Louis J. Gartner, Jr.
     Bottom: Rosetta Larsen

104. *Top left, bottom left:* Heirloom Needlework Guild, Inc.
     Bottom right: Woolworks, Inc.

105. Photographs—Sherman Deutsch

Fashion Accessories

106. *Top:* Designed and worked—Doris White
        Photograph—Sherman Deutsch
     Bottom: Woolworks, Inc.
        Photograph—Marian Stephenson

108. *Top left:* R. Mazaltov
     Center: John Dritz & Sons
     Right: Heirloom Needlework Guild, Inc.
     Bottom left and right: Heirloom Needlework Guild, Inc.
     Bottom center: Artbag, New York, N.Y.

109. *Top left:* Artbag, New York, N.Y.
     Top right: Artbag, New York, N.Y.
     Bottom: Ruth Cameron (Mrs. Freeland R.)
        Photograph—Sherman Deutsch

110. *Top* (*two*) and center: Alice Maynard
     Bottom: Designed and worked—Louis J. Gartner, Jr.

111. Hats—Alice Maynard
     Belts—Owned—Doris White
     Double eyeglass case—Alice Maynard
     Slipper, wallet, eyeglass cases—Heirloom Needlework Guild, Inc.
     Scissors and Seahorse cases—R. Mazaltov

112, 113. All accessories designed and worked—Doris White
       Photographs—Sherman Deutsch

115. Information and diagrams for measuring and mounting bags furnished by Louis Rosenberg, Artbag, New York, N.Y.
     Finished art—Charles Palmer

House and Home

116. Designed, pieced, and mounted—Rosetta Larsen

Worked—Mrs. Henry Pomeroy Davison
Owned—Mr. and Mrs. Henry P. Davison, Jr.
"Appledore," Locust Valley, N.Y.
   Photograph—Richard Fraser

118. Design—Alice Maynard
     Worked and owned—Mrs. Lowell Thomas

119. Lee Carpets—A Division of Burlington Industries

120. Designed and worked—Mrs. Paul C. Nicholson
     Owned—Mr. and Mrs. Stanley Livingston, Jr.
        Photographs—Val's Photo Studio, Coventry, R.I.

121. Russell Lynes
        Photographs—Richard Fraser

122. The D. M. C. Corporation

123. *Top:* Kugel Company, Inc.
     Bottom: Heirloom Needlework Guild, Inc.

Samplers, Mottoes, Monograms

124. Photograph—Sherman Deutsch

126. Alphabet designs—Claire Valentine
     Finished drawings—Charles Palmer

127. The Metropolitan Museum of Art
     Gift of Mrs. Russell Sage, 1909

128. *Top:* Designed and worked—Mrs. Reva DeBerry
     Bottom: Design—Alice Maynard
        Artist—Helen Disbrow

129. *Top:* John Dritz & Sons
     Center: Alice Maynard
     Bottom: Witte Museum, San Antonio, Texas

130. *Top:* Courtesy of the Smithsonian Institution
     Bottom: Museum of Fine Arts, Boston, Mass.

131. *Top left:* Kugel Company, Inc.
     Right (two): Courtesy—The Smithsonian Institution

132. *Top:* Heirloom Needlework Guild, Inc.
     Center: John Dritz & Sons
     Bottom: Heirloom Needlework Guild, Inc.
     Stitch designs—Claire Valentine
     Finished art—Charles Palmer

133. *Top:* Artist—Claire Valentine
     Bottom left: Bernhard Ulmann Co.
     Bottom right: John Dritz & Sons

134. *Top:* Artist—Claire Valentine
        Photographer—Sherman Deutsch
     Chair—Moravian Seminary for Girls, Bethlehem, Penn.
     *Bottom—*Design—Claire Valentine

135. Bell, clock—Paragon Needlecraft
        Photographs—Sherman Deutsch

136. Designs—Claire Valentine
     Compact slip-case—Designed and worked—Doris White

137. *Top:* Script—D. M. C. Library
     Designs—Claire Valentine
     Bag—Alice Maynard
     Paisley design bag—Gladys Mayes

Devotionals

138. Trinity Church, New York City.
     Advisor: Mrs. Bernard C. Newman, the wife of the former Vicar of Trinity Church.

140. Washington Cathedral Needlepoint Committee.
Advisors: Mrs. Houghton Metcalf, Chairman
Mrs. Kevin Keegan, Executive Secretary.
Mrs. W. Cole McCreery
Mrs. William J. Howard, Head Guide
We wish to express our deep appreciation to Mrs. Keegan for all the time, guidance, and cooperation she contributed. Also, special thanks to Mrs. McCreery and Mrs. Howard.
High Altar rug
Design by the Misses Tebbetts, Kent, Conn.
Chairman—Mrs. John F. Walton, Jr.
Contributed and worked by 23 women from the Diocese of Pittsburgh

141. High Altar kneelers.
Design—Mona Spoor, Edgewater, N.J.
Chairman—Mrs. Harold Talbott.
Workers—Mrs. Harold Talbott, Mrs. Charles R. Hook, Jr., Mrs. W. G. Mather, Mrs. R. H. Norweb, Mrs. George Humphrey, Mrs. Duddleson Brown, Mrs. Alfred W. Jones, Mrs. F. M. Thayer, Mrs. Charles Thomas, Mrs. George Mead, and Mrs. P. Schulyer Church.

142. *Top:* North Transept, West Wall.
Design—Mona Spoor, Edgewater, N.J.
Center:
Diocesan Seals of the Episcopal Church in U.S.
Designed by the Misses Tebbetts, Kent, Conn.
Worked in most cases, by residents of the individual diocese.
Honorary Chairman—Mrs. Harold Talbott
Chairman—Mrs. George A. Garrett
Advisory—Mrs. Sherman Adams and Mrs. George M. Humphrey
Diocesan Seals—Mrs. Herman Phleger, Mrs. Ray Atherton, Mrs. Charles Mills, Mrs. Kevin Keegan, and Mrs. David C. Stewart.
Bottom: Opposite side of North Transept.
Design—The American Needlework Center, Inc., Washington, D.C.
Three cushions worked by Mrs. Ralph Matthiessen, Mrs. Ross Thompson, and Mrs. Benjamin Thorom.

143. St. John's Chapel, Historic kneelers.
Design—The Needlework Studio, Bryn Mawr, Pa.
Chairman—Mrs. Daryll Parshall
Upholsterer—Seibert Decorators, Bethesda, Md.
Top row, left to right:
Mrs. William D. Duna, West Orange, N.J.
Mrs. W. R. Taliaferro, Rapidan, Va.
Mrs. A. Sidney Johnson, Jr., Swarthmore, Pa.
Center row, left to right:
Mrs. Hugh J. Chisholm, New York, N.Y.
Miss Elise Morrell, Knoxville, Tenn.
Alice K. Clark, Providence, R.I.
Mrs. A. Sidney Johnson Jr., Swarthmore, Pa.
Bottom row, left to right:
Mrs. Murray Danforth, Providence, R.I.
Mrs. Charles D. Dickey, Philadelphia, Pa.
Mrs. Leland G. Gardner, Washington, D.C.
Miss Frances McGrew, Gloucester, Mass.

144. Design—Eliza Miller
Teachers and Supervisors—Jane F. Burrows and

Bucky King (Mrs. Wilber)
Parish Administrator—Mary Swiss
Upholsterer—Center Arts Refinishing Company
Interior:
Janet I. Hamilton, St. Thomas' Church in the Fields
June C. LeBras, St. Catherine's R.C. Church, Wildwood, Pa.
Kneelers, *top to bottom:*
Roberta W. Gillen, Christ Episcopal Church, North Hills, Pa.
Dorothy J. Kort, Holy Sepulchre R.C. Church, Cooperstown, Pa.

145. Kneelers, *top to bottom:*
Jessie Smith, St. Thomas' Church in the Fields
Shirley E. Reed, Trinity Presbyterian Church, Mars, Pa.
Viola L. Wooler and Janne D. Wendahl, St. Thomas' Church in the Fields
Grace Church in Providence, R.I.
Donated and Worked—Mrs. Frederic B. Read, Jr. in memory of her father, William Studerbaker Innis
Photograph—Val's Photo Studio, Coventry, R.I.

146–147. Three of the photographs on these pages have been reproduced previously, and we appreciate being allowed to include them here. See title: *Embroideries and Fabrics for Synagogue and Home* in bibliography.

146. *Top:* Design—Mrs. Randolph Rothschild. The outline of all the symbols was worked by Mrs. Rothschild in order to achieve a uniform result. Worked by forty members of the sisterhood.
Bottom: Design—Bucky King (Mrs. Wilber)
Worked by Mrs. Sadie Shapiro.

147. *Top:* Design—Harold Haydon.
Worked by more than forty members of the sisterhood from adolescents to the elderly.
Bottom: Design—Bucky King (Mrs. Wilber)
Worked by Lillian Freehof (Mrs. Solomon B.)

148, 150. Heirloom Needlework Guild, Inc.

149. Washington Cathedral—Mrs. George A. Garret presented book used for the names of donors and workers.

Children

152. *Top:* The Metropolitan Museum of Art, Rogers Fund, 1946.
Bottom: Designed and worked—Mrs. Paul C. Nicholson
Owned—Mr. and Mrs. William Sayles Nicholson
Photograph—Val's Photo Studio, Coventry, R.I.

154. Kittens—Heirloom Needlework Guild, Inc.
Worked by Elizabeth Brooks Jankus
Kitten—Bernhard Ulmann Co.
Children Praying—Bernhard Ulmann Co.
Clown on Unicycle—Heirloom Needlework Guild, Inc.
Clown—John Dritz & Sons
Deer, Sailboat—Heirloom Needlework Guild, Inc.

155. Poodle—Heirloom Needlework Guild, Inc.
Frog—John Dritz & Sons
Geometric—R. Mazaltov
Motto Designs and Floral—John Dritz & Sons

156. Floral—Heirloom Needlework Guild, Inc.
Pincushion—Heirloom Needlework Guild, Inc.
Cushion—Worked by Mrs. Stanley Livingston, Jr.
Ballerina—Paragon Needlecraft

157. Gone Fishing—Heirloom Needlework Guild, Inc.
Sheriff and Indian—Paragon Needlecraft
Christmas Greeting—Doris White
Birthday Greeting—Claire Valentine
Motto—Heirloom Needlework Guild, Inc.

Men and Needlepoint

158. Historical Society of Old Newbury, Newburyport, Mass.

160. *Lower right:* Ben Shahn
Worked and owned—Russell Lynes

161. Design—Bernard Perlin
Worked and owned—Russell Lynes

162. Worked and owned—James De Weese

163. Designed and worked—Louis J. Gartner, Jr.

164. Owned—Mrs. Marcel Vertès, New York, N.Y.

The Hobbyist and The Collector

166. Tiger head, tiger slipper—Alice Maynard
Cushion—Designed and worked—Louis J. Gartner, Jr.

168. Designed and worked—Mrs. Paul C. Nicholson
Top: Owned—Mr. and Mrs. Paul C. Nicholson, Jr.
Bottom: Owned—Mrs. Raymond E. Ostby

169. Poodle, ducks—John Dritz & Sons
Horse—Heirloom Needlework Guild, Inc.
Dog—Bernhard Ulmann

170. Doves—Heirloom Needlework Guild, Inc.
Birds—The D. M. C. Corporation

171. Cushion—Designed and worked—Louis J. Gartner, Jr.
Picture—Woolworks, Inc.
Fish—Heirloom Needlework Guild, Inc.

172. Wild West Panel—Alice Maynard
Guns—Paragon Needlecraft
Soldiers—Paragon Needlecraft

173. Bell, clock—Paragon Needlecraft

174. Autos—Paragon Needlecraft
Locomotives—Bernhard Ulmann Co.

175. Rug—Paragon Needlecraft
Panel—John Dritz & Sons
Paddle cover—Alice Maynard

176. Bernhard Ulmann Co.

177. Venice, waterwheel, map (*right*)—Bernhard Ulmann Co.
Medieval couple—The D. M. C. Corporation
Map (*left*)—Heirloom Needlework Guild, Inc.

Advertising and Publicity

178. The Smithsonian Institution, Washington, D.C.

180. *Top:* Columbia Records
Bottom: Chase Manhattan Bank

181. *Top:* Copyright 1959 by General Mills, Inc.
Design and worked—Alice Maynard
Printed—Western Printing and Lithographing Company, New York, N.Y.
Bottom: Copyright 1959 by Esquire, Inc.
Design—Irene Haas
Canvas painting—Marcel Gengouldt
Worked—Frances Drury of Alice Maynard

Museum Treasures

182. Witte Museum, San Antonio, Texas.

184. *Top left:* The Metropolitan Museum of Art, Rogers Fund, 1925.
Right: The Metropolitan Museum of Art, Gift of Mrs. J. Insley Blair, 1950.
Lower left: The Shelburne Museum, Inc., Staff Photographers—Einars J. Mengis.

185. *Top:* The Metropolitan Museum of Art, Gift of J. P. Morgan, 1907.
Center: The Metropolitan Museum of Art, Fletcher Fund, 1929.
Bottom: The Metropolitan Museum of Art, Rogers Fund, 1925.

186. The Metropolitan Museum of Art, Gift of Charles Zadok, 1948.

187. The Metropolitan Museum of Art, Rogers Fund, 1920.

188. de Young Museum, San Francisco, California, Gift of Mr. Archer M. Huntington.
The Art Institute of Chicago, Gift of Mrs. Chauncey B. Borland.

189. The Metropolitan Museum of Art, Anonymous Gift, 1949.
The Cleveland Museum of Art, J. H. Wade Collection.

190. *Top and center:* The Metropolitan Museum of Art, Rogers Fund, 1929.
Bottom: Museum of Fine Arts, Boston, Mass.

191. *Top:* The Metropolitan Museum of Art, Bequest of Mrs. Maria P. James, 1911.
Bottom: Witte Museum, San Antonio, Texas.

192. *Top:* The Art Institute of Chicago, Gift of Robert Allerton.
Bottom: Courtesy, Henry Francis du Pont, Winterthur Museum.

193. Courtesy, Henry Francis du Pont, Winterthur Museum.

194. Philadelphia Museum of Art
Staff Photographer—A. J. Wyatt.
Museum of Art, Rhode Island School of Design, Providence, R.I.

195. The Smithsonian Institution, Washington, D.C.

196–197. Museum of The Voortrekker Monument, Pretoria, Union of South Africa
Designer—Mr. W. H. Coetzer

196. Both panels worked by J. W. Prinslor

197. *Top:* Worked by M. B. de Wet
Bottom: Worked by M. R. Oosthuizen

198. Outline for sewing instructions—Ann·Bozzi

Index

accessories for the home, 112
  address book, 101, 112
  bell pull, 101
  box, 112
  card table covers, 101, 137
  desk set, 89
  doorstops, 154
  glove box, 106
  hi-fi cover, 161
  luggage rack, 12, 101
  mail holder, making a, 90
  memo pad, 101, 106, 112
  straps for luggage rack, 101
  telephone book covers, 100
accessories to be carried, 112
  book cover with handles, 106, 113, 199
  brief case, 112
  compact slip-case, 106
  cosmetic bags, 111
  eyeglass cases, 91, 111, 113, 198
  needle case, 106
  tennis racket cover, 175
  wallet, 111
  zippered case, 91
accessories to wear
  cummerbund, 110
  hats, 111
  mules, 106
  scuffs, 111
  slippers, men's, 110, 166
  vest, 110, 160
  waistcoat, 110
acetate film, 35
adhesives, 206
allowance for finishing, 19
  for mounting, 19
  for shrinkage, 19
allover design, 134
  floral, 98
  patterns, 19
alphabets
  script, 127
  serifed block, 131
  simplified block, 157
  upright script, 137
animals, 16
  bears, 116
  big cats, 166
  cow, 145, 178
  deer, 154
  dogs, 116, 164
  donkeys, 116
  frog, 155
  goat, 163
  horses, 116
  Kheta and Alba, 168
  kittens, 103, 154
  lamb, 38
  lions, 11, 38
  Lucky, 168
  monkey, 100
  mouse, 161, 175
  poodle, 155, 169

  Samoyed dogs, 168
  squirrel, 145
  whale, 145
antique accessories
  armchair, 94, 96
  bench, 10
  boxes, 7, 190
  chair-back detail, 184
  chest, 190
  document case, 191
  settee, 96
  wall pocket, 182
area to be worked, 18, 112
Arey, Garrison Burdett, 158
Ark curtain cover, 146, 147
art needlework department, 15

background color, 23, 51–52, 101, 149, 171
background design
  checkerboard, 41
  continental stitch for, 54
  contrasting stitch, 147
  diagonal stitch, 143
  plain stitch, 45
  stitch for small areas of, 65
backing, 90, 99, 156, 190
backstitch with yarn, 112
backstitching for highlight, 135
bag maker, 86, 108, 115
bags, 91, 108, 199
  blocking, 86
  fitted travel, 109
  frame selection, 115
  luggage, 109
  marking area to be worked, 114, 115
  measuring for, 115
  monogramed, 137
  mounting costs, 109
  pattern guide for, 115
  travel, 109, 167
  wicker, 112, 114
  zipper, 91, 199
bargello stitch, 62, 90, 110
basic essentials, 26
basic materials required, 149
basket weave stitch, 56, 149
baste marking, 132
bias tent stitch, 56
Biblical scenes, 189
  Cain and Abel, 184
  Finding of Moses, 188
  "The Lord is my Shepherd," 157
  The Lord's Supper, 148
  Old Testament story, 188
  prayer, children's, 133
  "A Voice in the Wilderness," 146
birds, 16, 168
  bird of paradise, 158
  birds in flight, 170
  chickadee, 111
  ducks, 169

  eagle, 39
  owls, 17
  peacock, 161
  stylized bird, 170
Blair House, 9
  interior, 8
  President's Suite, 11
  Queen's Suite, 11
block around word, 129
blocking, 86
  board, 86
  drying, 87
  essentials for, 26
  plywood, 89
  professional, 86
  sizing, 87
  stiffening, 87
  uneven drying, 87
bolsters, 88
book covers, 106, 113, 147, 199
book sizes, 113
border designs, 40, 131
  apple blossom, 116
  decorative, 127, 181
  diagonal, 41
  evergreen and pine cone, 116
  four-color, 40
  leaf, 111
  on boxing, 142
  repeat, 36
  scroll motif, 41
  two-tone, 171
Boscobel, 5
box edge, 24
boxing, 24, 112, 142
braid and tacks, 118, 88
brief case, 107, 112
brush, soft, 149
  stiff, 45
butterflies, 17
buying needlepoint, 14
braid, see finishes
brick, 88
brick stitch, 47, 65, 106, 147

canvas, 18, 20, 21
  counting meshes, 48
  double-thread, 18, 21, 54
  enlarging, 74
  fraying, to prevent, 74, 88
  height, to add, 104
  large mesh, 91
  matching meshes, 75
  meshes per inch, 22
  overcast seam edges, 75
  piecing, 74, 75
  rug, 18, 98
  separating threads of double thread, 58
  silk scrim, 150
  single-thread, 20, 79
  sizes of mesh, 18, 20, 21
canvas edge finishes
  bias binding, 19, 156

canvas edge finishes (*cont'd*)
  glued, 74, 88
  hemmed, 54
  machine stitched, 88
  masking tape, 19
canvas, yarn and needle chart, 20–21
care and upkeep of needlepoint, 105, 149
centering a design, 44
  marking the center, 86
chairs, 12, 35, 96
  Adam-Hepplewhite, 185
  armchair, 11, 96, 185
  back, antique, 184
  Chippendale-type, 9
  dining, 9, 52, 163
  finishes for, 44
  French, 94
  Louis XV armchair, 185
  occasional, 96
  Queen Anne, 7, 184
  side, 7, 184
  slip-seat, 7, 96
  Victorian, 88
  wing, 7
Chase Manhattan Bank, 179
checking size of outline, 48
chevron stitch, 68, 106
Clay, Henry, 178
clipping canvas curve, 112
coat of arms, 116
Colonial Williamsburg, 7
color, 33, 50
  block of contrasting, 114
  fall colors, 123
  for outlining, 48
  receding, 51
  See also background colors
color cards, 52
colorfastness, 105
coloring a design, 45
color key, 48
color of yarn, 22
color symbols, 49
combining stitches, 112
computer numerals, 134
contemporary designs
  floral, 96
  kneelers, 144
  piano bench, 96
  prayer book cover, 147
  sampler, 131
continental stitch, 54
  accessories, used for, 106
  around gros point design, 31
  covering stitch, 134
  lettering, used for, 132, 134
  piecing, 74
  rugs, used for, 102
  yarn needed for, 22
contrasting stitch, 147
Cook, Inman, 159
corners
  design for, 131
  mitered, 198
  rounding, 112
  tailored, 76
cornice trim, 101

costs
  of mounting, 110
  prices for bags, 108, 109
  substantial investment, 102
costumes, 164
  ancient, 177
  Colonial American soldiers, 173
  Egyptian princess, 188
  Elizabethan, 189
cover designs, 101
  antique book, 190
  cookbook, 181
  magazine, 181
  prayer book, 147
  record holder, 180
cross-stitch, 53
cushions and pillows, 88
  backing for, 99
  box edge, 24
  chair, 139
  choir, 143
  fitted, 98
  fringed, 4, 11
  knife-edged, 24, 99
  measuring, 24
  pillow, 98, 171
  quick-point canvas, 90
  round, 166
  suede leather, with, 99
  zebra stripe, 98
cushion weights, 90

damaged area, 105
David, statue of, 42, 163
Davison, Mrs. Henry Pomeroy, 116
DeBerry, Reva, 124
design, 33
  adding details, 48, 135
  blocking in areas, 48
  chart, 14, 48
  choice of, 16
  coloring a, 45
  complex, 141
  creating a, 16
  develop, 34, 85, 141
  enlarging, 42, 43
  facial features, 48
  focal point, 48
  indefinite outline, 46
  made-to-order, 14
  positioning of, 105
  See also background design and design motifs
design effects, 193
  delicate, 18
  detailed motifs, 44
  different stitches, using, 144
  outlining, 48
  painted, 14, 111
  pencil drawing, 119
  petit point, 14
  reducing a, 42, 43
  repeat, 36
  reversing, 44
  scattered patterns, 37
  shaded, 64
  stitch for developing, 54
  trompe l'oeil, 103, 161
  variations, 38

design motifs
  block, 37
  famous Americans, 200, 201, 202
  figures, 48, 104, 143, 156, 173
  geometric, 98, 110, 111, 155
  octagonal dot, 96
  oriental, 103, 104
  paisley, 99, 111, 137
De Weese, James, 162
diagonal stitch, 66, 82
document case, 191
doorstops, 88
double-thread canvas, *see* canvas
drawing on canvas, 44
dyeing wool, 52

elongated simplified half-cross, 47, 61
emblems
  bank, 180
  eagles, 39
embroidery cotton, 135
encroaching Gobelin stitch, 47, 64
ending length of yarn, 57
enlarging canvas, 74, 104
  design, 42
  with fabric, 76
essentials for needlepoint, 26

facial features, 48, 58, 152, 162
family crest, 110
family tree, 128
fancy stitches, 44
fans, coquettes', 191
felt for finishing, 90
felt for lining, 198
figures
  cathedral workers, 143, 144
  filling in figures, 48
  full-length, 104, 164, 178
  nude human, 42
  outlining, 42
  primitive, 184
  See also costumes
filling in around a design, 30
filling in background, 113
finishing, 24
  allowance for, 19
finishing canvas edges, 19
finishes
  bias binding, 135
  braid, 114
  cord, velvet-covered, 156
  decorative braid and tacks, 185
  fitted facings, 76
  fold-under, 198
  ribbon, 190
  self-adhesive paper, 114
  self-stick tape, 90
  stitches on outside edge, 198
  upholstery nails and tacks, 88
fish, 145, 171
flame stitch, 62, 190
floral motifs, 98, 99, 187
  cutting garden, 116
  pansy, 89
  picture, 195
  rose, 96, 98, 111, 155
  wreath, 10

Florentine stitch, 62, 146
frames, 9, 92, 93
  one-handed use of, 93
"frame-stitch method," 76, 93
fraying canvas edges, 74, 88
fringed cushion, 4, 11
fringe on card, 157
fruits, 102, 187
furniture, 24, 88, 95
  benches, 10, 96
  cane-bottomed settee, 98
  covered stools, 96
  period, 52
  placement of needlepoint, 76
  replacing upholstery fabric, 88
  See also chairs

Gartner, Jr., Louis J., 163
geometric, 36, 98
  bands, 131
  border, 40
  designs, 98, 155
gifts, 101, 167
  children can make, 153, 155
  color for, 52
glue, 87
  fast-drying, 88
  mounting with, 89
  quick-drying liquid, 19
  solvents in, 89
  See also adhesives
glued canvas edge, 19
Gracie Mansion, 2
graph paper, 34, 127
  design on, 62
  detail on, 132
  enlarging on, 43
  Mylar film, 35
  reducing on, 43
greeting "cards," 135, 157
gros point background, 31, 58
gros point canvas, 18
gros point design, 15
gusset, 115

half-cross stitches, 59
Hammond, Natalie Hays, 33
handbags, *see* bags
handicapped, 91, 93
handwriting, 135
hangings, *see* wall hangings
Harper's Bazaar, 164
Harper's Magazine, 160
hats, 111
Haydon, Harold, 147
headboard, 164
Hebrew symbols, 147
Hicks, Edward, 38
hi-fi cover, 161
highlighting a design, 135
highlighting letters, 137
Historical Society of Old Newbury, Newburyport, Mass.,
  158
historic kneelers, 143
historic needlepoint
  American:
    18th Century, 4, 5, 7, 152, 184,
    190, 192, 193, 194

19th Century, 4, 131, 137, 178,
  182, 195
20th Century, 2, 133, 191
  English:
16th Century, 187
17th Century, 7, 188, 189, 190
18th Century, 6, 7, 185, 192
  Flemish:
17th Century, 189
  French:
18th Century, 185
  Spanish:
16th Century, 186
  Union of South Africa:
20th Century, 196
holding canvas in work, 32
horizontal stripe design, 36, 70
House & Garden magazine, 163
houses, *see* scenic designs
Hungarian point, 190

initials
  in boxing, 144
  in samplers, 131
  of needlepointer, 129
  of surname, 136
insects
  beetles, 98, 110
  butterflies, 103, 187
  caterpillars, 187
  moths, 187
interiors
  Ashlar Room, 5
  Blair House, 8
  La Banque Continentale, 94
irregular (uneven) bargello, 64,
  91, 106, 112, 136

jewel boxes or cases, 101, 107
Jewish religious symbols, 147
joining rug sections, 74

kneeler, *see* religious
kits, needlepoint, 15

La Banque Continentale, 94
large-mesh canvas, *see* quick point
  canvas
Larson, Rosetta, 116
left-handed stitches, 77
  basket weave, 80
  continental, 78
  diagonal, 82
  elongated simplified half-cross,
  85
  ending a length of yarn, 81
  petit point, 79
  regular half-cross, 84
  simplified half-cross, 84
Lella, Carl, 2
letters of the alphabet
  block with serifs, 126, 129, 132
  capital, 126
  computer numerals, 134
  condensed block, 132
  handwriting, 135
  in detail, 127
  legible, 137
  lower case, 127

made with backstitches, 135
  marking for light-colored, 132
  marking for very thin, 132
  on graph paper, 127
  script, 126
  shadowed, 136
  simplified block, 127
  stitches to use for, 132
  weight and width, 126
  upright script, 136
letters making words, 128, 129
  full name, 129
  greetings for various occasions,
  135, 157
  guide for working names, 134
  lay out on graph paper, 133, 134
  prayer, children's, 133
  styles of, 180, 181
linings, backings, finishes
  black cotton or nylon fabric, 26
  felt, 198
  leather or leather-likes, 99, 110
  moire, 191
  satin, 110
  suede boxing, 99
  upholstery fabric, 76, 99
  woven needlepoint fabric, 99
luggage racks, 101
luggage, *see* bags
Lynes, Russell, 121, 160

machine stitching canvas edge, 88
Madonna, 148
Madonna and Child, 48
making fashion items
  book cover with carrying handles, 199
  clutch bag, 91, 199
  compact slip-cases, 114, 198
  cushion weights, 90
  eyeglass case, 198
  holder for rain hat, 199
  mail holder, 90, 128
  needle book, 114, 198
marine plywood, 86
marking area to be worked, 19
  canvas for lettering, 132
  center, 86
  count of threads, 48
  outline on paper, 86
  small area to be worked, 53
Martin, Mary, 175
match adjoining stitches, 73
match meshes exactly, 75
materials for needlepoint, 26
Maynard, Alice, 159
Mazaltov, Robert, 159
measurements needed, 24
Menninger Clinic, 153
mitered corner on chair seat, 25
mitered corner on hem, 198
monograms
  block-letter, 137
  card table cover, 137
  initials framed in petit point,
  136. *See* center color spread
  on handbag, 137
  oriental script, 136

monograms (*cont'd*)
 unusual combinations of letters, 136
mottoes, 132, 148
 baste marking for lettering, 132, 133
 "God Bless Our Home," 132
 humorous, for doorstops, 155
 "The Lord is my Shepherd," 157
 Pennsylvania Dutch, 132
mounting
 allowance for, 19
 covering exposed thread of fold-under, 112, 198
 essentials for, 26
 fashion accessories, 26
 furniture, 88
 gluing method, 88, 89, 114
 on boxes, 92, 106
 on lead block, 88
 on memo pad cover, 92, 112
 on plastic briefcase, 112
 on wicker basket, 114
 pictures, 89
 revamping to fit new object, 74
 rugs, 89
 screens, 104
 slip-seat chairs, 105
 wastebasket, 89, 101
 with nonreflecting glass, 89
 with upholstery brass tacks, 96
mural-like hanging, 173
muslin cover, 86
muslin pattern
 for chairs, 25
 for fashion item, 107

name blocked on graph paper, 134
name stampings, 86
needlepainting, 119, 164
needlepoint for patients, 91
needlepoint technique, 161
needlepoint woven fabric, 99
needles, 20, 21, 23
needle size, 22
needle storage, 114
needle threader, 93
needle threading with one hand, 93
Nicholson, Martha F. Sayles, 121
noncolorfast wool, 105
nonglaring glass, 89
numerals, 126, 127

oil paint, 45
old needlepoint, reblocking, 105
one hand, use of only, 93
one-handed training, 91
outlined area, 54
outline letters or numerals, 135
outlining, 48
out-of-shape needlepoint, 32
overcast canvas edges, 75
overhanding with wool yarn, 199

painted canvas pieces, 111, 154
painting a design, 45
painting in needlepoint, 119

panels, 104, 173
 See also wall hangings
pantograph, 43, 162
paper pattern, 25
 for accessories, 107
 for brief case, 112
 for eyeglass case, 198
 for fabric piecing, 76
 for gusset, 115
paper method of threading, 27
Parisian stitch, 71, 91
patriotic emblems, 39
"Peaceable Kingdom," 38
Pennsylvania Dutch, motto, 132
perceptual training, 91
Perlin, Bernard, 161
permanent record of names, 149
personalizing a gift, 155
petit point
 applied to chest, 190
 applique, 58
 book cover, 147, 190
 canvas, 18
 design motifs, 14
 enlarging design, 43
 filling in around a petit point design with, 58
 floral, 150
 on silk scrim, 150
 picture, 163
 silk, 189
petit point stitch, 58
pictures
 cardboard for, 89
 framing, 24
 lacing the edges together, 89
 matting, 89
piecing
 abutted edge, 75
 enlarging with fabric, 76
 measured incorrectly, if, 74
 overlap, 74, 75
Pierce, Daren, 159
pillbox hats, 111
pillows, *see* cushions
pin cushion, 156
placement of design on canvas, 25
pointillism picture, 161
portraits, 152, 162, 178
pressing with steam iron, 198
protecting needlepoint in work, 32

Quaintance, Charles, 159
Quaintance, Linsley, 159
quality, 18
Queen Anne side chair, 7, 184
Queen Elizabeth I, 23
Queen Mary, 159
Queen Victoria, 51
quick point canvas, 18
quick point canvas cushion, 90

rain hat holder, 107, 199
random stripe, 36
record of donors and workers, 149
refurbishing needlepoint, 105
regular half-cross stitch, 59
reinforcing book cover handles, 199

rehabilitation therapy, 91
religious
 altar frontal, 189
 altar rug, 141
 All Saints Chapel, 139
 Ark cover, 147
 Ark curtain, 146
 Baltimore Hebrew Congregation, 146
 "Benedicte, Omnia Opera Domini," 144
 bishop's chair, 139
 Cathedral Church of Saint Peter and Saint Paul, 140
 Chelsea Old Church, Chelsea, England, 143
 communion kneelers, 141, 144
 cushions, 142, 143
 ecclesiastical needlepoint, 56
 "Flight into Egypt," 189
 "Forty Years—A Symphony in Needlepoint," 146
 Grace Church, Providence, R. I., 145
 kneelers, 138, 141, 144–146
 Lion and the Lamb, 38
 Lord's Supper, 148
 Madonna, 148
 Madonna and Child, 48
 National Cathedral, 140
 prayer book cover, 147
 Rodef Shalom Temple, Pittsburgh, Pa., 146
 St. John's Chapel, 143
 St. Thomas' Church in the Fields, Gibsonia, Pa., 144
 Temple Beth Am, Chicago, Ill., 147
 Trinity Church, New York, N.Y., 138
 "Voice in the Wilderness," 146
 Washington Cathedral, 140
Remington, Frederic, 162
removing a row of stitches, 73
repairing, 149
 damaged area, 105
 reinforcing a cut area, 105
 replacing stitches, 73
 See also piecing
repeat design formula, 63
reusing old needlepoint, 105
revamping to fit new object, 74
Rothschild, Mrs. Randolph, 146
rugs, 102
 antique, 5, 6
 binding, 89
 canvas, 18
 designs for, 102, 175
 finishing, 89
 fringed ends, 103
 high altar, 141
 joining sections by piecing, 74
 out-of-shape, 102
 room-sized, 175
 round, 103
 tasseled corners, 103
running stitches inside work area, 28

running stitches outside work area, 28

sample makers' working design, 16
samplers
    alphabetical, 125
    birth, 129
    contemporary, 131
    family tree, 128
    motifs, 130, 131
    period, 126, 127
    pictorial, 195
    silhouette, 133
    wedding, 124, 126, 129
Sayre, Dean, 143
Scandinavian Christmas greeting, 157
scenic designs
    Across the Orange River, 196
    Appledore, 116
    Athabasca Ranch, 116
    Birthday, 196
    brick houses, 117, 119
    country home, 121
    "Great Trek," 196, 197
    Harvesting, 192
    historic America, 176
    landscapes, 162
    modern design house, 119
    New York City, 2
    Prayers, 197
    Retief's Departure, 197
    rural scenes, 192–194
    seascape, 121
    Shepherd and Flock, 184
    swimming pool, 116, 120
    town house, 121
    "View of Delft," 72
    walled town, 186
scissors holder, 111
scissors, sharp-pointed, 73
Scotchgard Fabric Protector, 87
screens
    black lacquer, 104
    fireplace, 120, 164, 168
    folding panel, 2, 104
    French fireplace, 104
    hand, 191
    mounting, 104
    pole, 12, 121
separating strands of yarn, 23
sewing instructions, 90, 113, 114, 198
Shahn, Ben, 161
shrinkage, allowance for, 19
silhouettes
    animal and bird, 35
    "The Lord is my Shepherd," 157

making, 42
portrait, 162
sampler, 133
silk floss, 135
size
    of canvas mesh, 18, 20, 21
    of design, 18
    of design area, 22
    to fit specific area, 149
Smithsonian Institution, 143
sources of design, 18, 37, 131, 162
specialty shops, 15, 204
squaring a design, 42
starting and ending a strand of yarn, 28
stencils, 34, 44, 136
stitches
    alternating stitch, 65
    bargello, 62, 110
    basket weave, 56
    bias tent, 56
    brick, 65, 106
    chevron, 68, 106
    continental, 30, 54, 106
    diagonal, 66, 67
    elongated simplified half-cross, 61
    encroaching Gobelin, 47, 64
    flame, 62, 190
    Hungarian point, 190
    imperfect, 73
    irregular or uneven bargello, 64, 91, 106, 112
    "long bargello," 62
    Parisian stitch, 71, 91
    petit point, 14, 58
    plain, 44
    regular half-cross, 59, 73
    simplified half-cross, 31, 60
    tramé to indicate colors, 45, 72
    tramé, working over, 73
stitches made with only one hand, 93
stitches which make stripes, 45
stretching maximum, 87
    minimum, 86
stripes, 36, 45
symbols
    church and synagogue, 138–143, 144–147
    famous Americans, 143
    indicating yarn colors, 49
symbols, meaning of
    church and religious, 200, 202
    famous Americans, 200, 201, 202
    religious, 200, 202
synagogues, 146, 147

tapestry, 35
tapestry yarn, 22
tasseled corners, 103
teaching outline, 151
Tebbetts, the Misses, 141
templates, 44
therapy
    one-handed training, 91
    perceptual training, 91
threading needle, 27
    Styrofoam for, 93
    with one hand, 93
    with short length of yarn, 73
threads, cotton, silk, metallic, 48
    linen, 75
Thomas, Lowell, 119
trademarks that bleed, 86
tramé
    for color, 45
    indicates the design, 72
    working over, 73
transferring design to canvas, 43, 44, 134
trompe l'oeil designs, 103, 161
turning the canvas, 73
twisted yarn, 27

uneven (irregular) bargello, 91, 106, 112
uniform background color, 149
unifying design feature, 144
up-and-down motion for single stitch, 75, 93

vacuum cleaner, low-powered, 149
Vertes, Marcel, 104, 164
visual deception, 161
Voortrekker Monument, Pretoria, South Africa, 196

wall grouping, 174
wall hangings, 118
waste knot, 80
weight of yarn, 22
weights, drapery, 90
width of canvas, 18
working with a frame, 93
workmanship, evenness of, 52

yarn, 22, 23
    basic formula, 22
    dye lot, 23
    length to use in needle, 26
    number of strands per length, 22
    storage, 105
yarns, types of, 22

zippers, 112, 199